YES, VIRGINIA, THERE IS RIGHT AND WRONG

The following are endorsements of *Yes Virginia, There Is Right and Wrong!* Some of these appear in condensed form on the back jacket. They speak for themselves.

"This book is well written and provocative. Honest and open debate on the substance and origins of values is critical to both the present and the future. At our common peril, we ignore or evade their importance. Dr. Gow's book provides a springboard for educators and parents to examine where they are and where they need to be in teaching and guiding those young people for whom they have special responsibility." **Edwin F. Watson,** *Executive Director, Child Welfare League of America.*

"Cooly, judiciously, Dr. Gow picks her way through the enormously complicated and important subject of moral education in the public schools. Yes, Virginia's parents, your daughter is getting instruction in ethics, though in a way that would probably astonish you, to say nothing of most educators from McGuffey back to Socrates. A serious and sobering book." **William F. Buckley, Jr.,** *internationally renowned author, editor and broadcaster.*

"A penetrating and pleasant critical review of current moral values education 'packages.' This book shows how crucial it is to blend tradition and innovation in creating a system of values appropriate for this period of difficult transitions.

"These thoughtful pages have reminded me of the basic truth that it is we, the adults, who mostly need a solid moral values education if we are to help our young to face up to the challenges ahead." **Dr. Aurelio Peccei,** *Past President, The Club of Rome: an international organization of world leaders concerned with the world's most pressing long-term problems.*

"In an age in which everything seems to be shifting, it is useful to be reminded that certain values stand apart from pressures, fads and expedience. We are indebted to Dr. Gow for a book that reaquaints us with our foundations." **Norman Cousins,** *recipient of National and International Awards for Literature; Science; Law; Service to the Environment; Diplomacy and World Peace.*

"The quest for morality without God, for Eros without procreation, for happiness without tears, has led twentieth century Man into some bizarre and disastrous courses. Dr. Gow has charted one of them—the systematic debauching of children in the name of liberating them from bondage to Good and Evil. Her scholarly and exhaustive study of moral values education as it is developing public and private education, provides much needed guidance, equally for bewildered parents and teachers assailed by doubts about the validity of current syllabuses. They should read, mark and inwardly digest what Dr. Gow has to say on the subject." **Malcolm Muggeridge,** *World communications and literary figure.*

"The importance of Kathleen Gow's book, *Yes Virginia, There Is Right and Wrong!* is the attention it draws to the dangers of moral values education which is widely spread as a method, but while not focusing on special age groups, and while totally lacking content, seems to be more confusing than helpful for young people—especially as this method is used in schools without co-operation of parents and homes.

"While agreeing that moral values may differ and therefore are difficult to be imposed in one form, there are, however, nationally and internationally accepted values which should be taught. By this I mean national and state laws and national and international issues of human rights which both national and international laws contain as generally accepted standards. Action against national and international state laws may lead to punishment according to criminal laws, and there is no justification in not letting young people know the content of their own country's laws." **Helvi L. Sipila,** *United Nations' Assistant Secretary-General 1972-1980; internationally acclaimed lawyer; Secretary-General, International Women's Year.*

"The author makes a key point that our times need to hear: 'There is an inherent fallacy in emphasizing moral dilemmas and skills of problem solving and decision making as the primary components of morality and, therefore of values education' (page 221). Good decision making presupposes good moral character—traits such as loyalty, justice, and compassion are essential. This sort of person is not developed by a 'quick fix'—a course or two. There is no substitute for loving, caring and believing parents, and wholesome schools and communities. However, assuming that this character formation is taking place, you will surely want to have some courses in decision making in the educational process. *When a student has the course is a matter of discussion for educators and parents.* The author introduces us to this important debate." **Theodore M. Hesburgh,** *C.S.C., renowned educator and recipient of numerous Public Service and Civil Rights Awards.*

"Clinical evidence makes clear that a healthy mind comprises a sound consistent conscience with well defined moral precepts. The lack of a clear understanding of what is right and what is wrong for the individual contributes to the various forms of psychopathology observed today among our children and youth. A young person growing up in our society—a society which gives few moral guidelines—suffers a kind of culture shock within his own culture. If the home, the church and our mass media fail to give these guidelines, who can provide them? Can the schools? This book—a cogent, objective, critical assessment of a movement in the schools to inculcate moral values—perceptively analyses the more controversial aspects of this movement. Every person interested in education, the emotional health of young people and the future well-being of our society must read what Dr. Gow has written and noted carefully." **Armand Nicholi, Jr.,** *Department of Psychiatry, Harvard Medical School; international authority on children and youth.*

Yes, Virginia, There Is Right and Wrong

KATHLEEN M. GOW, PhD

Tyndale House Publishers, Inc. Wheaton, Illinois

To Jim and Kathleen
whose lives are
a constant joy and strength

First printing, Tyndale House edition, March 1985

Library of Congress Catalog Card Number 85-50046
ISBN 0-8423-8558-4, cloth
ISBN 0-8423-8561-4, paper
© 1980 by Kathleen M. Gow
Printed in the United States of America

Contents

Author's Note

"As youth go; so goes the nation."

All of us—educators, parents, citizens—are deeply concerned about escalating rates of teen-age crime, alcoholism, unwanted pregnancies, vandalism, suicide. It was, among others, the Community Mental Health Movement of the 60s which commissioned elementary and secondary schools to be "caretakers" of the mental health of their students. As everyone knows who works with youth, it is extraordinarily difficult for broken lives to be mended, and collision courses to be reversed. How much better if we could "educate" for mental health rather than undertake therapy after problems become full-blown. It seemed obvious that a key factor in this education would be helping youth to explore moral values issues. There was optimism that the infusion of such values education (variously termed "human relations" and "life skills") into all subjects of the school curriculum, from kindergarten to grade 12, would aid children and youth as they face a bewildering kaleidoscope of conflicting "facts," opinions, values, and decisions.

Yes Virginia is written from both the "inside" and the "outside":

- as a social scientist researching the Values Education Movement as a phenomenon of which the general public is chiefly unaware, yet whose directions have been shaping youth since the early 60s;

9

- as an educator and mental health practitioner and administrator directly involved with this movement from its beginning.

Academics and educational and research institutes produce texts, curricula, and "packaged" programs which federal, state and local educational authorities have bought and distributed for use in classrooms across the nation. Enormous effort and talent have been poured into developing these materials.

However, not everyone was, or is, prepared to accept this more explicit role of social and moral values educator to students. For one thing, some assert that professionals themselves differ far too widely in their values, let alone their opinion of what is "normal," to pretend to have a sound body of data on which to develop responsible programs.

Others counter that values education is not concerned with offering prescriptions regarding the "good" life, or the merits of specific life-styles, but merely provides an open forum in which children may freely discover and discuss their own values. Specifically, some stipulate that a teacher should not promote values such as justice, honesty or benevolence in the classroom for, in their view, this constitutes "indoctrination" of children, violating their moral freedom (pages 223-225).

Still others argue that this is irresponsible because even a society as pluralistic as our own must recognize a commitment to such core moral values, although these should not be taught in a dictatorial way.

For 20 years, academics, educational officials and teachers have been engaged in this very heated controversy. In the past decade in the U.S., well over 1000 books and articles have circulated among them on this issue. Depending on the personal views of the teacher and/or administrative pressures, the choice of values education exercises and philosophies put forward in the classroom is enormous. These range from the useful, to the potentially very damaging. However, because these materials are directed to educators, the public, for the most part, has been singularly uninformed about the values education movement, let alone the controversy and experimental programs which continue from kindergarten to grade 12. They have had, therefore, little in-put into the directions taken. *Yes Virginia* provides necessary documentation for teachers and parents so that they may carefully scrutinize the contentious and controversial aspects of current values education approaches.

Most of us, I believe, hope that children will grow up to be individuals of strong mind and heart who are their "own persons," but who will not live for their own benefit alone; who will be prepared to challenge what they see to be injustices and to contribute creatively to their society. The methods of values education which will best achieve this end is what the controversy and the experiments are all about, and I have found these a continuing challenge to my thinking and practice.

This book is directed to the "rational moderate" regardless of political, religious or non-religious persuasion, ethnic background, or economic status. It seeks to build on the dedicated work of present contributors. It cuts across the polarization of extreme positions, to emphasize a values education for our youth which outlines a middle road between totalitarianism and a moral vacuum.

1

So What's New?

"Moral values education in the classroom?"
   "Good! I'll buy that! Kids need all the help they can get these days."

For most of us, both question and answer sound a welcome note. And that's about as far as we look into the subject. Not so long ago a number of people bought property in Florida on a not dissimilar basis: sight unseen. Some of them lost assets it had taken a lifetime to build.

The idea that schools should be concerned with teaching moral values is anything but new. Ever since the days of the one-room schoolhouse, North American classrooms have provided a setting for transmitting values to students: values such as honesty, kindness, service to others, respect for the law, and so on. In the main, these values have been taught implicitly and transmitted informally as part of the day-to-day classroom experience. This traditional *ad hoc* treatment of widely accepted values has tended to be random and sketchy, and to provoke little discussion. In general, the public took for granted that moral values were implicit in education. Students, it was supposed, would absorb these values as their education progressed.

Today there is a new thrust in values education: it is commonly called "Moral Values Education" (MVE). Initiated in England and the United States in the early sixties, MVE has become an international movement. In July 1981, a

World Congress on "Values and the School" was held with forty-two nations participating and over 900 delegates in attendance[1]. This movement is redefining the place of moral education in many classrooms. In fact, in many classrooms it is totally revolutionizing both the methodology and the content of moral education. This new approach is making moral values not a general foundation of educational experience, but a highly visible part of its superstructure.

Why this increased concern to make moral values an explicit part of the school curriculum? The reasons are compelling. Frightening statistics highlight the need for immediate and effective action in the area of moral values: crime, alcoholism, out-of-wedlock pregnancies, and suicide escalate yearly among the teenage and preteenage population. Meanwhile the media court these same groups' every whim. Children and youth face a bewildering kaleidoscope of conflicting facts, opinions, values, decisions. Rock groups, street gangs, the cults—all compete for the youth vote.

The dilemmas and conflicts widespread in today's society make it plain that unless the rising generation is equipped with some tools for making its way through the confusion, we shall have left its members a very questionable legacy. As much as many of us as adults may be appalled at the tools some of our youth are choosing, we are all, in our own way, also struggling to find ways of coping. The speed and complexity of our society show plainly that our children and youth need more than ever to learn how to analyse moral issues and how to arrive at moral judgments. They need to find direction and meaning in their lives. They need to learn to deal constructively with value conflicts they encounter. Ironically, in our complex society, many religious institutions and families appear to have stopped discussing relevant questions and have forfeited their influence. The tragic result is that children and young people are often caught in a directionless backwash or a compulsive undertow in a sea of conflicting values and opinions.

Recognizing the current crisis, educators are attempting to step into the breach. Teachers and administrators are to

1   See Proceedings of The World Congress in Education, Values and the School. Serge Fleury (ed.), C.P. 668, Haute-Ville, Quebec, P.Q., G1R 4S2, 1981.

be admired for their concern and commitment. As informed citizens, they share the same conviction that there are compelling problems which must be faced. But do we all—school administrators, principals, teachers and parents—really understand what we are buying when we turn for help to the new moral values education? If we assume that we have put our hands on packages filled to the brim with the highest ideals and the finest moral values upon which our society has been built, we could be in for an unpleasant surprise. Consider the following examples of MVE material for classroom use:

- There is the *Values Clarification* exercise called "Life Raft" which is designed, among other things, to help participants consider their own self-worth. A group of ten students is told that they are at sea in a life raft which has a capacity for only nine people. One of the ten must be thrown overboard in order that the other nine may survive. Each participant in turn pleads his or her case to the group, arguing why he or she should be chosen to survive. Following this desperate "sales pitch," a vote is taken and, by group consensus, the least "worthy" is thrown out.[2]

- There is the *Moral Reasoning* exercise on the "Value of Human Life." It is based on Kohlberg's theory that individuals mature in their moral reasoning by sequential stages which are best worked through one stage at a time. This suggests that if a child makes a Stage 1 statement, "You should save a drowning man because he might be important or have a lot of money," a helpful response to stimulate him or her to move to Stage 2 might be, "You should save a drowning man because he might give you a reward for doing it."[3]

2 See documentation in chapter 2 from Maury Smith, *A Practical Guide to Values Clarification* (LaJolla, California: University Associates, 1977), pp. 120-121.
3 See documentation in chapter 3 from S. Barrs, A.L. McMurray, W.J. Stevenson, R. Wideman, "Cognitive Moral Development: Kohlberg," *Values Education: A Resource Booklet*, Ontario Secondary School Teachers' Federation (Toronto: 1975), p. 31. See also L. Kohlberg, "Moral Education in the Schools: A Developmental View," *School Review*, vol. LXXIV (1966), pp. 8-9.

- Then there is Beck's *Reflective Approach* which exhorts children to live by a philosophy of trade-offs and compromise: "that we should strive to be reasonably moral, but not extremely moral,"[4] and the conviction that "nothing is intrinsically good or bad."[5]

I am not speaking here of isolated "horror" incidents that can be dismissed as incredible or exaggerated and "certainly not happening in *our* area." These are specific exercises documented in moral values education textbooks and resource materials, written by internationally known "moral education experts," and designed for use in elementary and secondary schools. These books and materials are recommended on state and provincial department of education guidelines and are being widely used in classrooms across North America. In fact, the three illustrations above are taken from the three values education "approaches" which dominate the new thrust of moral values education.

1. The Values Clarification Approach;
2. Kohlberg's Moral Reasoning Approach (Cognitive Moral Development);
3. The Reflective Approach.

Behind these approaches are specific perspectives on morality, which will be examined individually in the next three chapters.

It is important to emphasize from the outset that the purpose, here, is not to condemn moral values education in schools, or to suggest that it should be eliminated. Neither will there be an argument for a return to the recital of lists of virtues and the sanctimonious nodding of heads about rules to match. To reduce values education to mere rule-giving and to define morality as obedient conformity, rather than compassionate and reasoned commitment, is to retard students' growth and development in moral sensitivity and

4 See documentation in chapter 4 from Clive Beck, *Ethics: An Introduction* (Toronto: McGraw-Hill Ryerson Ltd., 1972), p. 109.
5 See documentation in chapter 4 from "Sample of Class Discussion of Values," Appendix E, p. 4 of "Case Study: Grade 13: Integrated Literature and Values Course," Appendix 5, *The Moral Education Project (Year 5) Final Report: 1976/77*, eds. Clive Beck et al., Ontario Ministry of Education (Toronto: 1978).

to prevent them from thinking intelligently for themselves.

There are many approaches to moral values education currently being used, and all of them have positive aspects which, for lack of space, cannot be examined here. The above three approaches which, because of their popularity, I have chosen to examine in some detail, also have positive features, which many teachers are using to good advantage. But the other side of the picture can be ignored only at our children's peril—that is, the potential for incalculable harm which is also inherent in much of the current MVE material. This aspect of the new MVE approaches must be confronted and assessed.

None of us would buy an automobile without looking under the hood. When careful shoppers consider buying any "package" for consumption, they naturally focus their attention on those areas which are apt to create problems. So in this book. I have set out to look beneath the natural appeal of the label of moral values education and to "unpack" each of the three approaches in terms of its more controversial aspects. If these approaches are to provide the source material of moral values education in our schools, and if their message is to be infused into all subjects, as their proponents urge, the approaches surely merit the constructive scrutiny of every citizen.

OFFICIAL POLICY

The logical objective of MVE is to systematically integrate its materials into all subjects of the curriculum at all levels of education, from kindergarten to the final year of secondary school. This means, for example, that any one of the exercises we have just looked at might be integrated into the subject matter of an English, History, or Social Studies class.

Even in 1977, it was reported that "at least 40 states and countless local districts are developing or instituting moral-education."[6] There is ample evidence that the confusion, the variations in policy formulation, choice of materials and implementation, breach of legislation, heated political

6 "'Mind Bending,' in the Schools Stirs Growing Protest," *U.S. News and World Report* (Washington), 4 July 1977, p. 43.

controversy, lack of accountability, and apathy which surround the issue are of critical proportions. Perhaps the most
compelling fact is that with or without a defined official
stance, with or without policy or curriculum materials
approved by the local school board or even by the principal
of the school, many individual teachers—genuinely concerned about "doing something" in this crucial area and
encouraged by authors of MVE materials—are simply
experimenting with their own MVE strategies. Obviously, it
is virtually impossible to arrive at an exact count of these
experimentations, but the range of strategies is potentially
enormous.

Not surprisingly, some MVE approaches are causing
considerable controversy. Values education programs have
become the cause of lawsuits, court injunctions, and legislative rulings. One of the foremost texts in this field, *Values
Clarification: A Handbook of Practical Strategies for Teachers and Students* by Sidney Simon, L. Howe, and H. Kirschenbaum,[7] was introduced in the American Congress, along
with several other books, ". . . as an example of the decadent
immoral approaches being introduced in our schools."[8]
Over half a million copies of this book are in circulation.[9] It
is recommended in state department of education materials,
by many school boards and, almost without exception,
wherever the Values Clarification approach is being promoted. In fact, a survey of the use of values education
materials, conducted by one jurisdiction among some 10,000
teachers, 650 administrators and 550 teacher-educators
showed that the Values Clarification material was ten times
the most popular in the field.[10] In March 1976, *Newsweek*

---

7 S. Simon, L. Howe, and H. Kirschenbaum, *Values Clarification: A
   Handbook of Practical Strategies for Teachers and Students*, 1st ed.
   (New York: A & W Publishers Inc., 1972). (Rev. ed. 1978). Copyright©
   1972, A & W Publishers Inc. Copyright© 1978 Hart Publishing Co., Inc.
   Reprinted by permission of A & W Publishers, Inc.
8 See H. Kirschenbaum, *Advanced Value Clarification* (LaJolla, California: University Associates, 1977), p. 151.
9 See Introduction to "Moral Education and Secular Humanism," *The
   Humanist*, vol. XXXVIII, no. 6 (November/December 1978), p. 7.
10 *The Moral Education Project (Year 4): Annual Report 1975/76*, Ontario
   Ministry of Education (Toronto: 1978), p. 6.

reported that in audio-visual aids alone, Guidance Associates had distributed material on Kohlberg's approach to over 6000 school districts.[11] In the same year, the Ontario Ministry of Education distributed 5000 copies of *The Reflective Approach in Values Education*[12] to its own constituency and the book circulated across Canada and the United States.

These figures give us some idea of the coverage these three major approaches are enjoying in North America. To what extent are teachers actually applying these approaches? As far back as "the school year 1974/75, some 2400 courses were being offered across [New York] State in elementary and secondary schools."[13]

EVERYBODY'S IN IT

Some of us might assume that the new MVE "packages" are not being bought by any religiously based schools. But there is a great deal of documentation to the contrary in, for example, the national weekly, the *Catholic Register*, and in such articles as " 'Moral Education' and Values Clarification: Their Importation into the Catholic Schools".[14] Brian Hall, a past president of the Centre for the Exploration of Values and Meaning points out that the tendency of religious schools to "buy the label" without examining the contents is just as marked as in any type of school. He goes on to define the Values Clarification approach as:

> . . . strictly amoral. That is not to say it isn't useful, but I think that as a method it is very limited. I find it interesting that many religious educators pick up on the method, use it, and assimilate value clarification exercises into religious curriculum—without recog-

---

11 "Moral Education," *Newsweek*, 1 March 1976, p. 75.
12 *The Reflective Approach in Values Education: The Moral Education Project (Year 3)*, Ontario Ministry of Education (Toronto: 1976).
13 William R. Clauss, "New York State Education Department Fosters Inquiry about Values," *Moral Education Forum*, vol. 1, no. 3 (May 1976), p. 10.
14 James Likoudis, " 'Moral Education' and Values Education: Their Importation into Catholic Schools," *Newsletter*, Catholics United for the Faith Inc. (New Rochelle, N.Y.: July 1976), pp. 1-5.

nizing what the underlying value assumptions of its methods are![15]

In an article in *The New York Times* entitled "Prep Schools Explore Ethics," a spokesperson for the National Association for Independent Schools names values education as "probably the hottest issue in private education today."[16] In independent schools, in fact, just as in the public system, teachers are likely to decide individually on the extent and direction of their involvement with current MVE approaches, whether or not these have been discussed with or approved by the principal, the Board, or the students' parents.

None of this is intended as a condemnation of teachers in either public or independent schools. It *is* a questioning of our educational systems and their accountability in the area of moral values education. What is considered "moral" and what is defined as "education" and by what methodology "moral education" is to be achieved, stand, in current practice, as essentially open questions.

Because there is an obvious need to do something in the area of MVE, there is pressure to "buy," and "packages" are readily available. Education journals print articles exhorting teachers to jump on or off the new bandwagon or to adopt one particular approach instead of another. Newspapers run letters to the editor which alternately extol and denounce what is being done with our children in the name of MVE. Not only educators are caught up in this movement, but also psychiatrists, psychologists, sociologists, political scientists, philosophers, and producers of tapes, films, and records. Teachers' unions and MVE consultants are turning out handbooks, mini-courses, and resource lists; they are leading conferences and workshops and conducting numerous projects sponsored by school boards.

---

15 Brian P. Hall, "Values Education and Consciousness: The State of the Art, Challenge in Our Times," Inaugural Address delivered at Seattle University (November 1975).
16 Georgia Dullea, "Prep Schools Explore Ethics," *The New York Times*, 4 May 1975, Section 13, p. 26.

WHY GET INVOLVED?

Despite the fact that the values education movement has been described as the "hottest" and one of the most "explosive" in education today, it remains to many members of the public an unexamined and unknown issue. Understandably, we all tend to read our own interpretation into the words "moral values education" and to let it go at that. Some of us get caught up in the problems of defining the terms, "moral" and "values," and overlook the fundamental forest for the naming of the trees. Still further—and valid— confusion occurs when the "Value" or "Heritage" schools which have been established in different parts of North America are equated with the MVE movement. In fact, most of these schools have been established as a reaction *against* the "moral values" which are being taught through the new MVE approaches.

Most of us, however, simply have not yet realized that MVE is an issue which critically involves *us* as citizens. For example, we are unaware that material in present use ranges from the useful and noncontentious to that which has been ruled outside the law.[17]

Obviously, in a book of this length, it is impossible to attempt a complete analysis of each of the models we shall consider. I would urge the reader to evaluate this issue personally by reviewing classroom materials and the underlying philosophies which they represent. Some of these materials are presented in this book, and others are available through local school boards and libraries. Readers should expect to be favorably impressed by many of the arguments which MVE writers advance to support their particular approaches. Readers should also be sure to examine a broad enough range of the materials to judge whether, in their view, the underlying philosophies and fundamental assumptions are moral, immoral, or amoral.

In order to grasp more clearly the contentious issues which are at stake, it is enlightening to read the critiques which different value educators direct to each other's attention. Unfortunately, many of these critiques are written and read chiefly by academics. Meanwhile, the classroom

17 U.S. Public Law: 95-561, 92 Stat. 2143 (1978). See chapter 7.

material—some of it highly questionable—continues to be used by teachers who may consider that they have neither the time, the training, nor the experience in MVE to question its various approaches, or to question the "experts." Students, for various reasons, don't always tell their parents everything they do at school each day. Whether child or parent, all of us have been part of the suppertime scene which begins with the question,
"What did you do today?"
and ends with the answer,
"Nothing."
Following this familiar pattern, it can be a long time before parents or the general public have any idea of the actual dimensions of the issues and effects arising from MVE.

However, let it be most strongly stated: this is *in no way* a situation in which educators are on one "side" and parents are on the other. It *is* a situation about which all persons concerned with youth and education should inform themselves. It is for this reason that this book includes numerous direct quotations from classroom materials and from the stated philosophies of each of the three approaches examined. These sources are given here so that, at least to some extent, each reader may assess the original material from his or her own point of view.

A second important point must also be emphasized. The purpose of this book is not to condemn values education. For all its attention to the problematic aspects of MVE, the book is intended to be constructive—to suggest that we build on the efforts of those who have constructed present models, and be supportive of educators in their concern for youth, which we all share.

As noted earlier, ethical questions have always been an integral part of academic subjects, whether or not they were specifically articulated or discussed. Now, in a purposeful effort to activate value inquiry, emphasis is on specific examination of these questions. Most of us would be in support of such an educational objective responsibly handled. However few of us realize that for more than fifteen years, U.S. academics and educators have been engaged in heated controversy amongst themselves over what is considered "responsible": which values education strategies should be used with students, and which should not. In 1977 alone, they published an average of a book per week and 200 articles on this issue.[18] A conservative estimate of U.S. books and articles published in the past decade would be over 1000.

However, because these books and articles are chiefly written *by* academics *for* academics, the public, for the most part, has been singularly uninformed about the values education movement, let alone the controversy which surrounds it at its source. Only in 1981 did one government official concede that "the criticisms of the various approaches and their philosophies has been essentially an 'in house' affair."[19] In that our children are the consumers of the new values education, and in that United States taxpayers have been paying for its implementation since the mid 1960s, it is essential that they be party to this controversy. That is the purpose of this book.

Because *Yes Virginia, There Is Right and Wrong!* focuses—for the reasons I have explained—primarily on the contentious and controversial aspects of much current MVE practice, some readers could elect to make the book a vehicle for polarizing men and women of good will into extreme positions. This would be an unfortunate misuse of the purpose of the book. But far more importantly, it would misdirect the energies of those men and women whose contribution is so vital to what is easily one of the most crucial issues shaping the nation's legal, economic and social future. *Yes Virginia* is directed to the "rational moderate," regardless of political, religious or non-religious persuasion, ethnic background or economic status.

If, like many of us, you are inclined to dismiss this controversy as just one more unwelcome issue in an already troubled educational scene—and you are, frankly, feeling rather tired of it all—take a deep breath . . . and read on. The facts have more to do with knowing where your children are and where the nation is heading than most of us would ever suppose.

18 See Introduction to "Moral Education and Secular Humanism," *The Humanist* (November/December 1978), p. 7.
19 Donald M. Santor, Review of Books, *Canadian Materials*, Vol. IX, No. 3, 1981, p. 168.

2

The Values
Clarification Approach

We have always taught children that lying and cheating and stealing are wrong. Parents taught it. Teachers taught it. Not necessarily so anymore. At least not for teachers who follow the popular strategy of Values Clarification.[1] In this model, "right" and "wrong" are entirely relative depending on the situation and especially on the child's point of view at any given time. Most important of all, the child must be free to choose his or her own moral values without the encumbrances of adult "no-nos."

These are the contentions of Louis Raths and his colleague, Sidney Simon, associated with the National Humanistic Education Center and the University of Massachusetts. The Values Clarification programs that they have developed, along with Kirschenbaum, Howe, Harmin, Smith, and others have gained strong support among American, British, and Canadian teachers. Because the support for this model of values education is so strong—as noted earlier, one major study found it by ten times the most popular among

---

1 Two books regarded as basic texts of the Values Clarification approach to moral education are: L. Raths, M. Harmin, and S. Simon, *Values and Teaching: Working with Values in the Classroom*, 1st ed. (Columbus, Ohio: Charles E. Merrill Publishing Co., 1966) (2nd ed., 1978); and S. Simon, L. Howe, and H. Kirschenbaum, *Values Clarification: A Handbook of Practical Strategies for Teachers and Students*, 1st ed. (New York: Hart Publishing Co. Inc., 1972) (rev. ed., 1978).

educators involved in MVE,[2] and sales of one of its basic texts are well over half a million copies—it is the first model we will consider. We will examine the model's underlying philosophy, how this philosophy is translated into exercises in the classroom, and the fundamental questions which these raise.

The developers of Values Clarification maintain that the fundamental failing of traditional approaches to such behavior as lying, cheating, and stealing is that they deal in "indoctrination:" asserting to children that there are "right" and "wrong" ways of thinking and acting. These traditional approaches, they say, have the effect of arresting the development of a child's rational judgment, and can only be described as "totalitarian." Adults have made the mistake of trying to teach children certain moral values because, "to the dictator at least,"[3] such instruction seems more "efficient" than allowing children to choose or create values of their own.

> It is temptingly easy and insidiously gratifying to "mold" children or to "whip them into line" by exercising one's superior status and authority as an adult.[4]

This process, the advocates of Values Clarification maintain, has spawned generations of ethical retardates.

> For thousands of years, the long-term effects have been ignored and sacrificed to short-term adult advantages, most of the time. Probably it is no accident that there are relatively few people who are, or ever will become, psychologically and ethically mature.[5]

SEVEN STEPS TO MORAL VALUES

In the view of those who favor Values Clarification, the only "democratic" route to psychological and ethical maturity is to free children to choose and create their own

---

2 See footnote 10 in chapter 1.
3 Robert F. Peck and Robert J. Havighurst, *The Psychology of Character Development* (New York: John Wiley and Sons Inc., 1960), p. 191.
4 Ibid.
5 Ibid.

values. Specifically, Values Clarification prescribes a seven-step valuing process by which this aim can be achieved.

Choosing: (1) freely
            (2) from alternatives
            (3) after thoughtful consideration of the consequences of each alternative

Prizing: (4) cherishing, being happy with the choice
            (5) enough to be willing to confirm the choice to others

Acting: (6) or doing something with the choice
            (7) repeatedly, in some pattern of life.[6]

In the classroom, the teacher's role is to make this process easier by responding in such a way as to stimulate the child to apply these seven steps to whatever topic or issue the class may be discussing.[7] These discussions are to have no specific goals or purposes beyond offering each child a range of viewpoints from which to choose.

We all need to sort out preferences, feelings, and questions of self-identity, and Values Clarification suggests some classroom exercises which work toward this end in a positive way. For example:

Which do you like best in school?
_____ art
_____ music
_____ gym[8]

Which would you like least to do,
_____ listen to a Beethoven symphony
_____ watch a debate
_____ watch a play.[9]

Most of us would support this type of classroom exercise as being helpful. The issue under discussion is one of personal

---

6 L. Raths et al., *Values and Teaching*, 2nd ed., p. 28.
7 For an explication of this method, see "The Clarifying Response" in L. Raths et al., *Values and Teaching*, 2nd ed., pp. 54-83.
8 S. Simon et al., *Values Clarification: A Handbook*, rev. ed., p. 86.
9 Ibid., p. 65.

preference and feelings, and sharing these can promote understanding of individual differences among people—all opinions being equally valid. A boy, for example, might clarify for himself that it is equally "macho" to like art as it is to like gym.

However, there is a fundamental difference between the stance that all opinions are equally valid with regard to preferences among art, music, and sports (nonmoral issues) and identical treatment of questions concerning basic moral precepts. Regardless of the topic or issue in Values Clarification, laissez faire is the order of the day, and moral content gives way to a process without standards. Moreover, teachers must commit themselves to the view that there is no "right" or "wrong" answer to any question of value that the class may discuss. The teacher, we are told, "avoids moralizing, criticizing, giving values or evaluating. The adult excludes all hints of 'good' or 'right' or 'acceptable' or their opposites."[10]

This strategy provides a new and challenging experience for teacher and class: an exercise without restraint or the discipline of identifying any objective criteria for right and wrong.

THEFT: AN INDIVIDUAL CHOICE

Consistent with the Values Clarification model, let us consider how a discussion on stealing might be developed in a classroom of ten-year-olds. The object is to encourage the children to clarify their values about stealing so that they can be clear about their own individual choices concerning theft, and feel comfortable with these choices. A typical scene might unfold like this:

By way of introducing the topic, the teacher asks the children to compare stealing from Woolworth's to stealing from a boy's locker next to their own.[11] *Possible responses include:*

"I know the boy;" "I don't know the owner of Woolworth's."

10 L. Raths et al., *Values and Teaching,* 2nd ed., p. 55.
11 For a variation on this exercise, see Georgia Dullea, "Prep Schools Explore Ethics," *The New York Times,* 4 May 1975, Section 13, p. 26.

"Woolworth's counts on losing money from people stealing things. They charge me for that when I buy things there."

Next, the teacher asks the children to compare stealing from a likeable boy from a poor home with stealing from an unpopular boy from a well-to-do home, and with stealing from a blind man. The students are asked to weigh the pros and cons of each option and to rank the options on their own individual scale. (Individual responses will vary, but a sample is offered in table 1.)

Now follows free discussion of all opinions offered by the class, with no point of view treated as more "right" or "wrong" than any other. The teacher accepts every child's response as equally valid. The teacher has been told that his or her role is not to examine stealing in terms of right and wrong, but rather to provide a forum within which each student may clarify or create his or her own values. The emphasis is on helping the children feel comfortable with their own decisions. Then the consequences of each of these options are considered.

"The rich boy might steal from ME. But I'll take my chances. He's got better stuff than me."

"I might get caught at Woolworth's and probably get a warning. . . . Then again, I might not get caught. . . . It's worth a try."

The options are accepted without criticism.

One child—who, in light of the above discussion, would have to be particularly strong minded—might say:

"I think that stealing is always wrong."

The teacher may respond by introducing a further "clarifying" question.

"If you were a parent and your child was starving, would you steal food for him or her?"

"Of course," many of the children would agree.

Now to some ten-year-olds this newly discovered fact is revolutionary.

"It sure contradicts what Mom and Dad always said about stealing being just plain wrong!"

Discussion is not directed to the fact that although there are times when one moral value must take precedence over another, this does not negate the intrinsic goodness of not

Table 1. Sample of Values Clarification Exercise re: Stealing: Rating of Alternatives by One Child

PARENT STEALS BREAD FOR STARVING CHILD	+10
NOT STEALING AT ALL	0
STEALING FROM WOOLWORTH'S	−2
STEALING FROM RICH BOY	−5
STEALING FROM POOR BOY	−10
STEALING FROM BLIND MAN	−15

stealing. How are the children in this class clarifying their values? What are they learning? They are learning that the act of stealing should be considered relative to a particular situation, that the "right" or "wrong" of theft depends on the circumstances, the people involved, and the individual's point of view. They learn this through the very nature of the exercise administered by their teacher—and that is important, because the teacher thereby legitimizes this relativism. The teacher's uncritical acceptance of all points of view adds a very different dimension to the children's thinking than if the children were exposed to the same points of view, rapping with their peers in the schoolyard.

What is the likely result of this experience? Certainly the child's consciousness has been raised in terms of the options that relate to stealing. It is now clear in the children's minds that there are many levels of response to the concept of theft. They have certainly been left free to decide what point of view to adopt. It can, therefore, hardly be considered surprising if children decide that Woolworth's and the well-off boy are fair game:

"Woolworth's can afford it. They rip us all off, anyway."

"Peterson is a bully. Nobody likes him ... but I don't go for stealing from blind people."

The steps in the Values Clarification process have been followed meticulously. Values have been freely chosen. The class is dismissed. All that remains is for the students to act on their own individual decisions. It is quite possible that children may proceed to apply their new concepts of the relative value of theft to many situations. Taking fifty cents from Dad's bureau, for example, isn't as bad as taking a dollar ... and so it goes. In Values Clarification, the particular value the child adopts is not an issue. Raths, Harmin, and Simon put it this way:

> What the adult does do is create conditions that aid children in finding values *if* they choose to do so. When operating within this value theory, it is entirely possible that children will choose not to develop values. It is the teacher's responsibility to support this choice also. . . .[12]

> It is not impossible to conceive of someone going through the seven value criteria and deciding that he values intolerance or thievery. What is to be done? Our position is that we respect his right to decide upon that value.[13]

Some educators like Ivan Cassidy, Professor of Education at Acadia University, protest:

> This statement carries the ideal of individuality to the point where one can no longer distinguish between the moral and the immoral. Can an educational theory produce a dishonest person and then merely say that the choice of dishonesty is a legitimate expression of individual preference?[14]

---

12 L. Raths et al., *Values and Teaching*, 2nd ed., p. 48.
13 Ibid., 1st ed., p. 227.
14 Ivan Cassidy, "Values Educators Test the Spirits," *Journal of Education*, sixth series, vol. 3, no. 4 (Summer 1976), p. 25.

I do not intend to suggest that issues such as stealing should not be discussed with children. They encounter many situations in this and other areas of moral choice, and they must learn to confront and cope with what they encounter. Children are very discerning these days, and they generally "tell it like it is:"

"I saw you keep the wrong change."

"My Mom returned a dress she'd worn to two parties."

"Our Math teacher told us that he faked his ID at taverns when he was sixteen."

"My Dad set the mileage back when he sold our old car."

Directly and indirectly, theft is an increasing problem in our society. In his book, *Ripoff*, show business's Steve Allen documents the enormity of the issue. In the United States alone, petty thievery such as shoplifting costs retailers 15 billion dollars a year.[15]

Of course, theft and other moral issues must be faced and examined realistically. Of course, we need values education which calls a spade a spade and is willing to tackle *with* students the realities of their lives. Of course, children need to know and feel that they can say to teachers and parents what they are honestly thinking. And certainly children do *not* need an autocratic, preprocessed, prepackaged, dehydrated "obvious answer" laid on them in return.

All these possible objections to some of the mistakes of the past are valid, and it is these mistakes that Values Clarification sets out to counteract. But, as in many movements, the pendulum has now swung to the opposite extreme.

Consider the following Values Clarification session on cheating, which I have quoted here in full, and which is held by its authors to be exemplary. If, as an adult, *you* are confused as you work through this teacher's "rationale" on cheating, ask yourself where it would leave a child. Ask yourself to what degree this type of analysis contributes to the statistics on cheating and stealing, which are skyrocketing.

Teacher: So some of you think it is best to be honest on

---

15 Steve Allen, *Ripoff: The Corruption That Plagues America* (Secaucus, N.J.: Lyle Stewart, 1979).

tests, is that right? (Some heads nod affirmatively.) And some of you think dishonesty is all right? (A few hesitant and slight nods.) And I guess some of you are not certain. (Heads nod.) Well, are there any other choices or is it just a matter of dishonesty vs. honesty?

Sam: You could be honest some of the time and dishonest some of the time.

Teacher: Does that sound like a possible choice, class? (Heads nod.) Any other alternatives to choose from?

Tracy: You could be honest in some situations and not in others. For example, I am not honest when a friend asks about an ugly dress, at least sometimes. (Laughter.)

Teacher: Is that a possible choice, class? (Heads nod again.) Any other alternatives?

Sam: It seems to me that you have to be all one way or all the other.

Teacher: Just a minute, Sam. As usual we are first looking for the alternatives that there are in this issue. Later we'll try to look at any choice that you may have selected. Any other alternatives, class? (No response.) Well, then, let's list the four possibilities that we have on the board and I'm going to ask that each of you do two things for yourself: (1) see if you can identify any other choices in this issue of honesty and dishonesty, and, (2) consider the consequences of each alternative and see which ones you prefer. Later, we will have buzz groups in which you can discuss this and see if you are able to make a choice and if you want to make your choice part of your actual behavior. This is something you must do for yourself.

Ginger: Does that mean that we can decide for ourselves whether we should be honest on tests here?

Teacher: No, that means that you can decide on the value. I personally value honesty; and although you may choose to be dishonest, I shall insist that we be honest on our tests here. In other areas of your life, you may have more freedom to be dishonest, but one can't do anything any time, and in this class I shall expect honesty on tests.

Ginger: But then how can we decide for ourselves? Aren't you telling us what to value?

Sam: Sure, you're telling us what we should do and believe in.

Teacher: Not exactly. I don't mean to tell you what you should value. That's up to you. But I do mean that in this class, not elsewhere necessarily, you have to be honest on tests or suffer certain consequences. I merely mean that I cannot give tests without the rule of honesty. All of you who choose dishonesty as a value may not practice it here, that's all I'm saying. Further questions, anyone?[16]

The authors suggest that in such sessions, teachers help "students [to] develop an intelligent and viable relationship with their worlds, that is, develop clear values."[17] Can they be serious? Isn't the message many students would carry away from such a session rather: *On this matter of cheating, just do whatever you think at the time. There's nothing right or wrong about cheating in itself. But be cool. Check out the scene. Know your audience.*

Is this the best process that we have to offer our children for clarifying their values? Some adults may consider the seven steps of Values Clarification to be "clear," even "intelligent" ... but moral? Yet teachers who follow these strategies are caught. They must avoid giving moral justification for their positions because this would be tantamount to implying that the opposite position is wrong. Two Carnegie Council national surveys studied the incidence of admitted student cheating in 1969 and again in 1976. In the best known universities, the increase was 87%.[18]

"GETTING FURTHER INTO YOUR HEAD"

Because of general concern that many parents and religious institutions no longer offer children the right amount or kind of emotional and psychological guidance, a major emphasis in Values Clarification is on requiring children to

16 L. Raths et al., *Values and Teaching*, 1st ed., pp. 114-115.
17 Ibid., 1st ed., p. 115.
18 Cited in Edward A. Wynne, "Simple Honesty: A Complicated Matter," *Character*, Vol. 2. Number 2, December 1980, p. 10.

probe and question all aspects of their thoughts, feelings, and fantasies. Typical materials deal with developing one's identity and self-image, "getting in touch" with oneself, "feeling good" about oneself, the meaning of life and death, and so forth.

To promote being in touch with one's feelings and being clear about one's values—regardless of what these may be —Simon and his colleagues have devised many classroom "strategies" designed to open children up to themselves and to one another. These strategies include role-playing games, in-depth self-analysis exercises, sensitivity activities, contrived incidents, simulations, religious and self-doubts diaries,[19] in which students bring "an enormous amount of information about themselves into class to be examined and discussed."[20] They are advocated for children from kindergarten age onward.

If one accepts the premise that schools should be heavily involved in this area of children's development, some of these exercises are appropriate to the age and experience of the child. Others are shocking because of the naïveté with which they are proposed for use among children, and because of their potential for deep psychological harm. While literally scores of books and articles on Values Clarification are widely used, L. Raths' *Values and Teaching*[21] and S. Simon's *Values Clarification: A Handbook of Practical Strategies for Teachers and Students*[22] are considered the basic texts of the Values Clarification approach, the latter, as noted, having sold over half a million copies. The exercises in Values Clarification which I have chosen as examples of classroom materials are taken, with two exceptions, from these two books. This has been done in order that readers may see that these materials are not outside the mainstream of MVE strategies. They are not isolated horror exercises compiled over time from a wide variety of obscure sources. Rather, readers will find that either one or both of these books are recommended for classroom use in federal and

19 S. Simon et al., *Values Clarification: A Handbook*, (rev. ed.) pp. 390-391.
20 Ibid., p. 388.
21 By L. Raths et al.
22 By S. Simon et al.

state department of education materials, by values education committees of boards of education, by curriculum
consultants and, almost without exception wherever the
Values Clarification approach is being promoted. Even four
years ago, it was estimated that over 200,000 teachers and
other counsellors had been trained in Values Clarification
workshops,[23] and an indeterminate number have been encouraged in this approach outside formal sessions.

As we have noted, some of the exercises in this approach
are useful. The following are typical of those which were
discussed by Congress,[24] have raised public protest, brought
law suits[25] and suspended programs.[26]

LIFE RAFT

Consider the familiar dilemma called "Life Raft," which is
recommended to help children to clarify their self-worth.
There are many variations of this exercise and teachers are
encouraged to invent still others. Sometimes each child is
assigned a particular character to role-play in the situation.
In other versions, such as the following one, participants
keep their own identities. The process is quoted here in its
entirety.

   I. *(A) The facilitator instructs the group [of 10] to sit in the
   middle of the floor, in a formation resembling a life raft.
   He sets the scene by asking the participants to imagine
   they have been on an Atlantic cruise, that a serious
   storm has developed, that their ship has been struck by
   lightening, [sic] and that they have all had to get into a
   life raft. He explains that the major problem that now
   exists is that the raft has room and food enough for only
   nine persons and there are ten in the group. One
   person must be sacrificed in order to save the rest. The
   facilitator informs the group that the decision is to be*

---

23 See Introduction to "Moral Education and Secular Humanism," *The
   Humanist*, (November/December 1978), p. 7. The article first appeared
   in *The Humanist*, and is reprinted by permission.
24 H. Kirschenbaum, *Advanced Values Clarification*, p. 151.
25 See, for example, pp. 119-120, 153, 174-175, 201.
26 See, for example, " 'Values' Instruction Suspended," *The Milwaukee
   Journal*, 27 November 1975.

made by group consensus: each member is to "plead his case" to the others, arguing why he should live, and then the group is to decide who must go overboard. He tells the participants that they have one-half hour to make their decision. At the end of that time, the life raft will sink if there are still ten people in it. He puts a manual alarm clock near the participants so that they can hear it tick and sets the alarm to go off in one-half hour.

(B) At intervals during the decision-making process, the facilitator notifies the group of the time remaining.

II. The facilitator leads the group in processing the dynamics and the feelings that have emerged during the activity. Since the experience is powerful, sufficient time (one-half hour or more) must be allowed to complete this task successfully.

III. The facilitator then directs the group to brainstorm the values that are implicit in the situation they have just experienced. He asks the following questions:

1. What kind of value assumptions did members of the group make?
2. What values were the members acting on?
3. What did you learn about your values from an experiential standpoint?
4. In light of this experience, how do you value your own life and the lives of others?
5. What is your worth?[27]

What happens to the self-worth of the participant who—by the group's decision—is voted to be thrown out of the life raft and die? What happens to the self-identity of the others who, by aggression, grandiose promises, ability to "read" the group's sentiment, by emotive appeals, or by any other means, are voted to remain in the life raft and live? Are students to conclude that this is what "developing one's self-worth" is all about?

---

27 Reprinted from Maury Smith, A Practical Guide to Value Clarification, (San Diego, CA: University Associates, 1977), pp. 120-121. Used with permission.

The Life Raft

Instructions to the facilitators simply direct them to "lead the group in processing the dynamics and the feelings that have emerged during the activity." How simple life would be if the dynamics of such a powerful and dangerous session could be processed like so much cheese! And within the half hour or more that Smith recommends.

What happens to all ten of these students when the bell rings and they go out for recess together? Will this Values Clarification session be quickly forgotten? Or will it continue to haunt at least some members in the group even when they are adults?

THE FALL-OUT SHELTER PROBLEM

Strategy No. 48 in Sidney Simon's *Values Clarification: A Handbook of Strategies for Teachers and Students* is The Fall-Out Shelter Problem, "a simulated problem-solving exercise."[28] This exercise gives a group of six or seven children the authority, as members of a department in Washington, D.C., to decide which four of ten people will be driven out of a fall-out shelter as the Third World War breaks out and bombs are falling everywhere. The six who are allowed to remain may be the sole survivors left to perpetuate the human race. Again, the children have half an hour to choose the six most "worthy." Here is all the information about the ten people in the shelter which can be given to the six children who are to decide their fate:

1. *Bookkeeper; 31 years old*
2. *His wife; six months pregnant*
3. *Black militant; second year medical student*
4. *Famous historian-author; 42 years old*
5. *Hollywood starlet; singer; dancer*
6. *Bio-chemist*
7. *Rabbi; 54 years old*
8. *Olympic athlete; all sports*
9. *College co-ed*
10. *Policeman with gun (they cannot be separated).*[29]

28 S. Simon et al., *Values Clarification: A Handbook*, rev. ed., p. 281.
29 Ibid., p. 283.

Does such an exercise generate problem solving? Or does it encourage stereotyping on the basis of such characteristics as occupation or age? Because the students are given no information about the qualities of heart or the commitment to human service or even the level of occupational competence of the persons at their mercy, they can make nothing but totally superficial judgments. In fact, in a concluding note to the teacher, Simon appears to reinforce the process of stereotyping:

> If one of the fall-out shelter candidates that we have provided, or that you may create yourself, gets consistently eliminated, simply give that candidate(s) more skills, or make him more attractive in some way; for example, lower his age.[30]

CAVE-IN SIMULATION

Directly after the Fall-Out Shelter exercise, there follows Strategy No. 49, the Cave-In simulation. It is similar to the Life Raft, except that it makes the "grading" of the "worth" of each boy and girl in the classroom even more specific:

The teacher has the students sit close together in one corner of the classroom, on the floor, if possible. He turns out the lights and pulls down all the shades. He puts a lighted candle in the center of the group. Then he explains the situation.

The class, on an outing to some nearby caves, has been trapped hundreds of feet below the ground by a cave-in. There is a narrow passageway leading up and out of the cavern where they are trapped. Night is coming fast and there is no one around for miles to help. They decide they will form a single file and try to work their way out of the cave. But at any moment there might be another rock slide. The ones nearest to the front of the line have the best chances for survival. Each member of the class will give his reasons for why he should be at the head of the line. After hearing each other's reasons, they will determine the order by which they will file out.[31]

30 Ibid., pp. 285-286.
31 Ibid., pp. 287-288.

The guilt and confusion and the reported nightmares which this type of exercise leads to are not difficult to imagine. What *is* difficult to realize is the degree of naïveté required of an adult educator or parent who will agree that children should be put through such experiences in the name of values education. One's first reaction on reading that such materials exist is, quite naturally, "But they can't be using them!" "This can't be *actually happening!*" On November 28, 1981, *The Catholic Register* ran a 7-page Special Edition on Values Education, headed "Hottest Issue in Public Education." It gave numerous accounts by teachers, parents, students. Regarding the "Life Raft" exercise:

> *Ten students were placed on a "raft" in a swimming pool and asked to act out the dilemma. After some discussion, the students decided which two among them were least worthy to remain in the raft. Then they grabbed these two, fully clothed, and tossed them into the pool. One of the boys ejected was colored; the other was an epileptic who had been in a special education class.*

> *The mother of the epileptic student told* The Register *she was "terribly upset" by the incident. "The principal didn't even want to talk to me about it. I asked him: Suppose my son had a seizure?"*[32]

Parents and teachers should check out state and local board of education guidelines and actual resource materials in use. Many State Curriculum Guides (Maryland to name only one[33]), recommend Simon's *Values Clarification: A Handbook* for children of all ages from kindergarten forward. This is the book which includes: *Fall-Out Shelter* (Strategy No. 48); the *Cave-In Simulation* (Strategy No. 49); and *Obituary* (Strategy No. 56). It is designed to help ten-year-olds clarify the quality and meaning of their lives.

---

32 Stan Koma, "Hottest Issue In Public Education," *The Catholic Register*, November 28, 1981, p. 1.
33 "New Perspectives in Inter-Group Education," (Resource Materials), *Maryland State Department of Education*, September, 1975.

OBITUARY

The teacher says, "We are going to look at life by viewing it again from the perspective of death. I am going to ask you to write out your own obituary. Here is a simple format, although you are free to write your obituary in your own form. You can use as many of these suggestions as you wish, or add your own."

James Clark, age 10 died yesterday from . . .
He was a member . . .
He is survived by . . .
At the time of his death he was working on becoming . . .
He will be remembered for . . .
He will be mourned by . . . because . . .
The world will suffer the loss of his contribution in the areas of . . .
He always wanted, but he never got to . . .
The body will be . . .
Flowers may be sent . . .
In lieu of flowers . . .

When everyone is finished, students may volunteer to read their obituaries out loud, or they might share their obituaries in smaller, more personal and supportive groups. . . .

To The Teacher

Try not to generate a lot of anxiety about this exercise. Treat it matter-of-factly, but seriously. Give some comfort to the few students who will be very resistant. Let them know that this is not everyone's cup of tea; but also support those students who really get into the exercise and are trying to learn from it what it has to teach.[34]

That this is surely not every 10-year-old's "cup of tea" is a devastating understatement. In fact, it may be a very questionable activity for many highly vulnerable teenagers. One department of education has recommended that: "Having students write their own obituaries is a useful exercise to help them discover who they are, what they

34 S. Simon et al., *Values Clarification: A Handbook*, 1st ed., pp. 311-313.

want, what they can offer...."[35] But if the objective is to consider such possible directions in life, why is it useful to "view [life] again from the perspective of death?" Wouldn't it be a more positive, up-beat activity to ask students to write their own press releases 5-10 years from now? "Pat Smith is entering architecture...."

It must be asked: What mandate have our schools been given to undertake such exercises? How many parents have been consulted about the inclusion of such material in their children's program? Consider the load of individual anxieties which can be aroused through probing such topics as self-worth and death to the depths suggested by exercises like these. Add to this hazard the enormously complex influences of group dynamics. Put in charge a teacher—no matter how well intentioned—who has had no special training for directing this mixture of psychodrama and group therapy and, according to many child psychiatrists, you have enormous potential for inflicting lasting psychological damage on children.

RANK ORDERING

So far, we have looked at some examples of Values Clarification strategies with regard to issues such as stealing, cheating, self-worth, survival, and decision making. Another major category of exercises claims to help students clarify their values by requiring them to rank order their choices among several possibilities. For example, Simon suggests the following situation be discussed by "you and your family at the dinner table, or your friends across the lunch table."[36]

Your husband or wife is a very attractive person. Your best friend is very attracted to him or her. How would you want them to behave?

☐ *Maintain a clandestine relationship so you wouldn't know about it.*

---

35 "The Valuing Process: Developing a Personal Value System," *Guidance: Curriculum Guideline for the Senior Division*, Ontario Ministry of Education (Toronto: 1977), p. 11.
36 S. Simon, *Meeting Yourself Halfway* (Niles, Illinois: Argus Communications, 1974), p. 44.

☐ *Be honest and accept the reality of the relationship.*
☐ *Proceed with a divorce.*[37]

In a critique of Values Clarification in *The Public Interest,* the authors argue that in these exercises, Simon repeatedly fails to honor his claim to encourage free choice. The range of options he offers for conduct is so severely limiting and misleading that it implicitly promotes "hasty, ill-informed, ignorant and precipitous judgment [rather] than any kind of informed free choice."[38] Concerning the example quoted above, they point out:

> Typically the spouse and best friend are presented as having desires they will eventually satisfy anyway. The student is offered only choices that presuppose their relationship. All possibilities for self-restraint, fidelity, regard for others, or respect for mutual relationships and commitments are ignored.[39]

Despite their claim to value neutrality, the Values Clarifiers seem oblivious to the fact that they continually build their own values into the very methodology of their strategies. For even though, in another book, Simon mentions that students might wish to add additional alternatives to the choices given by the teacher, he stipulates that this offer should be made "after the initial ranking is completed".[40]

VOTING

Both the Simon and Raths books recommend the Voting strategy, the purpose of which is to bring "to the verbal level issues and ideas that might otherwise be difficult to make public."[41] (Why it should be necessary for these issues and ideas to be made public is another question.) The teacher asks a number of questions and students show their

37 Ibid., p. 49.
38 William J. Bennett and Edwin J. Delattre, "Moral Education in the Schools," *The Public Interest,* no. 50 (Winter 1978), p. 86. Reprinted with permission of the authors. Copyright© 1978, by National Affairs Inc.
39 Ibid.
40 S. Simon et al., *Values Clarification: A Handbook,* rev. ed., p. 60.
41 L. Raths et al., *Values and Teaching,* 1st ed., p. 152.

answer by raising their hands. Simon suggests the following questions for "General Use with All Ages:"

How many of you
. . . have ever had problems so bad you wished you could die so you wouldn't have to face them?
. . . think that most students feel free to talk with their parents?
. . . would like to have different parents?
. . . would like to have a secret lover?[42]

Raths comments: "A simple vote, with no one talking but the teacher, can lead to a lot of clarifying thinking."[43] How so? By allowing each student to see the number in the class who agree or disagree with his or her view? Why do students need to discover whether or not they are with the majority? Should this knowledge affect their thinking? If influencing the child's thinking is not one of the purposes of the exercise, then why the "vote" in front of the class?

In spite of its proposed emphasis on individuality and its statements about avoiding peer pressure, many Values Clarification strategies make very questionable use of the group as a powerful tool. Raths points out, for instance: "Sometimes a view of another's life removes guilt from our own lives; this happens when we find that what we think or do is not so terrible or unusual."[44] Depending on the particular issue involved, freedom from guilt may be very healthy—or very dangerous. But then, in the Values Clarification philosophy, the child's own preference (or those of peers?) determines what constitutes "health." In either case, such "group-share" exercises, which ask students to bare their most intimate thoughts publicly can be a gross exploitation of the vulnerability of children and youth, and a direct violation of their right to privacy.

THE CLARIFYING RESPONSE

A basic technique in Values Clarification, the clarifying response, can imply another bias. For example, in response

42 S. Simon et al., *Values Clarification: A Handbook*, 1st ed., pp. 41-46.
43 L. Raths et al., *Values and Teaching*, 1st ed., p. 153.
44 L. Raths et al., *Values and Teaching*, 2nd ed., p. 171.

to a student who makes a direct statement of conviction, the teacher might ask: *"Do you think that people will always believe that?"* or *"Would Chinese peasants and African hunters also believe that?"* or *"Did people long ago believe that?"*[45]

Thus the concepts of cultural and moral relativism are introduced, and the students are encouraged to apply these criteria to their value formation—"Such questions," say the value clarifiers, "are useful to suggest to a student that his beliefs may be unknowingly influenced by his surroundings, by his social milieu. It helps him gauge the extent to which he may be conforming."[46] But, by encouraging students to conform to the criteria of cultural and moral relativism, are educators not running the risk of imposing *this* set of values on them?

THE PUBLIC INTERVIEW

Another technique for "opening up" students is the "Public Interview." A student chooses to be interviewed in front of the class. Either the student or the teacher may pick the topic for the interview, and the questions asked are intended to "clarify" the student's values related to this topic. The student who does not wish to answer a particular question during the interview may say, "I pass." The student may also terminate the interview before the allotted time, by saying, "Thank you for your questions."

The following interview, which appears in *Values and Teaching*, is an example of this technique in the classroom. The teacher has chosen Paul as the first student to be interviewed; she describes him as "a rather secure boy, a safe bet for a new venture."

Teacher: Fine, Paul, now on what topic would you like to be interviewed?

Paul: My sister.

Teacher: Would you care to tell us something about your sister, Paul?

45 L. Raths et al., *Values and Teaching*, 1st ed., p. 62.
46 Ibid.

Paul: Not especially. Except that we hate each other. I want to be interviewed, asked questions, rather than just to say something.

Teacher: O.K., Paul. What do you hate about your sister?

Paul: Well, she is two years younger than I am, and she is always in the way. Like she argues about what TV program to watch, and she hangs around me when I'm playing, and she . . . she is just a nuisance.

Teacher: Are there some times when you like having her around?

Paul: No, absolutely not. (Laughter.)

Teacher: How do you define hate? What do you mean by that word?

Paul: Terrible. Like I want to murder her. She should go away.

Teacher: What's the difference between hate and dislike?

Paul: One is stronger. Hate is stronger.

Teacher: What is the difference between hating someone and hating things that the person does?

Paul: Hmm. I just thought of a time when I didn't hate my sister. Once we were walking along and someone said how nice we looked together, we were younger and were walking hand in hand. It was a good feeling. But, I don't know. If you hate enough things a person does, I guess you end up hating the person. Is that right?

Teacher: What do you think?

Paul: I don't know.

Teacher: Paul, what are you going to do about the situation between you and your sister? Apparently you don't like things the way they are.

Paul: What can I do? I know what I'd like to do . . . (Laughter.)

Teacher: Well, one thing you can do is keep away from her. Another is to try and work things out so that there is less *argument and conflict between you. What other alternatives are there?*

Paul: I don't know. I don't know. But thank you for your questions. Can I go now?

Teacher: Certainly, Paul. That's the rule. Whenever you want. Thank you. (Moving to the front of the class.) Maybe we'll ask for another volunteer for a public interview tomorrow, but now let's get ready for our arithmetic work.[47]

Promoters of this technique see its purpose as giving a feeling of importance to the student who is interviewed and, more important, giving "the classroom teacher a vehicle for getting lives revealed to each other in more than a superficial what-did-you-do-over-the-weekend fashion."[48] No consideration is given, however, to the possibility that although Paul may appear to be "a rather secure boy," he may, in fact, be extremely anxious about his hatred for his sister and his feeling of wanting "to murder her." Shortly after he has made this statement he terminates the interview abruptly by saying, "I don't know. I don't know . . . Can I go now?" This response to his teacher's probing questions may well indicate Paul's inability to handle the feelings with which the experience of the interview has confronted him.

In the opinion of many child psychologists and psychiatrists, teachers, who are generally totally untrained in diagnostic assessment, despite their best intentions, play with fire when they employ these techniques. They do not understand the implications of unleashing such highly charged emotions, or the results which can follow outside the classroom. If a student decides to let the teacher choose the topic of the interview, Raths points out:

> then a good part of the excitement is to see what topics the teacher hits upon. . . . Some questions that have proven provocative are:
>
> > *Are there things you would not tell even best friends?*

47 L. Raths et al., *Values and Teaching*, 2nd ed., pp. 170-171.
48 Ibid., p. 171.

What kinds of things, and why?
Would you bring up your children differently from
the way you are being brought up? How and why?[49]

Technically, the student being interviewed has the option
to "pass" on a question. But as a teacher in one survey
points out:

> The "I pass" strategy doesn't serve its intended purpose
> [to give students freedom to say nothing without
> consequent pressure from others]. Outside of class,
> kids apply pressure. [It] goes into personal areas which
> teachers can't handle. Values seem to be relative.[50]

There is also some question whether Values Clarifiers
invariably accept a nonresponse. In discussing the filling
out of Daily Reaction Sheets, Raths points out:

> It is important to realize that there will be some
> resistance from students who feel that this kind of
> questioning borders on prying or invading privacy. We
> inform students that they have the right to leave any
> questions blank any time. (However, to leave any
> particular question blank for three or more times may
> also bring forth a gentle "why" from the teacher.)[51]

In these strategies of group confrontation, confession,
role playing, and the use of the group to "get lives revealed
to each other," many readers will recognize the techniques
of group therapy[52] and sensitivity training. Even a cursory
review of the contents of the popular *Humanistic Education
Sourcebook* edited by Donald Read and Sidney Simon
shows the reliance on these techniques:

> "Letting Go: Emotion in the Classroom," by Kent
> Owen;

49 Ibid., p. 172.
50 Appendix C, *The Moral Education Project (Year 3)*, (Spiral Bound
    Edition), Ontario Institute for Studies in Education (Toronto: 1976),
    p. 6.
51 L. Raths et al., *Values and Teaching*, 2nd ed., p. 161.
52 For a systematic comparison of Client-Centred Therapy and Values
    Clarification, see Alan L. Lockwood, "A Critical View of Values Clarifi-
    cation," *Teachers College Record*, vol. 77, no. 1 (1975), pp. 35-50.

"Depth Unfoldment Experience: A Method for Creating Interpersonal Closeness," by Herbert A. Otto;
"Sensitivity Modules," by Howard Kirschenbaum;
"Encounter Groups . . . May Loom as a Potential Source of Salvation," by John D. Black;
"Education and Therapy," by Walter M. Lifton.[53]

In the late 1960s many adults learned from painful experience that to take part in sensitivity training and encounter groups led by untrained people can be disastrous. Literally thousands of people laid themselves open to enormous psycho-social damage. Recognizing this, many are concerned that now, in the name of values education, the same techniques are being applied to children in the classroom, often without parents' knowledge or consent.

For all that has been said—and much of it has been valid—to the effect that it is better for teachers to discuss moral issues with children in the classroom than to leave them to discuss the same issues with their classmates in the schoolyard, there is another side of the matter to be considered. If the teacher is merely going to throw issues such as stealing, cheating, and lying wide open for discussion and *leave* them wide open, with no reference or deference to the consideration of right and wrong, chances are that many adults would definitely opt for the rap in the schoolyard. For whether or not Simon and his colleagues wish to recognize it, what teachers stand for can have enormous influence on students. In the Values Clarification approach to moral education, the position of teachers plainly is: "Values are relative, personal, and situational."[54] Can our society afford—or even survive—this potentially fragmenting indoctrination of its young people?

REACTIONS FROM TEACHERS

What do teachers think of the Values Clarification approach? In 1974/75, a government-sponsored Moral Educa-

---

53 Donald A. Read and Sidney B. Simon, eds., *Humanistic Education Sourcebook* (Englewood Cliffs, N.J.: Prentice Hall Inc., 1975). (Table of Contents).
54 S. Simon and H. Kirschenbaum, *Readings in Values Clarification,* (Minneapolis: Winston Press, 1973), p. 11.

tion Project undertook to poll some reactions. Structured interviews were conducted with classroom teachers, principals, and co-ordinators who were participating in moral education programs under five different school boards. Here are some of the teachers' comments quoted in that year's annual report of the project:

> One of the things that Simon and Kirschenbaum tend to leave us a little uneasy with is that they are concerned with process; content seems to be almost irrelevant. You can teach the process in any content ... anything goes. Our commitment is much more to content than that. DR

> FOUND USEFUL—to ... raise questions and get the kids to think them through and hopefully go through a process and also to learn some content as they go through it.

> ... in the beginning it was a handle that I could take and use right away. I have found it really works ... gives background to handle situations. GB

> I think it takes a really skilled person. It's the humanitarian approach that I like but it can go farther than that if a person wants to go down that route and I think you get into a lot of situations where maybe you're really opening kids up and I wonder whether ... people ... really know what they're getting into. RB

> The reaction to those kind of techniques (clarification) was really positive. I didn't believe that ... they were really enthusiastic and wanted to do more. The only negative thing is that a lot of them (students) think it's a waste of time ... isn't strictly history, or geography ... but I think they still enjoy it. PE

> I use Simon in Grade 9 to help to learn to work together in groups ... I've tried to use it to improve self-image but found it difficult to cut out killer statements. RW

> I've had students argue that it's right to steal ... you can identify the issues, you can do that; there's no

conviction there. You begin with the principle that a leader is amoral, that he can do what he wants to. How do you argue with that? You can clarify the issue ... you can be as logical as anything and come up with all kinds of evil conclusions. PVH[55]

The Association for Values Education Research at the University of British Columbia describes the reaction of one teacher whom they had instructed in the Values Clarification approach as part of a comparative study they were undertaking to assess the effectiveness of various MVE approaches.

This teacher's initial reactions to the materials and approaches were most enthusiastic; here was something eminently *practical*—in the sense in which that term is used by the student teacher faced with his first practicum. Two weeks later his response was much the same: the strategies really do work, they really get the students making choices and discussing their values. After a further fortnight, however, his comments were much mellowed. He still saw the values clarification strategies as being tremendously effective in getting value issues onto the table and in stimulating discussion about them, but the more he applied the strategies in his classroom the less he could see any worthwhile point being achieved: the students list their preferences, they take sides, they discuss and discuss, and they tell how they feel about things. But all the talking seems just so much babble which, though enjoyable in itself, leads no place.[56]

Despite its controversial aspects, the widely differing opinions of educators, and the imprecise instruments that are available to measure its results,[57] Values Clarification

55 Appendix C, *The Moral Education Project (Year 3)*, (Spiral Bound Edition), pp. 6-7.
56 Murray Elliott, "Clarity Is Not Enough," *Four Papers on Moral Education*, Association for Values Education Research, Faculty of Education, University of British Columbia, Report no. 3 (Vancouver, B.C.: 1974), p. 70.
57 See D. Superka and P. Johnson with C. Ahrens, *Values Education: Approaches and Materials* (Boulder, Colorado: Social Science Education Consortium and ERIC Clearinghouse for Social/Science Education, 1975), p. 142.

remains the preferred approach for an overwhelming majority of teachers involved in MVE. One reason may be that many Values Clarification exercises are clearly laid out, appear easy to apply, and seem to require the minimum of study or preparation. In the already crowded schedule of most teachers, these are very positive advantages. In the February 1978 edition of the *Moral Education Forum*, the editors make an important observation:

> The Values Clarification approach continues to draw heavy criticism and despite less than convincing rebuttal, the movement's momentum continues quite unaffected. Such a phenomenon raises interesting questions of its own.[58]

The strong point of the Values Clarification approach is that it is useful in helping students to become aware of their own values. It can be useful in cautioning us anew against restrictive forms of moral education. Feelings, preferences, and emotions are a very important part of life. However, they should not be construed as being more fundamental than rational clarity and moral principles when it comes to distinguishing right from wrong. In its moral and individual relativism, Values Clarification fails to distinguish the fundamental difference between a moral and a nonmoral question. It treats issues such as stealing and lying in the same way as preferences in sport or recreation. This gives the individual the illusion of possessing expertise and power in decision making without helping him or her to recognize or examine the responsibilities involved. For example, as Alan Lockwood explains,

> The advocates of values clarification do not seriously entertain such fundamental questions as: assuming Adolf Hitler, Charles Manson, Martin Luther King, and Albert Schweitzer held values which met the seven criteria, [see page 26] are their values equally valid, praiseworthy, and/or good?[59]

58 L. Kuhmerker and D. Cochrane, "From the Editor's Desk," *Moral Education Forum*, vol. III, no. 1 (February 1978), p. 1.
59 Alan L. Lockwood, "A Critical View of Values Clarification," *Teachers College Record*, vol. 77, no. 1 (1975), p. 46.

Lockwood strikes at the very heart of the matter. The method of dealing with stealing and cheating; the question of self-worth as opposed to the survival of others; decision making with regard to the Fall-out Shelter and with regard to other open-ended group exercises such as class voting and the public interview all reinforce Lockwood's point. Further, we have noted that the Values Clarification model does not require students to confront the process of justifying the values they hold, or of learning how to evaluate or analyse critically a situation where two or more values conflict. For many, these factors confine the positive aspects of Values Clarification to far more superficial limits than responsible value inquiry demands.[60]

In contrast to the weakness of the positive aspects of Values Clarification methods, the negative possibilities of these methods are substantial, and the risk of using them is high. Many hold that Values Clarification not only strikes at the very foundation of our system of justice, but also undermines the highest ideals upon which viable societies have been founded. They take this position because this model suggests to our youth that whatever values each person chooses will be right for him or her because he or she chooses them. This teaching in our schools is unprecedented—if not revolutionary. It offers us all the dangers of uncharted entry into an orderless moral environment, which may be irreversibly damaging.

---

60 For further discussion, see John S. Stewart, "Clarifying Values Clarification: A Critique," *Phi Delta Kappan*, vol. 6, no. 10 (June 1975), pp. 684-688.

3

Cognitive Moral Development: The Moral Reasoning Approach

CHOICE OF CHILDREN

Suppose that your house is on fire and two young children are in two adjacent rooms. You know that it is only possible for you to save one child.

1. What would you do?

2. On what basis would you make your choice? Why?

Suppose the situation were somewhat different. Suppose that you were a Jewish individual living in Nazi Germany. The Germans ordered the Jewish children to be shipped away. You had two children and they were put on a truck. (This is a true story.) The mother pleaded with the Germans to let her keep at least one of her children. A German officer felt sorry for her and told her that she could take one child. She went over to the truck and both of her children begged her to choose him.

1. How does this case change the situation?

2. *What should the woman do in this case?*
3. *What would you do? Why?*[1]

Asking students to solve this type of dilemma is characteristic of Lawrence Kohlberg's classroom approach to fostering the development of moral reasoning in children. It is a widely accepted model in values education. *Newsweek* reported even in March 1976—that in audio-visual aids alone—Guidance Associates had distributed material on Kohlberg's approach to over 6000 school districts. Regular school textbooks, such as the Holt Social Studies curriculum, edited by Edwin Fenton, are based on Kohlberg's theory. With its vast impact on children, it qualifies as our second model for evaluation. As with the first model, we will examine the underlying philosophic and theoretical stance of the approach, how these are integrated into exercises for the classroom, and the fundamental questions which arise from the approach.

Kohlberg, of the Center for Moral Development at Harvard University, claims to have gone beyond what he considers to be the limitations of the relativism of the Values Clarification approach. Like Simon, however, Kohlberg has been adamant in his rejection of traditional moral education as useless and totalitarian. He has "objected to the deliberate effort to inculcate majority values ... [as a] ... violation of the child's moral freedom."[2] Kohlberg has stated that his approach to

> the stimulation of moral development defines an educational process [which respects] the autonomy of the child, whereas any other definition reflects indoctrination. The constitutional issue arises from the point of view of the child's parent, who can object to the teaching of values other than the parent's own. Respect for

1 M. Blatt, A. Colby, and B. Speicher, *Hypothetical Dilemmas for Use in Moral Discussions*, no. 23 on the list, *Kohlberg Reprints Available from the Center for Moral Education*, Moral Education and Research Foundation, Harvard University (Cambridge, Mass.: 1974). Copyright© 1974 Moral Education and Research Foundation.
2 L. Kohlberg, "Stages of Moral Development as a Basis for Moral Education." *Moral Education: Interdisciplinary Approaches*, eds. Clive Beck et al. (Toronto: University of Toronto Press, 1971), p. 71.

the parent's rights is not respect for child's autonomy, a more legitimate concern.[3]

SIX INVARIANT STAGES

Kohlberg focuses on the development of moral reasoning: values as cognitive concepts. Drawing on the tradition of Dewey and Piaget, and on his own cross-cultural studies, Kohlberg contends that an individual's thinking about moral situations matures according to a specific six-stage sequence.[4] These six stages are divided into three levels: (See also appendix I of footnote 2.)

- *The Pre-Conventional Level*, in which the individual is chiefly oriented toward obedience and avoidance of punishment (Stage 1) and personal interest (Stage 2);

- *The Conventional Level*, in which the person is oriented toward a desire to receive approval from others (Stage 3) and toward authority, fixed rules, and maintaining the social order (Stage 4);

- *The Post-Conventional or Autonomous Level* (Stages 5 and 6), where moral reasoning becomes more comprehensive, and reflects self-chosen ethical principles which are universal in nature.

Kohlberg asserts that human beings begin their moral development at Stage 1 and progress, one stage at a time, by being exposed to and stimulated by the reasoning of the next stage. He contends that it is not educationally sound to skip stages of development. In fact, Kohlberg has maintained, it will retard or even halt moral development to

---

3 Ibid., p. 72.
4 More recently, Kohlberg has introduced a seventh stage which addresses the questions "Why live?" "How face death?" (See L. Kohlberg, "Continuities in Childhood and Adult Moral Development Revisited," *Life-span Developmental Psychology: Personality and Socialization*, eds. P.B. Balters and K.W. Schaie (New York: Academic Press, 1975), pp. 202-203. Kohlberg does not include these questions as moral, but rather as ontological questions. For a discussion of this, see Edmund V. Sullivan, *Kohlberg's Structuralism: A Critical Appraisal*, The Ontario Institute for Studies in Education (Toronto: 1977). (Chapter VI.).

introduce a child to a level of response more than one stage higher than his or her current stage. Not everyone progresses through all six stages, since any person can become "fixed" at any level. In fact, fewer than 20% of all adults, says Kohlberg, ever develop beyond Stage 4.

The classroom exercise most characteristic of Kohlberg's approach is the presentation of hypothetical moral dilemmas. Students are asked to state what they think the person in the dilemma should do, give reasons for their point of view, and discuss it with others in the class. According to each child's response to such dilemmas, the teacher may "chart" him or her on a scoring manual. This "score" represents that child's current stage of moral development. It is the teacher's responsibility to assess the child's current stage of thought and stimulate his or her response by a reply based on the reasoning of the next stage. For the teacher to make such critical judgments is an onerous responsibility. The teacher must decide to what degree a moral principle should be shared with a child at any given time, and when the child is ready for the next stage.

For example, Kohlberg has outlined the stages of reasoning and accompanying value statements relative to the question of "The Basic Moral Worth of Human Life."[5] Reflecting this formulation, Table 2, taken from the Kohlberg section of a teachers' union manual on MVE, presents a sample of typical value statements which would be made in Stages 1 to 6 about the value of human life and the reason a person should save a drowning man.

If a child made the remark,

(Stage 1) *"You should save a drowning man because he might be important or have a lot of money."*
will that child be challenged to re-consider that remark by a "questioning" response which, in essence suggests the next step "higher" reasoning:

(Stage 2) *"You should save a drowning man because he might give you a reward for doing it."* What happens when

---

5 L. Kohlberg, "Moral Education in the Schools: A Developmental View," *School Review*, Vol. LXXIV (1966), pp. 8-9.

Table 2. Kohlberg: Cognitive Moral Development: Sample Chart of Typical Comments

Level	Stage	Value of Life
PRECONVENTIONAL	I. Obedience-punishment orientation	You should save a drowning man because he might be important or have a lot of money.
	II. Personal interest orientation	You should save a drowning man because he might give you a reward for doing it.
	III. Good-boy, good-girl orientation	You should save a drowning man because his family will appreciate it and your friends will congratulate you for doing it.
CONVENTIONAL	IV. Authority and social-order-maintaining orientation	You must try to save a drowning man because the law requires you to give help to people in distress.
POSTCONVENTIONAL	V. Social contract orientation	You should try to save a drowning man because it's important that everyone in our society be concerned about the welfare of others.
	VI. Conscience orientation	You should try to save a drowning man because every individual human life is important and is worthy of respect and protection.

Source: S. Barrs, et al., *Values Education: A Resource Booklet*, Ontario Secondary School Teacher's Federation (Toronto: 1975), p. 31.

we leave a child with that Stage 2 statement? How does he or she know that the teacher does not believe that this response is the final reasoning on the matter and the best thinking our society has to share? Does giving the child a Stage 2 statement or even a Stage 3 statement such as, *"You should save a drowning man because his family will appreciate it and your friends will congratulate you for doing it,"* really give that child a vision of the fundamental value of human life and of helping others? But these latter considerations Kohlberg has called "conventional right answers" and he wants us to give children "food for thought" instead of conventional right answers. He encourages freeing the child for the natural development of individual moral judgment, "rather than imposing an alien pattern upon [the child]."[6]

There is no question that to help a child develop moral judgment is fundamental to his or her growth. Unless this help is given, and given honestly—that is, not simply by making a patronizing gesture which camouflages what is, in fact, a no-win situation for the child who dares to question or think independently—we systematically thwart growth toward analytical thinking and therefore toward responsible adulthood.

But are we really giving the child food for thought if we follow Kohlberg's stage approach? If *choice* is to be the order of the day in values education, why (under Kohlberg's staging) must the child wait until adulthood—or forever—to be introduced to universal ethical principles and thereby begin to consider a "conscience orientation?" Can this be construed as responsible moral education or even moral freedom? Surely there is a vast difference between dogmatically insisting on a child's automatic and unquestioning compliance with the highest moral principles and never even offering these ideas as possibilities. Surely there is a difference between rigidly programing the child for mindless conformity and offering the child a moral vision.

In fact, many Kohlbergian moral dilemmas, in themselves, impose an alien pattern upon the child. For instance, one

---

6 L. Kohlberg, "Stages of Moral Development as a Basis for Moral Education," *Moral Education: Interdisciplinary Approaches*, p. 71.

book for classroom use entitled *Hypothetical Dilemmas for Use in Moral Discussions*[7] is a case in point. It presents 111 moral dilemma situations. These concentrate heavily on violence and death: personal survival at the cost of others' lives; cannibalism among survivors of a disaster; and, as we read at the beginning of this chapter, choosing one child's life over another. Here are two further examples of the dilemmas this book presents.

THE DONNER PARTY

In 1841 large numbers of Americans decided to emigrate westward to Oregon and California. A severe depression that hit the western part of the United States in 1837 slowed down business throughout the Mississippi valley. Because of widespread unemployment and poverty the thoughts of the more adventurous turned more and more to the tempting stories of lush valleys beyond the Rocky Mountains that they had heard from the trappers, propagandists, and missionaries who had ventured to the Far West during the previous two decades.

One of these groups of emigrants who desired to migrate to the West was the Donner Party, which was organized in Illinois by two brothers, Jacob and George Donner. This group experienced no unusual hardships until it reached Fort Bridger, an outpost west of the South Pass that had been built by an old mountain man. There eighty-nine of the emigrants were persuaded to follow a new trail just opened by Lansford Hastings, a promoter of westward expansion. He told them the new trail would shorten their journey by three hundred miles. Turning southward, the Donners and their followers wasted a month trying to find a pass through the Wasatch Mountains and then gambled away still more precious time crossing the eighty-mile alkaline desert that lay south of the Great Salt Lakes. By the time they reached the old trail along the Humbolt the scant grass had already withered away and further delays resulted as

7 M. Blatt et al., *Hypothetical Dilemmas*, no. 23 on the list, *Kohlberg Reprints Available from the Center for Moral Education*, Copyright© 1974 Moral Education and Research Foundation.

draft animals grew so weak that they could scarcely draw the wagons. Stark tragedy was the result, for the party began their assault on the Sierra Mountains as the gray clouds of winter already whirled about the mountain peaks. When they were still well below the summit they were trapped by a furious storm and with neither food nor shelter to protect them. A few members of the group volunteered to seek aid and formed a smaller group called "The Forlorn Hope." The smaller group finally reached the California settlements, but only after they committed acts of cannibalism in order to survive. When rescue parties finally reached the remainder of the Donner Party, only forty-five of the original eighty-nine were still alive.

1. Do you consider cannibalism the same as murder? Why or why not?

2. Would it make any difference if certain members of the party agreed to be sacrificed so that the others would have an opportunity for survival and possible rescue?

3. Could cannibalism in the above case be considered self-defense? Why or why not?

4. Should all of the surviving members of the Donner Party be held equally responsible for the atrocities committed during their struggle for survival?

5. What would you have done if you had been a member of the Donner Group?[8]

Many other dilemmas involve sexual conflicts, extramarital and premarital sex, partner swapping.

"SWAPPING"

A number of married couples who knew each other were thinking of "swapping" (changing partners for sexual intercourse). The couples lived in the same neighborhood and knew each other quite well. They were people in their late thirties or early forties. They felt that they would like to have new sexual experiences. They felt that after being

8 Ibid.

married for so long and having sex with the same person,
sex had become quite dull.
   1. *If all the couples agreed to it, would it be all right for*
      them to change partners? Why or why not?
   2. *Recently there have been a number of "swapping"*
      cases reported in the newspapers. The public's general
      reaction is very negative. Why do you think people
      react this way? Do you agree or disagree with them?
      Give your reasons.
   3. *If the couples had children, would this make any dif-*
      ference? What effect do you think "swapping" would
      have on the children?
   4. *What could some of the possible positive effects be?*
   5. *What could some of the possible negative effects be?*[9]

These are not isolated or extreme examples of the 111 moral
dilemmas in *Hypothetical Dilemmas for Use in Moral*
Discussions which is on the list of *Kohlberg Reprints*
Available from the Center for Moral Education Moral
Education and Research Foundation, Harvard University;
they are clearly representative. While Kohlberg himself now
recognizes (personal communication with author[10]) that
some of these dilemmas have "proven unsatisfactory," and
does not now use them in the four schools with which he is
personally involved, nonetheless these materials continue
to be listed, recommended and used by other educators
across the country.

The popularity of Kohlberg's approach stems from its claim
to be neither indoctrinative nor morally relativistic (e.g.
Values Clarification), in that each Kohlbergian stage is
considered to be "higher" or more "just" than the pre-
ceding one. Notwithstanding this and other major theoretical differences between Simon and Kohlberg,[11] Robert Hall
still contends that:

   ... [Kohlberg's] techniques for classroom use of the
   moral dilemma strategy are just as likely to convey the

---

 9 Ibid.
10 Communication with author, February 4, 1982.
11 See "An Exchange of Opinion between Kohlberg and Simon," in H.
   Kirschenbaum and S. Simon, eds., *Readings in Values Clarification*,
   (Minneapolis, Minn.: Winston Press, 1973) pp. 62-64.

impression that morality is all a matter of one's own opinion.[12]

For virtually a decade, Kohlberg's theory enjoyed relatively uncritical acclaim. From a practical standpoint it is, at least initially, appealing to many classroom teachers because of the security which seems to be offered in its highly structured process of "matching" the child's statement and the teacher's reply. In fact, the skills required to discuss, observe, interpret, and chart individual student responses and the procedures for scoring have proven to be highly complicated, often confusing, and currently, are both defended and criticized.[13]

Also latterly, the fundamental validity of Kohlberg's theory has been questioned on empirical grounds—that is, the existence and order of the six stages are being called into question by other researchers whose findings contradict Kohlberg's structured formula for the development of moral reasoning.[14]

JUSTICE

It is an important part of Kohlberg's theory that a person at Stage 6 chooses certain courses of action because it can be proved to that individual's satisfaction that the principle behind them can be applied universally, that justice— Kohlberg's all-inclusive moral principle—has been logically identified for all those concerned in that particular issue. Such a course of action qualifies as just, even though it may conflict with the laws of society. Kohlberg's Stage-6 person

12 Robert Hall, "Moral Education Today: Progress, Prospects, and Problems of a Field Come of Age," The Humanist, vol. XXXVIII, no. 6 (November/December 1978), pp. 12-13.
13 See James R. Rest, "Moral Judgment Research and the Cognitive-Developmental Approach to Moral Education," The Personnel and Guidance Journal, Vol. 58, No. 9, (May 1980), pp. 602-605. See also, Marvin W. Berkowitz, "A Critical Appraisal of the Educational and Psychological Perspectives on Moral Discussion," The Journal of Educational Thought, Vol. 15, No. 1, (April 1981), pp. 20-33.
14 See Jennie Nicolayev and D.C. Phillips, "On Assessing Kohlberg's Stage Theory of Moral Development," eds. D.B. Cochrane, C.M. Hamm and A.C. Kazepides, The Domain of Moral Education, (New York: Paulist Press, 1979) pp. 231-250.

is autonomous, a sovereign being, apparently above the value of society's rules. Society's rules apply to the person oriented to the law-and-order stage of morality (Stage 4). To be above the law has a certain appeal to us all, because some of our laws are imperfect, and a democratic society should develop individuals who can reason and question and challenge, rather than merely conform.

But while Kohlberg's Stage-6 individuals can reason about universal principles of justice, they may not necessarily believe in *compassion* for others or in *commitment* to them. Edmund Sullivan, a scholar of Kohlberg's work, identifies this missing factor: "We can see a person completely lacking in 'imagination'—an attribute that I would deem essential to effective moral commitment."[15] Pressing this point further, Sullivan pinpoints the critical distinction between thought and action, and the danger which lies in focusing on philosophical reasoning to the virtual exclusion of personal commitment:

> If there is a place for Kohlberg's postconventional man in contemporary culture, he will not represent un-equivocal virtue. He will ultimately have to face the dilemma that thinking thoughts of universal brother-hood and sisterhood is a far cry from the passion, care and commitment that will bring that ideal into being. Given a passion for principles and an aversion to his-tory, it would seem to be a much easier task to get to Stage 6 than to be involved in the creation of a caring society.[16]

True. Genuine morality among persons requires more than a legalistic and impersonal exercise of the mind put into action stage by stage. It requires personal commitment. There is more involved in moral maturity than mere ration-alism and justice put into action stage by stage. There is spontaneous compassion.

---

15 Edmund V. Sullivan, *Kohlberg's Structuralism*, p. 23. For a further exposition of the relationship between morality and the faculty of imagination, see especially chapter V.

16 Ibid., pp. 31-32.

THE "JUST COMMUNITY SCHOOL"

Over the past decade, Kohlberg has broadened his focus beyond "stimulating [moral] discussion"[17] in the classroom, to emphasize the importance of also "deal[ing] directly with moral behavior:"[18] this within the context of a democratic "just community school."[19] In these schools, which Kohlberg has developed, policies concerning behavior such as stealing, cutting classes, and the question of enforcing such policies if they exist, are determined with students and teachers each having one vote. While teachers will speak for the basic ideals of the (larger) community, in the role of community advocate,[20] and will attempt through discussion, to stimulate movement to a higher stage of moral reasoning, the majority vote rules. This is based on the concept of democracy and the conviction that the group must function at its own stage of cognitive moral development until it elects to adopt a higher one. This theory and its practice has been challenged on various grounds[21] and research findings on its effects on students are conflicting.

At the same time, it should be recognized that both praise and criticism of the "just community" approach has focused more and important attention on present educational structures which operate on one-way edicts "from the top down." Hopefully a re-examination of more growth-producing ways in which students may participate will be precipitated, together with the conviction that schools can and should reflect a sense of shared community.

17 L. Kohlberg, "Moral Education Reappraised," The Humanist, vol. XXXVIII, no. 6, p. 14.
18 Ibid., p. 15.
19 See L. Kohlberg, "Education for Justice: A Modern Statement of the Platonic View," Moral Education: Five Lectures, eds., N.F. Sizer and T.R. Sizer (Cambridge: Harvard University Press, 1970) pp. 57-83.
20 See L. Kohlberg, "High School Democracy and Educating for a Just Society," R. Mosher, ed., Moral Education: A First Generation of Research, (New York: Praeger, 1980).
21 For a critical discussion of the application of Kohlberg's principle of the "just community school" at the Cluster School in Cambridge, see William J. Bennett and Edwin J. Delattre, "Moral Education in the Schools," The Public Interest (Winter 1978), pp. 94-97.

COMMITMENT RE-VISITED

In the just community school, commitment to the group norm appears to be primarily grounded in the fact of the group *contract* and not so much in the conviction that, including, but also *beyond* contract, commitment—to be fully alive—is an attitude of the heart as well as of the mind. Apparently, still so concerned not to pick out "right" answers from what Kohlberg has disparagingly called the "bag of virtues" and "pin" these on children (an approach which has been in disrepute as effective pedagogy for some years), he takes an over-size conceptual leap to reduce moral virtues to "habits of action."[22] Again this is a very technical treatment of a phenomenon which is exceedingly dynamic and inextricably involved with the rational as well as the affective moral endeavor. O'Leary states the inter-connection clearly:

> Kohlberg's assimilation of the virtues to habits of action has obscured an important element in moral education by leading us to an unjustifiable separation of morally relevant cognitive development from the development of moral virtues. The development of the latter is important if we are to enable children to overcome the obscuring force that the passions have upon our judgments as to what is the right thing to do. Without the virtues and their development it is difficult to see how appropriate judgments can ever be made. On the other hand, without the development of moral judgment it is difficult to see how the virtues could ever come to be exercised since to say a virtue has been exercised requires a right judgment. The moral virtues and moral judgment are indispensible to one another and to the morally educated person.[23]

Current applications of the Kohlbergian approach are so

---

22 For an incisive discussion of this concept, see R.S. Peters, "Virtues and Habits in Moral Education," eds. D. Cochrane et al, *The Domain of Moral Education*, pp. 267-287.

23 P.T. O'Leary, "Moral Education, Moral Character, and the Virtues," *The Journal of Educational Thought*, Vol. 15, No. 1, (April 1981), p. 46.

diverse and so open-ended,[24] both as regards teacher training and classroom techniques, that it emerges as absolutely crucial for educators and parents to confront its basic position. Unlike Simon and his colleagues, Kohlberg operates from a base of the existence of objective ethical principles. Yet we must ask: to what extent is this base actually evident to most students, given the commitment to the methodology of staging? With its major emphasis on examining moral dilemmas, Kohlberg's approach can become what has been termed "Quandary Ethics."[25] Without, for example, more central importance afforded to caring and compassion, the essence of life can evolve around never-ending quandaries of competing contracts and rights. Is this the vision of morality we would choose for our children?

24 "Kohlbergiana," D. Craig, ed., Ethics in Education Vol. 1, No. 5, (December 1981) p. 3.
25 E. Pincoffs, "Quandary Ethics," Mind, vol. LXXX, no. 320 (October 1971), pp. 552-571.

4

The Reflective Approach

The third package for consideration is the Reflective Approach of Clive Beck, director since 1969 of the Moral Education Project at the Ontario Institute for Studies in Education (OISE) in Toronto. His work includes *Ethics: An Introduction*,[1] a high school text; *Moral Education in the Schools*;[2] extensive annual reports of the activities of the Moral Education Project[3] and *Reflecting on Values: Learning Materials for Grades 1-6*.[4] The Moral Education Project was funded by the provincial government's Ministry of Education who themselves distributed over 5000 copies of Beck's *Reflective Approach in Values Education*. Beck's work is widely known and has considerable influence among academics and values educators in the United States and thereby qualifies as our third model for examination.

1 Clive Beck, *Ethics: An Introduction*.
2 Clive Beck, *Moral Education in the Schools*, The Ontario Institute for Studies in Education (Toronto: 1971).
3 Clive Beck, *The Reflective Approach in Values Education: The Moral Education Project (Year 3)*, Ontario Ministry of Education (Toronto: 1976); Clive Beck, *The Moral Education Project (Year 4): Annual Report 1975/76*, Ontario Ministry of Education (Toronto: 1978), and Clive Beck, *The Moral Education Project (Year 5): Final Report 1976/77*, Ontario Ministry of Education (Toronto: 1978).
4 Clive Beck, Norma McCoy and Jane Bradley-Cameron, *Reflecting on Values: Learning Materials for Grades 1-6*, Ontario Institute for Studies in Education, (Toronto: 1980).

Beck's approach aims at values education which is grounded in the process of reflection, standing back, as it were—

1. to consider all relevant facts;
2. to "bring values one is not sure about into line with the values one is more sure about;"[5]
3. to "bring means-values into line with end-values"[6] (i.e., to consider the age-old issue of whether the end justifies the means);
4. to consider one's "ultimate life goals . . . such as survival, happiness (enjoyment, pleasure, etc.), health, fellowship (friendship, love, etc.), helping others (to some extent), wisdom, fulfillment of our capacities), freedom, self-respect, respect from others, a sense of meaning in life, and so on."[7]

Certainly one would agree with Beck that reflection, as a method by which values are scrutinized, analysed, and evaluated, must be an important part of values education. Any process which excludes reflection would surely not qualify as an educational experience, but would, rather, be an exercise in automatic and blind passivity. But Beck's Reflective method has begged certain questions. As Jerrold Coombs of the Association for Values Education Research points out:

> Still, Beck's account is not satisfying. Reflection if it is to be worthy of the name, must be disciplined. That is to say, it must be conducted in accordance with rules or standards of relevance and adequacy. Beck has virtually nothing to say about the standards that might guide reflection about values. He does not tell how one determines which facts are relevant, how one is to resolve the conflict of means-values that are out of line with end-values, or what establishes the soundness of an ultimate life goal.[8]

5 Ibid., p. 2.
6 Ibid., p. 2.
7 Ibid., p. 1.
8 J. Coombs, book review of Thomas C. Hennessy, *Values and Moral Development* (New York: Paulist Press, 1976), in *The History and Social Science Teacher*, vol. 13, no. 1 (Fall 1977), p. 63.

Quite correctly, Beck states that developing sound values is important. However, he leaves the definition of "sound" entirely open. In fact, says Beck, "the feature that distinguishes moral decisions from other personal life decisions is not a particularly important one."[9] In his text for high school students, Beck makes his position quite clear:

A view commonly expressed by moral philosophers is that moral principles are distinctive in that they are overriding: if a moral principle applies in a particular situation, then it overrides all other principles— economic, political, social, medical or whatever. When two moral principles conflict, of course, one is in difficulties. But at least it is clear that moral considerations always prevail over non-moral considerations.

If my account of the purpose of morality is sound, however, we should no longer look at morality in this way. There are many areas of value apart from the moral, and all areas of value are equally subordinate to the ultimate life goals that lie beyond them. Morality, like other types of value, is a *means* toward "ultimate" ends; and moral principles, such as "Be humble," "Be patient," "Don't steal," and so on, are *intermediate* principles, serving these ultimate ends. . . .—moral considerations must be weighed against others—and the overriding consideration is the promotion of ultimate life goals, not the promotion of moral principles . . .[10]

If moral values have no greater, and even less, moral legitimacy than any other life goals such as survival or happiness, then it becomes entirely conceivable, as Coombs points out, that "one could have the ultimate goal of pleasure (one of Beck's examples) take precedence over the life goal of not hurting persons, and still have sound values."[11]

9 Clive Beck, *Moral Education in the Schools*, p. 29.
10 Clive Beck, *Ethics: An Introduction*, p. 13.
11 J. Coombs, book review of Thomas C. Hennessy, *Values and Moral Development* in *The History and Social Science Teacher*, (Fall 1977), p. 63.

Moreover, if moral judgments are no more or less important than other personal life decisions, then, presumably, moral values can become merely tools or instruments. They are to be assessed and used if, as, and when they may be effective in helping to achieve any personally desirable goal. On this basis,

> all so-called moral values are means values, and ... they are justified in the same way as are all other means values, *viz*, by determining whether or not they are part of the most effective way of achieving one's ultimate life goals. On this construal, values generally regarded as moral values, e.g. treating persons fairly, are justified to the extent that their adoption is effective in attaining ultimate goals such as survival, health, happiness, friendship, freedom, self-respect, et cetera.[12]

Surely, to teach students that moral values are intermediate in nature, and that the "ultimates" in life are essentially private, personal aspirations is to affirm as, in fact, Beck maintains, that "nothing is intrinsically good or bad."[13]

THE TRADE-OFF

One of the faults of modern Western society, says Beck, has been our tendency

> to encourage children and youth to adopt a strongly idealistic and sentimental approach to values. This has not been to the advantage of our culture or of our young people. The net result of the attempt to keep them innocent has been to deprive them of the opportunity to deal with values problems realistically and satisfactorily and to initiate them into our own system of hypocrisy. Through the presentation of appropriate information, ideas and examples, value materials can be used to put values issues in a more

---

12 Ibid.
13 "Sample of Class Discussion of Values," Appendix E, p. 4 of "Case Study: Grade 13: Integrated Literature and Values Course," Appendix 5, *The Moral Education Project (Year 5): Final Report 1976/77.*

realistic light, make students more aware of the trade-
offs that are necessary in value situations, and hence
place their valuing on a solid footing. . . .[14]

Beck's emphasis in classroom materials tends to be on
"necessary trade-offs" rather than on exploring the intrinsic
value of any ideal. He appears to disregard the fact that
many of us do not attempt to "keep [young people] innocent" and thereby "initiate them into our own system of
hypocrisy." Actually, many of us talk through a wide range
of value issues and their options with our children. We
readily admit the fact that as adults, we constantly fall short
of what we know to be right, that we are often torn between
the "right" and the "half-right" or the "expedient," and
that we sometimes give in to the last two. We share these
experiences as fellow human beings who make many mistakes and who live in a society which often entices us to be
hypocritical. But this reality does not mean that we relin-
quish our moral standards, that we—along with our children—no longer strive either to recognize what is right or
attempt to accomplish it.

In Beck's view many young people are carrying around a
load of guilt because many moral standards are impossible
to maintain consistently. Since aspiring to these moral values
is likely to make young people feel guilty, the way to lessen
their burden, Beck explains, is to focus on what people
actually do, rather than on what they should do. He has
discussed, for example, the hypothetical situation of a car
accident where the question arises as to whether to intervene to save another's life at the risk of one's own. In this
discussion, "The Case of Either My Life or His," Beck concludes: "Perhaps I should sacrifice myself for him; but certainly I might refrain from doing so and still be quite a
moral person."[15] While Beck's point of view may be rational
enough, it is a question of whether there is moral value in
making such a statement from the front of the classroom. If
personal happiness and personal survival are to be equated
with, or placed higher than, "doing to others what you

---

14 "The Nature of Learning Materials," *The Moral Education Project
(Year 5): Final Report 1976/77*, p. 26.
15 Clive Beck, *Ethics: An Introduction*, p. 20.

would have them do to you"—a moral precept held by religious and nonreligious alike—do we, in making—and living by—such pronouncements stand in danger of forfeiting the essence of what it means to be human?

But Beck claims that compassion is not a sufficient motivation to action; enlightened self-interest is also necessary. Given this mental set, can we be surprised if students of this approach join the ranks of those people who stand by, idly, as they witness violence done to a fellow human being? Incidents like the one described in this article are becoming more and more prevalent:

Dozen Watch, Offer No Help As Boy Drowns

MONTREAL (CP)—About a dozen people watched a 7-year-old boy drown Saturday and refused to jump into the Riviere des Prairies to save him, some saying the water was too polluted.

Police said Martin Turgeon of Montreal slipped off a wharf near a spot where untreated sewage is dumped into the river.

"We're not going in there—the water is much too dirty," witnesses quoted one onlooker as saying. Some people even left the scene as the boy's father, a nonswimmer, thrashed about in the water and screamed for help. A boater fished the boy's body out of the river about 25 minutes later.

"It makes you wonder about how human people are," a policeman remarked. "The boy probably would have been saved."

The boy's family said they were too shaken up to talk about the incident.[16]

Is the function of moral education in the classroom to mirror this type of contemporary behavior "because it is real" and to make it more understandable to youth so that they may find it less guilt-producing to act in the same way? Certainly, in his text for high schools, Beck stresses the importance of nonmoral values.

16 "Dozen Watch, Offer No Help as Boy Drowns," *The Globe and Mail* (Toronto), 6 June 1978, p. 2.© The Canadian Press.

As has been noted previously, moral value is just one area of value among many, and the moral values in a situation must be weighed against the non-moral values.

But does this not mean that, in some situations, where a happy compromise cannot be arrived at, we will end up acting in a less moral manner than we would have if we had only taken account of moral values? In my view, yes. And there is an important general principle here. We must not become so fanatical about moral values that we pursue them regardless of other values. The point is that, as total human beings, we should strive to be reasonably moral but not extremely moral. Extreme morality—extreme unselfishness, extreme humility, extreme honesty, and so on—may be justified in some situations but in general it is not something people should aim at.[17]

THE CHALLENGE

It is as if fundamental moral values such as courage, kindness, honesty, and compassion are, in themselves, a real burden: a psychological "heavy," a negative imperative to be approached and skirted gingerly. Is this how most of us regard moral values? If it is, this is most certainly the message we will deliver to youth.

But is there not the thrill of challenge and, paradoxically, a sense of freedom—as well as some pain—in aspiring to such values as courage, kindness, honesty, and compassion? Is youth, by nature, oriented to qualification, compromise, and trade-offs? Do we really believe that focusing on compromise and trade-offs and directing and initiating students into these mental sets will make them more truly and fully human?

Take the analogy of teaching archery. Is an instructor to identify the bull's-eye to the novice archer, recognizing that it is a difficult target to hit? Or should the instructor just casually observe that "most archers hit the canvas on the

17 Clive Beck, *Ethics: An Introduction*, p. 109.

outside rim?" In many of his classroom materials, Beck deals with those moral tenets to which our society has traditionally held for inspiration and direction, encouraging students to critically examine them. While this is a valid endeavor, the identification of a target remains crucial. Whether by design or not, the child's eye may be averted from the bull's-eye until the focal point becomes the outer rim.

In the following excerpts from Beck's classroom materials, we will examine his treatment of some of these moral principles to which society has traditionally held.

On Helping Others:

Moral principles that require us to treat everyone alike are seldom useful. Students should learn how to determine the population to which particular acts of kindness and unselfishness ought to be directed....[18]

It seems to me that *we must favor an "inner group"* ... [which] will consist of close relatives and friends and a few acquaintances (perhaps in far off countries) whose needs we know well and whom we have decided to help in a continuing way. The main reasons for concentrating on a group that is close to us, are, first that we best know how to help these people, and, second that such an arrangement will promote our own welfare in various ways, since we will develop enjoyable and enriching personal associations and establish relationships of mutual help.[19]

"Realistic," utilitarian, reciprocal, shrewd: all these measures of behavior offer restricted moral vision. Again, in a classroom unit for nine- to twelve-year-olds, entitled *Self and Others*, Beck emphasizes:

How do we decide just what balance there should be between helping ourselves and helping others? It is a very rough-and-ready process. It depends on how we were brought up, what is expected in our society, how

---

18 Clive Beck, *Moral Education in the Schools*, p. 33.
19 Ibid., pp. 30-31.

we are feeling at the moment, what principles come to mind, what alternative compromises we can think of.[20]

Practical, "sensible," focusing on compromise. The statement comes with built-in rationalizations about parental and cultural relativism and the individual's mood. It doesn't demand too much. It's easy to live with. No ideals are imperative. No standards are necessarily required.

On Rules

In a course unit called "Rules People Give Us," which Beck wrote for ten- to eleven-year-olds, the "Principle for Discussion" is: "Rules and principles given to us by other people are not always very good."[21] Here is one idea presented for consideration:

Sometimes, perhaps, bad rules are given to us for self-centered reasons. People want us to do something which is good for THEM; so they persuade us to follow a rule which will help THEM, without really caring about us. For example, commercials on television and in the newspaper are often like that. The person who makes the toothpaste or ballpoint pen or chocolate bar may be more concerned with selling his product and making money than with satisfying us. Or again, sometimes when adults give children rules of behavior, they are more concerned with their own comfort and convenience than with the happiness of the children. Of course, adults should look after themselves. But sometimes, perhaps, they go too far. What do you think?[22]

Before immediately discounting this exercise, could it be that it is simply defensiveness and even a measure of guilt which causes some parents to take issue with the school if it implies to their ten-year-olds that parental rules may be as empty and self-serving as the claims of T.V. commercials? Is it simply the parents' compulsive need for authority which

---

20 Clive Beck, "The Self and Others," Topic 6 in "Man in Society," A Discussion of Ideas about Human Life in Society, Humanities Enrichment Course for the Middle and Upper Elementary School, Ontario Institute for Studies in Education, Mimeo, p. 16.

21 Clive Beck, Appendix 1, *Moral Education in the Schools*, p. 37.

22 Ibid., p. 38. (THEM in italics in original.)

causes them to suggest that such exercises may be under-mining and indoctrinating for children of this age? Many values educators would support this view. But to what degree should this questioning be carried?

Beck holds that a prime objective of moral education is to move students to a level of personal autonomy. To this end, the child must be encouraged to develop a critical attitude toward conventional right answers, rules and authority, whether they appear in the form of the Ten Command-ments or of parental guidance. All of these must be open to serious scrutiny and discussion, and the classroom, in Beck's view, should provide this type of forum.

I believe that critical, analytical scrutiny of values is vital to moral education—provided the age-topic match is ap-propriate. The objective of moral education should certainly not be to program automatic rule-followers who comply with value pronouncements without thought or question. However, if values are scrutinized from the basis of subjec-tive life-goals, with little deference to objective moral crite-ria and standards—then the quality of the analysis will be questionable indeed.[23]

Beck has held that nonauthoritarian teacher-training institutions, nonauthoritarian schools and nonauthoritarian teachers would provide for children the climate most con-ducive to moral development.[24] Student involvement in curriculum planning and school disciplinary procedures are specifically stressed and strike a responsive note in the important effort to promote students' active participation.

Most of us respond to the plea for nurturing sound rea-soning skills in students rather than unquestioning confor-mity to authority. If it is argued that fewer of today's teachers rely on authoritarian measures in the classroom, let me say that I hold no particular brief for the old days and that I am

23 For a useful distinction between "value criteria" and "value principle," see Jerrold R. Coombs, "Objectives of Values Analysis," Values Educa-tion: Rationale, Strategies, and Procedures, 41st Yearbook, ed. L. Met-calf (Washington, D.C.: National Council for Social Studies, 1971), pp. 1-27. Used with permission.

24 See Edmund V. Sullivan and Clive Beck, "Moral Education in a Cana-dian Setting," Phi Delta Kappan, vol. 56, no. 10 (June 1975), pp. 700-701.

not advocating a return to them. But it is a fact that in times of change and innovation, we tend to adopt one of two stances with regard to what was done in the past. We may see the methods we used in the past through such a haze of sentiment that we can neither recognize nor admit their faults and inconsistencies; or we may go to the other extreme and downgrade all that was done. It is too easy to conclude that horrendous things were done to students in the past and decide that everything related to past methods has to go.

It is easy to see the advantages in a relationship of trust and co-operation between student and teacher, and the creation of an atmosphere of mutual respect and mutual willingness to admit ignorance and acknowledge mistakes. But there is nothing revolutionary about such a situation. I believe that for generations, the best teachers have *not* used sheer maintenance of law and order or arbitrary exercise of authority as their chief working tools. Moreover, to implicitly equate such qualities as ridicule, rigidity, and condemnation with an authoritarian approach to students, and caring, warmth, and empathy with a nonauthoritarian approach is to create a false dichotomy for both teachers and students.

Yet much of current MVE implies an out-and-out conflict between Authority and what is often seen as its opposite, Individual Autonomy. These two concepts are constantly portrayed as incompatible in current practice models. However, it is possible that in pitting Autonomy against Authority, we create a false opposition. It is not the existence of authority which dehumanizes children—or any group of people, for that matter—and renders them unable to reason and develop judgment. It is the way in which authority is exercised that can be dehumanizing. By setting up authority per se as the factor which must be eliminated, we take ourselves down a long and winding road only to discover anarchy at its end. Surely we need to examine both authority and autonomy for the essential good in each so that we may combine those elements. Whenever we stubbornly pursue one to the exclusion of the other, not only are we destructive, but we also obscure or even obliterate the possibility of establishing true democracy.

THE HIDDEN CURRICULUM?

The argument which is most frequently advanced in favor of the new movement in values education is that schools have always been in the business of transmitting values—and this is unquestionably valid. These values were usually implicit, often subliminal, and not always open to question.[25] Now they are to be made explicit and open to scrutiny. This statement sounds a positive note for most of us. But study the fine print on the package. Beck proposes that

> the teacher should deal with value topics—content—explicitly and should feel free to express his views on these topics and present arguments for them ... if all teachers adopt this approach, students will be impressed with the diversity of viewpoints on various value topics throughout the school and will learn to pick and choose among them.[26]

Too frequently, however, no distinctions are made concerning the age group involved or the nature of the topic. For students to hear diverse opinions from teachers on some topics is helpful and stimulating, and an essential part of learning to evaluate complex issues. The use of land for industrial expansion versus agriculture is one case in point, and there are countless other value issues which, according to age-appropriateness, may be debated responsibly. But to hear diverse opinions from teachers on the morality of, for example, suicide,[27] and to encourage students to pick and choose among these opinions is of questionable value.

On what basis will students choose? On the basis of which teacher argues more convincingly at the given moment? On the basis of which teacher has a more attractive personality? On the basis of peer consensus? Beck makes quite an astounding statement. Given the classroom and school

---

25 Beck and others refer to this as the "hidden curriculum." For discussion on this, see *The Reflective Approach in Values Education: The Moral Education Project (Year 3)*, p. 5.

26 Ibid.

27 See Deanne Bogdan, "Values and Literary Criticism: Case Study: Grade 13: Integrated Literature and Values Course," Appendix 5, *The Moral Education Project (Year 5): Final Report 1976/77*, p. 7.

atmosphere he prescribes, he claims that students "will be stimulated by the class-room 'teaching' and will make progress toward sounder value positions."[28] Beck's contention that students will progress toward sounder value positions is a highly questionable assumption. Is it not equally possible that after class discussions of the types described, some students may *regress* to less sound value positions? Consider, for example, the following account of a values education session led by Beck. This session was one of a series held with grade thirteen students at St. Michael's Choir School (Roman Catholic) in an integrated Literature and Values course.[29] The discussion turned around a study of Miller's play, *Death of a Salesman*, in which the hero, Willy, commits suicide. This account was written by the students' English teacher:

> It became increasingly apparent that the ideological differences between Clive's reflective but pragmatic philosophy . . . was bound to clash sooner or later with the students' "idealistic" application of traditional moral principles. Notwithstanding their avowed sympathy for Willy's plight, the boys were judgmental both about him [Willy] and about Clive's "condoning" his suicide as an act of prudence and of freedom. Students' rebuttals included an affirmation of the doctrine of natural law by Ken . . . a reminder from Henry that the will must be subject to reason and a frontal attack by Michael on the destructive influence on moral ideals of looking at what people *do* do rather than what they *should* do . . . Clive was impressed with the students' background knowledge and undaunted by their vehemence and their tenacity.[30]

These particular students—well above average in their facility for moral-ethical dialogue because of their background of explicit teaching in the nature and function of moral principles—offered a major challenge to Beck's util-

28 Clive Beck, *The Reflective Approach*, p. 4.
29 For an account of this course, see Deanne Bogdan, "Values and Literary Criticism," Appendix 5, *The Moral Education Project (Year 5): Final Report 1976/77*, pp. 1-20.
30 Ibid., p. 7.

itarianism. One wonders, however, how students less firmly grounded in specific moral teaching would be affected by his determined assertions. Further dialogue between Beck and this class centered around Beck's contention that "nothing is intrinsically good or bad."[31]

ENDS AND MEANS

In summary, Beck's emphasis on reflection as an approach to values is clearly valid. Any values education process which excludes personal reflection would surely not qualify as an educational experience: it would not touch lives and would often be irrelevant. In Beck's more recent writing, he proposes that moral education should encompass "instruction [non-indoctrinative] and reflection, affective components and the institutional context of moral learning."[32] Validly, he sees this as a more comprehensive approach than either the Simon or Kohlberg models. Also, at first reading, Beck's emphasis on considering one's "ultimate life goals" strikes a responsive note. For many, the word "ultimate" carries the connotation of an "absolute," an objective moral truth, and it is easy to assume that this is what Beck is implying. It is, therefore, crucial to understand that in his model, moral principles are reduced to the intermediate level of means-values. Although latterly Beck has stated that "the traditional moral virtues [honesty, self-control, courage, truthfulness, generosity, loyalty etc.] can and should be fostered in the schools,"[33] he stresses the importance of pointing out to students that these moral values "*serve*" (his emphasis) other life goals.

> Moral values . . . are appropriately seen, to a degree, as ends in themselves. The point is simply that we must stress the *further* ends they serve . . . seeing moral virtues [such as unselfishness and fairness] as means to other values [such as happiness, fulfillment, health,

31 Ibid., Appendix E of Appendix 5, p. 4.
32 Clive Beck, "*Moral Education: A Comprehensive Approach*," Proceedings of the World Congress In Education, *Values and the School*, Serge Fleury (ed.), C.P.668, Haute-Ville, Quebec, P.Q., G1R 4S2, 1981, p.41. Used with permission.
33 Ibid.

survival, friendship and freedom] ... enables us to show students the significance of moral virtues in the contemporary world. Having explored [this], students will see more clearly the point of morality and be more inclined to commit themselves to it. . . .[34]

If Beck's point were that honesty, for example, should not be taught purely as an abstract moral "ideal," he would have few objectors, and one attempts to specifically address this issue in chapter 10. However, it is clear that Beck's essential point, as in his earlier work, is that he

do[es] not wish for one moment to subscribe to the view that morality is an entirely autonomous domain of values, whose principles and precepts override all others. . . .[35] Morality to a considerable extent serves basic human values which lie beyond morality and help give it form and purpose. Unless school students see this they will not know how to be moral and will not have any reason to want to be moral.[36]

Given his emphasis on the pragmatic gains of morality, it remains for Beck to grapple with the realistic fact that to "promote" the moral values of honesty, courage, generosity as serving utilitarian ends and personal "benefits" is to suggest a connection which does not necessarily follow. To hold out the "carrot," as it were, that there are positive "spin-offs" to the practice of morality in the non-moral domain is tempting, and sometimes true. However, it is not by any means dependably true, and therefore such an expectation can be not only misleading, but can also confuse primary motivational ends and means.

Young people are quick to recognize that for many people in our society, happiness, fulfillment, meaning in life and freedom are *not* served by, for example, honesty and generosity. Quite the reverse, their "fulfillment" and "meaning" derives from being, quite unabashedly, dishonest and selfish. Thus a pragmatist might render honesty and generosity quite irrelevant in the scheme of life. Indeed,

34 Ibid.
35 Ibid., p. 34.
36 Ibid., p. 41.

it is perhaps precisely because young people so often see that there are no dependable "pay-offs:" that "good guys" do not necessarily "profit" and that "bad guys" are not necessarily "brought to justice," that it becomes exceedingly important to consider moral values for their own sake. William Bennett picks this up:

[It should be shown] that morally right and even praiseworthy conduct does not always result in benefits to the agent or to society in a contingent world . . . [It should be understood] that excellence of character is an end in itself.[37]

This is not to imply that students should be "indoctrinated" in this view or required to accept it as an abstract dictum. "Excellence of character" and moral values should be explored from all aspects, including the reality that there may or may not be "rewards" in the non-moral domain: that indeed there may be the very reverse.

Yet again, we must ask: is there not the thrill of challenge and, paradoxically a sense of freedom—as well as some pain—in aspiring to such moral values as courage, honesty and compassion on their own merit? Is youth, by nature, oriented to qualification and compromise? Do we really believe that in encouraging them to be "reasonably moral—but not extremely moral"—we do justice to their capacity for living life?

LIFE AT HIGH RISK

I shall pass through this world but once. Any good therefore that I can do, or any kindness that I can show to any human being, let me do it now. Let me not defer or neglect it, for I shall not pass this way again.[38]

Adults and young children and youth alike are highly aware of just how difficult it can be to live this philosophy. The caring, sensitive individual with moral ideals who genuinely wants to "give [to others] and not count the

37 William J. Bennett, "The Teacher, the Curriculum, and Values Education Development," *New Directions for Higher Education*, 31, 1980, p. 32.

cost,"—whose first, automatic reaction is not to analyse the situation on a personal "cost/benefit" basis before moving in to help—is open to hurt. People like this live life at high risk. Their philosophy can result in a sense of alienation from much that characterizes life in today's society. It can also, paradoxically, result in more liberating personal autonomy and authenticity than is being suggested to many, if not most, students of current moral values education.

5

What Messages Are Getting Through to Our Youth?

The three most popular approaches to values education in North American school systems—Values Clarification, the Moral Reasoning approach, and Reflective Approach—are the three models most frequently recommended in official educational documents as resource materials for teachers. And it is these three which are the source of the most widely used exercises in the classroom.

The obvious question is whether these classroom exercises and the philosophies they represent are actually having an impact on students. From there we can proceed to look at these models within the context of the major social movements of the sixties and seventies, and return again to consider the current response of youth.

A newspaper piece, entitled, "If It Gets You through the Night It's Alright, Grade 11 Student Says,"[1] gives us some indication of the extent to which current MVE approaches have become part of youth's life-view. Forty-one grade 11

---

1 T.W. Harpur, "If It Gets You through the Night It's Alright, Grade 11 Student Says," *The Toronto Star*, 18 March 1978, p. A8.

pupils were responding to an earlier article in which editorialist T.W. Harpur had argued against approaches which communicate no basis for differentiating between right and wrong: that it is impossible to teach morality without some agreed universal standards. Teacher Wilf Hughes of Lakefield District Secondary School encouraged his students to express their views by writing to the paper:

> The opinion of Dave Vandendort ... sums up pretty well what the majority of his classmates think about morality today.

> [He wrote:] "Moral values cannot be taught and people must learn to use what works for them. In other words, 'whatever gets you through the night, it's alright.' The essence of civilization is not moral codes but individualism.... The only way to know when your values are getting sounder is when they please you more...."

> Ralf Dietart wrote: "Values cannot be taught as the individual must individually get his values. There can be no systematic, equational approach ... because each person has his own varying set of morals."

> Linda Ball said: "I don't think anyone can say what human values are because everyone has their own viewpoint. Although I agree the word value can be defined, each value cannot be clearly defined. So if you can't say what the values and morals are, you can't teach them."

> Charlotte Flagler agreed: "What one person thinks is bad or wrong, another person might think that it is good or right. I don't think morals should be taught because it will cause more conflicts and mess up the student's mind."

> Don Hunt put it this way: "In your article you state that you can't teach right and wrong without standards. I disagree with this because I feel that everybody has their own set of standards and values; thus, everybody will have their own set of morals and ethics...."

While a few of those who wrote said they would welcome courses on morals and values in school, most were critical of [educational] programs of this kind. Two said they feared conflict with parental values and undue pressure from teachers to put across their own views of morality.

Sheri Hutchinson commented: "I think that the only one who decides what one's morals should be is oneself."

Janice Ferguson agreed: "[One] approach says that the teacher's opinion on any moral topic would simply be that of a class member. This would not work because the teacher will always have a great influence on the students."

Only a couple of the 41 students who wrote agreed that there are some moral absolutes and that the future itself is in jeopardy unless these can be somehow communicated to the young.

Andy Rafton wrote to say: "I do agree that we are facing a moral vacuum of crisis proportions, but to instruct classes in morals is not the answer."

He went on to argue that moral teaching is the responsibility of parents "from the crib on" and of the various churches or synagogues.

Bob Donaldson added: "I do think we are facing a moral vacuum. . . . In today's generation there is less and less respect for morality and in some cases none at all."[2]

Harpur's conclusions provide us with an interesting commentary:

The youngsters of Lakefield Secondary School who wrote to the Star, like the vast majority of our youth, have many high ideals. In some ways they are more sensitive to injustice than their elders. Yet, the logic of their letters, taken to its conclusion, is the logic of a

2 Ibid.

moral jungle in which each person does that which is right in his own eyes. . . .

There was a time when people held some basic absolutes of right and wrong. They did not always keep them, but they knew when they had missed the mark.

The best of our civilization, not to mention the law, was built on this. Morality was based on shared values of love, truth, honesty, fidelity, generosity, self sacrifice, etc.

The new morality, however—the sexual revolution is but a small part of its real impact—has changed all that. Today, the individual is the center of his universe and the emphasis is on what seems right or wrong to him alone. . . .

The new, would-be moral teachers, in their anxiety to escape the "indoctrination" of traditional values fall into an indoctrination which threatens to be worse. Free of the burden of old authorities they introduce a tyranny of the authority of the self.[3]

It is time to find out where this new thrust is taking us. What is its origin and its destiny?

THE SICKNESS OF THE SEVENTIES

It is not mere coincidence that, in the past few years, numbers of articles in popular magazines and daily newspapers and programs on television have called the public's attention to the "sickness of the seventies." This sickness, they claim, is narcissism: preoccupation with self, neurotic individualism. In a stunning article by Stephen Williams entitled, "Me: A Magnificent Obsession," the author documents the clinical evidence and conclusions of an increasing number of modern thinkers:

A new vanity has become a social pathology, a veritable political crisis in North America. . . . [Social analysts are] pointing with alarm at the emergence of a dominant

3 T.W. Harpur, "This Is the Logic of a Moral Jungle," *The Toronto Star*, 18 March 1978, p. A8.

personality type, a new character, who, when scrutinized closely, is frightening in the extreme. . . .[4]

He is impervious to traditional appeals to right or
wrong, his romance of the self having obliterated his
sense of the past upon which judgments must be based
. . . . Because his values are tailor-made to fit the moment, the individual suffering from a pathological
preoccupation with the self is generally fickle. A *mea
culpa* today is a *felix culpa* tomorrow.

He makes of the self a subject, a discipline, thereby
transforming the subject into an object to which all
things must relate. "Is it relevant to me?" is the
question put to the mirror on the wall. The mirror
answers: "Good is what is good for me" and "one
man's opinion is as good as another's." His ethics *must*
rationalize self-interest. When what is outside the self
seems to be impossible to change, our man adopts the
"what's-one-vote?" attitude. In fact, most narcissists
are, when all is said and done, politically apathetic. The
Narcissus is a technician of the self: a therapist per-
petually analyzing himself. Therapy replaces religion
in the Narcissus' society. Being of little faith, he must
find help within the social sciences to rid himself of his
guilt.[5]

When we place the values education instruction and
exercises we have just seen beside the profile Williams has
drawn, do we recognize the logical result of following some
MVE approaches? Much MVE material is anti-historical,
choosing not to draw insights from the past or even to
consider the future, but to focus on *present* wants, fulfill-
ments, preferences, gratifications, to focus on one's own
life goals, rather than on moral precepts as the "ultimate"
criteria for life-style. Such MVE approaches encourage each
child, despite the very limited span of his or her life and
experience, to choose the course of action which, at this
moment, seems most personally advantageous. Can we be

4 S. Williams, "Me: A Magnificent Obsession," *Toronto Life* (December
1977), p. 41.
5 Ibid., p. 42.

surprised by the vast majority of youth's response to the Harpur article? As Williams points out, the person who approaches life in this way is

> located totally in the present, he is where it's at. *Cool in the extreme.* Because it has become impossible for him to take seriously the mystery of the universe, he settles for a mystique of the self, seeking to compensate for the dangers of an external reality. . . .[6] [He is characterized by] a withdrawal of interest in others and the world at large.[7]

What are the rewards of this self-focus? Often the self-focused person is admired for being confident and self-sufficient. However, this person is often fundamentally lonely, rootless, apathetic, adrift, "immobilized by a lack of core strength."[8] Such people are crowding into psychiatrists' offices at an unprecedented rate.[9] As summarized in a CBC television program: "The point here is not that the search for inner awareness is bad—there is such a thing as healthy inwardness—yet everything does contain its opposite. . . . Narcissism in the end, is a defense mechanism, a retreat. A failure of nerve. Inwardness minus courage."[10]

There is documentation on all sides to attest to the fact that our youth are confused and alienated, even despondent. Those of us who taught university students in the sixties were constantly being confronted. There were sit-ins, stand-ins, marches on the dean's office if students didn't like a question on the exam or, in fact, if there *was* an exam at all. But there was vigor and fire in what students said: they were against hypocrisy; the chasm between the ideal and the real; the sell-out of the right to the expedient; corruption in high places and in bureaucratic systems which excuse, rationalize, and qualify their mediocrity in terms of

6 Ibid., p. 69.

7 Ibid., p. 42.

8 L. Hurst, "Loneliness Hits 'Me' Generation," *The Toronto Star*, 2 October 1978, p. C1.

9 See transcript of the CBC television program, "The 'Me' Decade," in the *Man Alive* series, as reported in "Narcissus of the Seventies," *The Globe and Mail* (Toronto), 17 June 1978, p. 10.

10 Ibid.

National Survival

the compromises which are seen as inevitable in the "real" world. Perhaps some of you were part of that student movement, which had its less constructive aspects, but which at its best was a positive assertion that ideals should not be compromised. It is therefore all the more disastrous that the seventies spawned such phenomena as the punk rock movement. This may be what happens when moral relativism is pushed to its final conclusion. If there are no ideals, then perhaps no cause is really worth taking up: nothing is that important. In fact, maybe there is just nothing. The hippy of the sixties dropped out of society, but he dropped out in protest. The punk rock fan just drops out.

SOMETHING'S MISSING

Dr. Saul Levine, a Professor of Psychiatry and syndicated columnist, is an internationally recognized clinician and researcher in the field of youth and their belief systems, their involvement in mass movements, fringe religions, and cults. On the matter of moral values education, he maintains:

> If in this era of rapid technological change, hyper-stimulation, constant gratification, materialism and superficial relationships, a child is taught that there are no rights or wrongs, no do's and don'ts, no limits or restrictions; that there is justification for *any* behavior given the right circumstances—then (paradoxically) we stand the risk of having that child when an adolescent or adult gravitating to social groups or movements that *do* provide absolute answers, authoritarian leaders and rigid intolerance of others.[11]

The studies of Levine and others have shown that many, if not most, adolescents "have a great need for absolutes, to counter ambiguity, fluidity, and the indeterminable."[12] As we have seen, many MVE proponents insist, however, that adults must not, under any circumstances, try to promote in

---

11 Saul Levine, Interview with author, December 1978.
12 Saul Levine, "Adolescents: Believing and Belonging," *Adolescent Psychiatry*, vol. 7 (1979), p. 45.

youth even universally proven human values because to do so is to be totalitarian. This position surely denies youth access to a resource that could be vital to them and may, therefore, be totalitarian in its own right.

Referring to the young adherents to fringe religions, Levine points out:

> Individuals who feel that they are drifting aimlessly and that there are so many imponderables confronting them in our urban technological society, are often pleased when "Structure" is given to their lives. There are rules and regulations, definite do's and don'ts, stringent punishments for their contravention, rewards for adherence. It is paradoxical that in the swinging seventies these religions espouse a rigid "Puritanism," and attract thousands of young members to moral codes with strict prohibition of drugs and restriction of sexual activity.[13]

Clearly, many of the supporters of MVE would take the position that if some youth seek and respond to such structure and rules, it is precisely because they have not learned to be independent. Thus proponents of these models become even more confirmed in their determination to throw children and youth back on their own resources to "choose and create their own values" and thus become true individuals. These supporters of MVE are totally justified in their objective that youth learn to think for themselves and so be self-actualizing. However, they appear not to recognize with equal conviction what have been defined as the two basic psycho-social needs of adolescents:

1. a *belief system*, something intense to believe in, and
2. a *sense of belonging*, of community.[14]

Dr. Levine continues:

> We have a mandate in society to provide alternatives for those increasing numbers of young people who

13 S. Levine and N. Salter, "Youth and Contemporary Religious Movements: Psychosocial Findings," *Canadian Psychiatric Association Journal*, vol. 21 (1976), p. 415.
14 Saul Levine, "Adolescents: Believing and Belonging," *Adolescent Psychiatry*, p. 41.

are floundering and who cannot achieve belief and belonging by themselves; or for those who might find their salvation, their meaning in life, their relationships, from groups which might have less than salutary effects on the young people or society.

This latter possibility poses a danger that the movements the young choose might be exploitative (some fringe religions—Lefkowitz 1971; Levine and Salter 1976) or even destructive (Bugliosi 1974). Adolescents have achieved belief and belonging in large social movements which can be seen to be bad (or good) depending on what side of any fence you happen to be on (e.g. Red Guard, Hitler's Yugend, Mussolini's Brown Shirts, or the U.S. antiwar movement, the civil rights movement)....[15] These issues are becoming increasingly vital in a society where many normal adolescents are significantly alienated and vulnerable.[16]

"JUST TO SEE WHAT WILL HAPPEN"

In light of this very fact that many normal adolescents feel significantly alienated and vulnerable, it is startlingly ironic that—under the aegis of "enhancing self-worth"—students are being given "you or me" survival exercises of the type described in chapters 2-4. Again, we must ask, "What messages are getting through to our youth?"

The following is a transcript of a nationally aired interview with a grade 12 student. He describes his several experiences in being given the Life Raft exercise. In this exercise, the reader will recall, ten students are told that their life raft, afloat on the Atlantic, can only hold nine. "[Each] member is to 'plead his case' to the others, arguing why he should live."[17] In half an hour, a vote is taken among the ten, and the student with the least votes is thrown overboard to die.

Student: I'd done the Life Raft before. I'd seen its effects ... people are just different. I've never been

15 Reprinted from "Adolescents: Believing and Belonging," *Adolescent Psychiatry*, p. 48 by S. Levine by permission of the University of Chicago Press.
16 Ibid., p. 49.
17 For documentation of the "Life Raft," see Chapter 2, pp. 35-36.

thrown overboard. I know how I'd react if I was.

Interviewer: You told me yesterday that the last time you did it, you ended the game rather abruptly by saying, "I'll be the one to be thrown over." Why did you do that?

Student: It's a feeling that you simply—you go into class expecting to learn about Shakespeare and you come out with the feeling that you have no friends and sort of, to avoid that happening—and to let the teacher know, in I guess the only way that a teenager thinks is possible, I guess I decided I'd create a direct confrontation by simply ending the game and telling her that I would dive overboard.

Interviewer: How did she react?

Student: She reacted just as I thought she would. She got mad. She took me out of the game, took me aside, told the others to keep playing the game. She asked me why I did it, told me that I was wrong to do it; that I should have played the game, just to see what would have happened.[18]

This account portrays a devastating sequence: students in an English-MVE class asked to lobby against their classmates for life and death survival; a student sufficiently traumatized by these exercises which, as he says, "leave you feeling that you have no friends" (alienation), that he concludes that freedom lies in destroying himself (suicide) and hopefully the exercise. The teacher, in spite of these cues, is angry; requires that the exercise be continued by the others, and argues to the student that he should have remained in the exercise "just to see what would have happened."

Given this scenario—and others similar to it, documented in chapter 7—can we find it surprising that the messages getting through to many youth translate into: preoccupation with self; alienation; suicide; violence; assault?

Assault on fellow students, for example has reached crisis proportions. (And isn't a survival exercise of the above type a blatant form of assault: not only to the victim but to all those who are instructed to victimize?) Even in 1976, a National Institute of Education survey established:

18 CBC Radio FM, "Sunday Morning," June 29, 1980.

An estimated 282,000 secondary school students reported that they were attacked at school in a typical one month period ... 800,000 students stayed home from school at least once in the previous month because they were afraid; 12 percent of the secondary school teachers (or 120,000) said they were threatened with injury by students at school; a similar number said they hesitated to confront misbehaving students because of fear....[19]

A study of one school board's high school teachers breaks cases of assault against teachers down into the categories of common assault, indecent assault, and assault causing bodily harm. The study recommends danger pay for teachers and leaves of absence for victims of the "battered teachers syndrome."[20]

At the same time, this has led some to inquire if the sometimes permissive attitude of educational institutions to underage drinking and use of drugs has not merely reinforced students' general apathy and disregard for the law.

The administration of George Brown College showed stunning complacency in turning its back on the open use of drugs on its campus....

While no one expects professors and deans to go sniffing around student lounges like policemen, it was nevertheless wrong for the college's administrative vice-president, John Stephens, to say that George Brown accepts the use of marijuana and hashish by students and will do nothing to suppress it.

Whether the vice-president likes it or not, the college has a responsibility to help maintain the law ... until the day the law is changed ... the college cannot regard itself as an island of law unto itself ... until the day the law is changed no [government] institution can decide to disobey it.[21]

19 Cited in Edward G. West, "Education And Crime: A Political Economy Of Interdependence," Character, Vol. 1, No. 8 (June, 1980), p. 6.
20 Howard Fluxgold, "School Needed for Unruly, North York Teachers Say," The Globe and Mail (Toronto), 16 May 1979, p. 1.
21 Editorial, "Right or Wrong It's the Law," The Toronto Star, 28 May 1979, p. A8.

But in those very educational institutions, from kindergarten to the final year of high school, we are plunging deeper and deeper into a presentation of morals and values based on the philosophy of relativism and individual functionalism. Are current statistics on the values of our youth, therefore, so surprising? In his analysis, Williams makes a telling point:

> The development of civilizations and the development of individuals runs parallel. The civilization that has abandoned its past and is vague about its future mirrors the personality it has created—the Narcissist in limbo, without family, without community and finally, without hope.[22]

Perhaps we need to examine the history of those civilizations which opted for "Good is what is good for me." We need to discover that over the long march of human history, civilizations which have tried to sustain themselves by moral relativism or individual utilitarianism have simply not survived. This is not a matter of conjecture: it is historical fact. This is why many opponents of moral and individual relativism contend that to uphold such life views from the front of the classroom begs the question not only of responsible citizenship, but also the question of national survival. It does not follow that the people who oppose such teaching are ultra-conservatives who want to preserve the status quo at all costs, or that they are all Jews and Christians—an assumption which is made frequently. The critical question about specific content in moral values education, they contend, is not whether your politics are to the right or to the left, or whether you are Moslem, Jew, Christian, or Atheist. The essential question is whether you are concerned for the sheer survival of the future generations of your nation. Developments in the late seventies and early eighties cause us to heed an Eastern intellectual's reading of the impoverished spirit of America today. Aleksander Solzhenitsyn sounds this warning:

> The Western world has lost its civic courage, both as a

22 S. Williams, "Me: A Magnificent Obsession," *Toronto Life* (December 1977), p. 70.

whole and separately, in each country, in each government, in each political party, and, of course, in the United Nations. Such a decline in courage is particularly noticeable among the ruling and intellectual elites, causing an impression of a loss of courage by the entire society. ... Must one point out that from ancient times a decline in courage has been considered the first symptom of the end? ... It is time, in the West, to defend not so much human rights as human obligations.[23]

23 Specified brief excerpts from, *A World Split Apart* by Aleksander I. Solzhenitsyn. Copyright© 1978 by Aleksander I. Solzhenitsyn. English language translation copyright© 1979 by Harper & Row, Publishers, Inc. Reprinted by permission of the publisher.

6

The Self-Serve Cafeteria

The problems discussed in the previous chapter would be considered by numerous advocates of the three models discussed earlier, as exactly those which they have identified and which they are making every effort to rectify. There is no question that their motivations are well intentioned. The question is: Where do these approaches actually lead us? As we have noted, there are variations in each of their formulations and while these will not be constantly reiterated, their differentiations should be kept in mind as we consider more general questions related to MVE practice.

In the Values Clarification arena, for example, supporters would argue that they are not actively working against moral precepts; that there is room for anyone who really wishes to take the stand that basic moral precepts do exist. All points of view are acceptable, after all. True, but supporters of these models present "moral precepts" as if they were only *one* of many equally acceptable "dishes" on the menu of values in a self-serve cafeteria. Further, if you do claim that your choice is "right" you will, in all probability, be directed to see that in the final analysis, all precepts must be qualified. "You *would* steal for your starving child, wouldn't you?" "You sometimes *have* to tell a lie, don't you?" And so on.

Of course extenuating circumstances do occur. Of course there are times when one moral value must take precedence over another, as in the example of stealing food for a starving child or lying to conceal a Jew in Nazi Germany. But does this change the inherent goodness of the moral precept per se? To jump from the fact that there are extenuating circumstances to the conclusion that there are, therefore, no basic moral precepts, is to fall far short of logic.

Children may become so confused by all the qualifications and situational dilemma exercises—many of which are extreme and very far removed from everyday life—that they will decide that the world is totally without moral or social order. As one grade seven student asked, "Isn't there *anything* you can count on?"

When we are caring for babies, we do not give them a whole apple to eat. We know that their digestive systems are not sufficiently sophisticated to process the skin, the flesh, and the core. The risk that they will choke is very high. So instead of the whole apple, we give them applesauce—the essence of the apple. This does not mean that we are cheating them of their independence.

COPPING OUT

Is it possible that parallels exist in the area of morals? Do we consider with as much concern the age-appropriateness of values education material presented through such courses as English, History, and Family Life Education, which holds out open values and "free" choice in the name of producing independent thinkers? But we adults like to believe that we are "with it" when it comes to contemporary thinking, that we are meeting kids "where they are at." And probably, if polled, most youth would opt for wide-open choices, at least as preteens and teenagers. One of the most jolting comments on this issue comes from a twenty-five-year-old high school dropout, now enrolled at university.

Ten years ago when I was in high school and we were asked our opinion [about the academic program], we were all in favor of the move to a permissive, no standards, "student directed" academic program. Who wouldn't be at that age?

But ask those same people now—*after* the fact. Many of us feel cheated and ripped off. "Whatever you choose will be right for you—just because you choose it" didn't turn out to be true. It was our teachers and parents who copped out.[1]

We need to be very sure that we are not copping out in MVE. For there is a popular notion that tends to imply:

- Parents and teachers who hold that there are core moral precepts and wish to share these with children are authoritarians. They tend to turn out children who are unimaginative, intellectually inhibited and dependent.

- Parents and teachers who hold that there are no core moral precepts are free thinkers. They turn out children who are creative, independent, and self-actualized.

Is it not ironic that those who support this notion find it necessary to believe that no middle ground can exist between these two extremes? But many parents and teachers have bought this notion. They have come to believe that it is best for them to opt out of influencing children, since to exert such influence amounts to "a violation of the child's moral freedom."[2]

Our society has long recognized that the school plays a major role in the socialization of children. The school's mandate, as set forth in education acts across the United States is to commend to students the moral values and conduct that previous generations have approved: honesty, justice, courage, and service to others, for example. Pupils, the Acts have stated, are to be encouraged to pursue and prize these ideals for their intrinsic goodness.

AFTER THE FACT

So far, for example, we have valued our system of jurisprudence, which is based on definite moral precepts. Now

---

1 K. Gow, "What Every Parent Should Know," *The Canadian*, 21 May 1977, p. 7.
2 L. Kohlberg, "Stages of Moral Development as a Basis for Moral Education," *Moral Education: Interdisciplinary Approaches*, p. 71. Reprinted by permission of University of Toronto Press and Paulist Press, Copyright© University of Toronto Press, 1971.

major forces in the values education movement assert that to teach a child moral precepts—that stealing is wrong, for example—is totalitarian and counterproductive to the child's moral development.

At a recent seminar on MVE, one of the participants, a social worker in a penal institution, pointed out what seemed to her the ultimate irony.

> We hold that to inculcate moral precepts—such as honesty—in the school classroom, is authoritarian and indoctrinating. As Values Clarification instructs: If a child "decide[s] that he values ... thievery ... we respect his right to decide upon that value."[3] After the fact, and if the child is caught stealing, we send him to training school. Only then is he taught that our society is founded on core moral precepts.

Behind this approach—whether the link is consciously recognized or not—is a theory of the basic nature of human beings and a theory of deviance which throws into question traditional approaches to crime and to individual responsibility. Even twenty years ago, Barbara Wootton, in *Social Science and Social Pathology*, identified sectors of the medical profession who seek to equate antisocial/criminal behavior with mental illness, and would treat them both alike.

> [They] are in fact prepared, either explicitly or by implication ... to obliterate the distinction between criminality and illness altogether. For them the line between the sick and the healthy either does not exist or is irrelevant to problems of social behavior; and they are prepared accordingly to treat all offenders as "patients" and to dispense with the concepts of responsibility altogether.[4]

This means that the concepts of "right" and "wrong" are no longer socially relevant. The individual offender is no longer held responsible for the morality of his or her own actions,

---

3 L. Raths et al., *Values and Teaching*, 2nd ed., p. 227.
4 Barbara Wootton, *Social Science and Social Pathology* (London: George Allen and Unwin, 1959), p. 227.

but is simply "ill." Guilt is merely a religious concept relevant to a few. The question of existential guilt is not even raised.[5] Behind such theories is the underlying assumption that human beings are moral rather than moral/immoral and rational rather than rational/irrational.[6] In moral education, this means that if we simply provide a permissive, nonauthoritarian environment which outlines all possible moral options, the child will rightly evaluate them and make the right choice. Thus it becomes the school's responsibility to children to simply "open up" all the choices. Any other procedure would purposely and automatically close minds.

The following editorial spells out what this philosophy means in terms of MVE:

> For six to seventeen year-olds, all value systems are to be presented—the Christian, the Marxist, the nihilist, even . . . the satanist, the sadist and the sick. All would be spread, as it were, upon a table so that the young-sters can pick and choose for themselves. "Now it is true," the child will be told, "that in the Christian and the Jewish traditions the individual acquires a signifi-cance because Christians and Jews believe in what they call 'God'. . . . But by contrast look over here at this part of the table. These people in this dish are called fascist, and they believe that a thing is right insofar as it serves the cause of a master race. And over in that bowl are what are called communists and they believe that any-thing is right if it serves the cause of the proletariat. And on these glittering platters are hedonism and sen-sualism and these people think anything is right that turns your crank. So you see, dear children, there are all kinds of ways of living. The one your parents happen to have chosen need not restrict or confine you. . . ."

5 For an explanation of existential guilt, see Rollo May, Ernest Angel, and Henri Ellenberger, *Existence* (New York: Basic Books Inc., 1958), p. 55.

6 For a discussion of various MVE approaches and the underlying assumptions they make concerning human nature, see D. Superka et al., *Values Education Sourcebook* (Boulder, Colorado: Social Science Education Consortium and ERIC Clearinghouse for Social Studies/So-cial Science Education, 1976).

Since no one can really know whether any doctrines be true or false, whether any forms of conduct be good or bad, right or wrong, why not dish them all out and let the kiddies pick for themselves. . . ? If all systems are laid out impartially before the child, he will be bound to come up in the end with the right one. The child once given the Case for Goodness as written by, say, Dickens versus the Case for Drugs, as written by, say, Leary, will inevitably opt for Goodness. No need to emphasize, no need to exhort, no need to prejudice, no need even to distinguish. Just present all the viewpoints and virtue is inevitably bound to result. It is a beautiful philosophy. It is also insane.[7]

But surely it is not a matter of whether moral issues should be put on the table or not. Of course they should. It is not a question of students knowing that people hold different views. Of course they know this. It *is* a question of whether the teacher asserts that any one view is as morally right as any other. It is not a matter of whether the dimensions of an issue and the choices available should be uncovered and discussed. It *is* a matter of whether the issue will be examined in relation to any evaluative standards. It is not a question of whether children should be allowed or encouraged to question or disagree. This is the essence of mature communication. It is not a question of ultimately allowing children freedom of choice; they have it. It *is* a matter of determining from what "tables" moral values should be offered, what issues should be discussed, at what age, and what objectives should be established.

TOPIC TIMING

In fact, one of the astounding features of many values education strategies is that the topics advocated for class discussion and the methods employed seldom offer any suggestion at all about the age at which these topics and methods might or might not be appropriate. For example, Simon's book, *Values Clarification: A Handbook of Practical Strate-*

7 T. Byfield, "Letter from the Editor," *Edmonton Report*, 6 March 1978, p. 2.

gies for Teachers and Students, is recommended with no qualifications by officials in *Career Education Activities: Teacher Handbook for Kindergarten*: "An excellent set of strategies for student use . . . offers a variety of techniques and topics . . . for all age groups."[8] Yet this is the book examined in chapter 2 in which Strategy Numbers 48, 49, 50, and 56 are the Fall-Out-Shelter Problem, the Cave-In Simulation, Alligator River, [see chapter 9] and the Obituary. It may be, in part, such lack of consideration of age-topic appropriateness in MVE that has led Brian Hall, past president of the Center for the Exploration of Values and Meaning to advocate restricting its use:

> Value education is an integrative, holistic discipline: it integrates science, religion and the social sciences. If it has any place as subject matter, it belongs in late high school and college. It should then be seen as an opportunity for students to integrate and bring together all the things they are learning, and to translate them in terms of their own behavior.[9]

Even taking into account the apparent sophistication of today's youth and the very real necessity for them to confront and learn to deal with conflict, there is little doubt that premature exposure to some issues leads to unnecessary anxiety, confusion, and even miseducation. For example, consider the "Devil's Advocate" exercise in the popular text, *Values and Teaching.* While it could be stimulating for older children, this particular example involves eight- and nine-year-olds in a discussion about the first heroes of the space age.

> [*Teacher:*] *I want to play the devil with you. I'll screw on my horns and get ready to jab you with my pitchfork. Watch out.*
>
> *You know all that stuff you've been reading about these heroes who go up in space ships? Well, this devil*

8 *Career Education, Activities: A Teacher Handbook for Kindergarten: Division I and II,* The Saskatchewan Department of Education (Regina: September 1979), p. 153.
9 Brian P. Hall, "Values: Education and Consciousness: The State of the Art, Challenge in Our Times," Inaugural Address delivered at Seattle University (November 1975).

thinks they're not heroes at all. What's so heroic about going up in a space ship? Why, they have those things so carefully figured out that nothing can go wrong. With all of those movie cameras grinding and all of those TV cameras focused on them, you don't think our government could afford to have the bad publicity of anything going wrong, do you? This devil thinks that your walk to school every morning has about as much danger in it as the danger those so-called heroes had to risk. And to ride in a car without seat belts is twice as dangerous as that. But no one calls you a hero when you do that.

Anyhow, if there is such a risk, what kind of person would leave a spouse and children to do something a monkey could have done? Finally, you foolish children, this devil wants to raise the question about all that money that goes into space projects. Did you know that we spend over a billion bucks a year, and that money could easily wipe out the slums, build new colleges, work productively on cancer and mental illness research?

So speaks the devil.

What a lively class session followed the devil's discourse. Few students take that kind of confrontation lying down, and the alternatives to consider filled the room. It was value clarifying on a high level, for students were forced to examine what they prized and cherished, and consider affirming it in front of the entire class. There was no right answer with which even the devil wanted each student to agree. But the teacher, not the devil, wanted to make sure that students considered alternatives to the popular notions that are so easy to leave unexamined, thus encouraging misunderstandings and lazy thinking habits.[10]

Are eight- to nine-year-olds ready for this kind of experience? Do they really understand the concept of the Devil's Advocate? Were they really making "choices from among alternatives which they fully understood?" Do the "facts"

10 L. Raths et al., *Values and Teaching*, 2nd ed., pp. 193-194.

that the space trip required neither courage nor risk and could have been accomplished equally well by a monkey— which many children would accept as true—create a basis for sound value clarification? Further, what purpose is served in levelling that weight of negativism against the exploration of space to children of this age? How will the arguments be likely to affect their budding scientific imaginations? Must all the heroes of nine-year-olds be called into question? And if we insist that children need experiences like this to help them confront "reality," are we not in grave danger of spawning a lot of jaundiced, turned-off, tuned-out young minds?

We must also consider the extensive and far-ranging area the cafeteria covers. MVE strategies are geared to be integrated as a prime objective into any educational subject at any time. This means, of course, that a student can scarcely be exempted from MVE because it is so fully integrated into all offerings in the cafeteria. One has only to run down the list:

Value Topics for Language Arts and Literature;
Value Topics for Social Studies;
Conflict in the Family (Family Studies);[11]
Teaching Science with a Focus on Values;
The Search for Values with a Focus on Math;
Teaching History with a Focus on Values;
The Use of Selected Value-Clarifying Strategies in Health Education.[12]

GROUP PRESSURE

Undoubtedly, the most effective way to help students appreciate that questions of value enter into every aspect of life is to purposely recognize and integrate the value dimension into their regular classroom subjects. Few would quarrel with that fact. The most important question is *How*

---

11 Listed on *The Moral Education Project: Materials List/Order Form*, pp. 4-5. Available from The Moral Education Project, OISE, 252 Bloor Street West, Toronto, Ontario, Canada.
12 Selections from section entitled, "Values Clarification and School Subjects," *Readings in Values Clarification*, eds. H. Kirschenbaum and S. Simon (Minneapolis: Winston Press, 1973), pp. 111-222.

is this integration being accomplished, and with what objectives? Earlier we saw that many MVE strategies are modelled on sensitivity training and encounter group methods. The group is used to unfreeze a child's existing value system so that new attitudes and values may be injected and adopted. Accordingly, department of education guidelines for family life education, for example, have made specific reference to "the process whereby the individual's emotional defense mechanisms are deactivated so that he may look at new facts, new ways of behavior and new attitudes without having to lower his self-esteem."[13] What happens, as Clifford Edwards points out in "Sensitivity Training and Education: A Critique," is that

> beliefs long accepted as true by the individual are exposed to cursory examination by the group. Such items as loyalties, family relationships, and religious convictions become subject to change. The person may then suffer disassociation from parents and others as a consequence of his altered beliefs.[14]

> The implication played upon is that values which one cannot defend must be worthless and in need of change. Judgments concerning change are ordinarily made in terms of emotional criteria only. Pressure from the group may thus supply adequate leverage to alter values which are rationally superior to those which the group advocates. . . . The major consequence is really one of evolving common values, with the more influential members supplying the direction.[15]

When one adds to this Sidney Simon's affirmation [regarding sex education], that "the schools must not be allowed to

---

13 *Family Life Education Guideline for the Development of an Elementary School Program*, British Columbia Department of Education, Division of Instructional Services Curriculum Development Branch (Victoria, B.C.: 1973), p. 24.

14 Clifford H. Edwards, "Sensitivity Training and Education: A Critique," *"Educational Leadership*, vol. 28, no. 3 (December 1970), p. 261. Reprinted with permission of the Association for Supervision and Curriculum Development and Clifford H. Edwards. Copyright© 1970 by the Association for Supervision and Curriculum Development. All rights reserved.

15 Ibid., p. 260.

continue fostering the immorality of morality. An entirely different set of values must be nourished ... ,"[16] we must ask ourselves whether the cafeteria is actually offering a "free" choice at all. Moreover, it is when this "entirely different set of values" is nourished without prior discussion with parents that students can become confused and pulled between the values of home and school. In terms of the cafeteria's offerings, the question of what constitutes "nourishment" is vital.

SEX EDUCATION

Michele Dore, a counsellor with the Toronto Birth Control and VD Information Centre, described in *Maclean's* magazine as "intent on waging her own little war against what she sees as middle-class values," urges:

> If [the educational system] is so concerned about pregnancy, why don't they teach teens more about oral sex and mutual masturbation? Why don't mothers teach their daughters to masturbate?[17]

Some would go further than that. *Time* magazine reports on the "propaganda campaign" which is being mounted with regard to supporting "consensual incest" and "positive incest." Wardell Pomeroy, whose books entitled *Girls and Sex* and *Boys and Sex* appear on many school guides (see page 194) (the latter which includes discussion of intercourse with animals) now states his views on incest quite clearly:

> "It is time to admit that incest need not be a perversion or a symptom of mental illness," he says. "Incest between ... children and adults ... can sometimes be beneficial."[18]

In fact increasing numbers of family life educators and researchers—after years of basing their rationale for sex

---

16 M. and S. Simon, *Sexuality and School*, paper available from the National Humanistic Education Center, Springfield Road, Upper Jay, New York 12987, p. 3.

17 Judith Timson, "Teen Sex," *Maclean's*, 31 March 1980, p. 45.

18 "Attacking the Last Taboo," *Time*, 14 April 1980, p. 60.

education programs on the "fact" that they would reduce escalating rates of illegitimacy and VD—now argue the reverse. They are now supporting the purpose of sex education as defined in such directives as "Preparing Professionals for Family Life and Human Sexuality," issued by the Michigan Department of Public Health:

> "[Few] people today take seriously the assumption that sex education will lower rates of illegitimacy, venereal disease or promiscuity.... The more viable assumption behind an interest in sex education is that it should work to make sex a more rewarding part of people's lives—to make sex education impart competence and not necessarily constraint...."[19]

Not surprisingly, given this objective, numerous tests and questionnaires are designed so that students may become more aware of various techniques and the matter of "competency." Thus, in a book entitled, *Education for Sexuality*, which is widely used in North America, students from grade 7 up are given the task to "analyse ... and differentiat[e] the effect of each [of touch, smell, sight ... pornography] on the sex drive of the male and of the female,"[20] and to fill out the following Sexual Behavior Chart (Table 3) in order to clarify their own individual choice of sexual life-style.

Since 1978, U.S. citizens have had a federal law which prohibits—to the extent of withdrawal of federal funds from that school—the formal testing of students "in which the primary purpose is to reveal information concerning ... (3) sex behavior and attitudes ..."[21] Fully documented and discussed in chapter 7, the Hatch Act is, however, scarcely utilized to protest such activities.

"What's Right for the Individual"

In Arcata, Humboldt County, California, "the curriculum guide for seventh and eighth grades advises, 'stress what is

---

19 Cited in *Life Advocate*, April 1980, p. 7 (4901 Richmond, Houston, Texas, 77027).
20 John J. Burt and Linda Brower Meeks, *Education for Sexuality: Concepts and Programs for Teaching* (Toronto: W.B. Saunders Co., 1975), pp. 354-355.
21 Public Law, 95-561, 92 Stat. 2143 (1978).

Table 3.   Sexual Behavior Chart

Code	Male Commitment Additional Criteria	Female Commitment Additional Criteria	Code
	Sexual Behavior Chart		
	light embracing or fond holding of hands		
	casual good-night kissing		
	intense (French) kissing		
	horizontal embrace with some petting but not undressed		
	petting of female's breast from outside her clothing		
	petting of female's breast without clothes intervening		
	petting below the waist of the female under her clothing		
	petting below the waist of both male and female under clothing		
	nude embrace		
	sexual inter-course		

Personal Commitment	Code
Casually attracted	A
good friends	B
going steady	C
tentatively engaged	D
officially engaged	E
married	F

Source: John J. Burt and Linda Brower Meeks, *Education for Sexuality: Concepts and Programs for Teaching,* (Toronto: W. B. Saunders Co., 1975), p. 379.

right for the individual.' "[22] In light of this, the following comments from a school psychologist are worth consideration:

> We have overemphasized the role of the school in "freeing" young people to "be themselves." The majority of our youth are immature and inexperienced and somewhat confused about their sexuality, and their values related to sexuality. Often regarding intercourse they are told either directly or indirectly in the course of MVE sessions that "if you respect each other, if no-one will be hurt, and if you feel ready for it—it's O.K."

> But these criteria are almost impossible for a kid to evaluate. What *does* "respect" mean? As long as the other is willing? How can you know who is going to be hurt in the short run *or* the long run? And how do you tell when you're ready? Being "ready" has a positive implication to it which kids interpret as an expectation of them.

> Other than the possibility of unwanted pregnancy—is equal time—if any—spent on looking at possible negative *psychological* effects of this degree of intimacy? With how much conviction? The usual introduction to discussing intercourse with a class of kids is "If you're going to be *sexually active.* . . ." But what is the reverse? Sexually passive. What normal teenager wants to see him or herself as sexually "passive"—dead from the ankles up?!

> These aren't real choices being put out. They don't "free" kids at all. Most kids just feel more pressure to shed their apparent "hang-ups" and "get on with it."

But even putting psychological and moral factors aside, in two stunning articles in the *Journal of the New York State School Nurse-Teachers Association*, Dr. Lorand provides multiple documentation of the fact that in this self-serve

---

22 Jacqueline Kasun, "Turning Children into Sex Experts," *The Public Interest*, no. 55 (Spring 1979), p. 9. Reprinted with permission of the author from *The Public Interest*. Copyright© 1979 by National Affairs Inc.

moral values cafeteria we have been examining, the *medical facts* necessary to responsible decision making are not being given to students. Documented in British and American medical journals over the past 30 years, Dr. Lorand points out that such vital scientific findings as the link between early repeated sexual intercourse and cervical cancer are very often "screened out" in classroom presentations. For example, an article in the *Journal of the American Medical Association* by I.D. Rotkin of the Kaiser Foundation Research Institute reports:

> These several studies are concerned with causation of cancer of the uterine cervix, and results are all in the same direction. . . . All studies agree that cervical cancer risk is increased by . . . first coitus at early ages[23] . . . by observing abstinence the adolescent female is on reasonably valid biological ground, which requires no moral or religious support.[24]

Similarly, Dr. Lorand points to the omission of vital information regarding venereal disease.

> For example, several films and leaflets, including the latest from the American Foundation for the Prevention of Venereal Disease, written with the cooperation of the New York City Health Department, as was the TV program VD BLUES, all reveal unquestioning acceptance of promiscuity and state that VD is curable. None mentions that the painful and dangerous venereal disease, genital herpes is *not* curable, nor that some strains of gonorrhea are penicillin-resistant and sterility may occur during the time a cure is sought. Nor do any of these sources take note of the fact that Cytomegalovirus, another sexually transmissable disease which cripples and retards more infants than German measles, is also incurable.[25]

---

23 I.D. Rotkin, "Relation of Adolescent Coitus to Cervical Cancer," *Journal of the American Medical Association*, Vol. 179 (17 February 1962), p. 486. Copyright© 1962, American Medical Association.

24 Ibid., p. 491.

25 Rhoda Lorand, "The Betrayal of Youth," *Journal of the New York State School Nurse-Teachers Association* (Spring 1978), p. 14.

Can youth be expected to make "free," informed, and responsible judgments when such facts are withheld? One of the basic questions in MVE, then, is not only whether the self-serve moral values cafeteria offers the most nourishing diet, but whether in many cases the cafeteria is actually making available an equally balanced selection of real alternatives, equally prominently and attractively displayed for equally thoughtful examination. Sex education is, of course, only one section of MVE's multisectioned cafeteria where this question must be considered.

DEATH EDUCATION

More recently, a new section has been added to the cafeteria. Values educators are placing increasing emphasis on death, dying, and survival, especially among children in the elementary grades. We have already seen ample evidence of this emphasis in many Values Clarification exercises: the Life Raft; the Fall-Out Shelter; the Cave-In Simulation; the Obituary; in Kohlbergian dilemmas concerning the drowning man, cannibalism, and choosing one child to live over another; and in the Moral Education Project materials concerned with murder and suicide.

Death and dying are realities of life, and it is true that as a society we often appear to do all in our power not to recognize their existence. We are particularly negligent in working through these issues with children when so many teachable moments are naturally available, if we adults feel comfortable with them. From my experience as founding director of Medical Social Work in the largest children's hospital in North America and from the number of years I have spent in teaching and in international research concerning children and youth, I know only too well the trauma which occurs when the need of children to talk about death has not been recognized.

It has also been my experience that unless one knows each child and his or her parents' convictions very well, one can, without knowing it, unleash immeasurable distress by choosing to give a classroom of young children the cafeteria-style unit on death and dying. Consider this account of such a unit conducted by a fifth-grade teacher and originally published in the October 1978 issue of *Phi Delta Kappan*, a highly regarded American journal for educators. Following the account is a response from another teacher, which also appears in the journal.

I Taught About Death and Dying[26]

by James M. Mueller, Jr.

Funereal facts for fifth-graders.

For three days I taught a group of 26 fifth-graders about death and dying.

On the first day, the students were allowed to do extra-credit reports on a choice of topics: mummies, pyres, cryonics, cremation, embalming, and stone for graves. For spelling, a pretest was given using such terms as undertaker, morgue, corpse, dying, tomb, wake, cemetery, bury, mourn, mortician, life, grief, etc. In language class the pupils viewed and discussed a filmstrip titled *Life-Death: Perspectives on Death*, in which living things are compared with nonorganic objects. Math class involved working out funeral-related written problems. For social studies it was discussion time. We talked about how we begin to die as soon as we are born. The class compared the seasons to the life cycle.

They discussed pacemakers and modern science. They decided we should enjoy each day we are alive. They discovered that death not only brings sorrow but sometimes happiness. Then the whole class listed all the ways to die—e.g., disease, suffocation, suicide, murder, old age, drowning, earthquake, and 40 other ways. (The children voted that the best way to die is of old age in bed. The worst way to die is by beating or whipping, a choice probably influenced by viewing *Roots*.)

During health study the children were split into many small groups to discuss these topics: Why do we have death certificates? Should a person donate parts of the body to science? Should the casket be open for viewing or closed? Should flowers be sent to the funeral? Do we need

26 *Phi Delta Kappan* (October 1978), p. 117. Reprinted from *Phi Delta Kappan*. Copyright© 1978, Phi Delta Kappan, Inc.

funeral homes? Which is better, cremation or burial? What is better, knowing or not knowing that you are going to die? What would happen if no one died for one full year? Music time allowed the students to hear a song about death. "You and Me Against the World," by Helen Reddy, is a song about a mother and her daughter enjoying life but knowing that someday one of them will die and the other will remain behind.

The second day began with spelling. The pupils were told to write a 75-word story using some of the spelling words. The title was "How I Died." Many of the stories told of violent deaths, heroic deaths, and experiences after death. In handwriting class the children were to write all the spelling words in a special format: lower-case print, then upper-case print, then lower-case cursive. Next we viewed a filmstrip titled "Facts About Funerals." The story line began with a student who visited a funeral home and wrote a report about what he saw. The funeral director showed the viewing room, the casket room, the embalming room, and the garage area. We discussed the needs of funeral services, and the pupils took a quiz about the filmstrip.

During language period small groups discussed and recorded idiomatic statements related to death and dying. Examples: starving to death, over my dead body, catch your death of pneumonia, I'll skin you alive. After lunch the students had to write death-related math problems. One example: Forty-five people died each day. How many died in 27 days? They also had to measure their own coffin, using metric and English units. In social studies the pupils were assigned the task of role-playing a life situation. Three of the seven groups acted out a death-related situation. One was about an "Operation Death," one about someone dying in a car accident, and one concerned a person being shot in a fight. The day was completed with music class. The pupils listened to two records. "Deep Blue Sea," an American folk tune, is about a person who drowns and is buried in the ocean. "Alone Again (Naturally)," by Gilbert O'Sullivan, is about a person who loses his girl friend, then remembers how his mother and father died.

The children then compared and contrasted all the songs heard thus far.

On the last day the class took a short bus trip. When the bus stopped for a red light, some of the children called attention to a hearse by a local church. Just as we all glanced in that direction, the flower-covered casket was removed from the hearse. The comment (from a little girl), "We know what's going on over there," seemed to make all my work worthwhile. Later that morning the pupils were asked to give meanings for spelling words related to death. There was also a discussion based on these questions: What would you die for? What do you live for? The responses were varied. The children replied that they would die for their parents, their families, their friends, to protect someone special, and for their country. They said that they would live for enjoyment, to continue the family, and to learn about life. In language class, the students had to choose two of three activities. They could write their own obituary (using newspaper examples), write their own wills, or draw their own tombstone.

In the afternoon the class greeted the guest speaker, a local funeral director invited to discuss funerals and answer any questions that the children might have about death and dying. Hands shot up from nearly every desk for about an hour. Questions ranged from unusual funeral arrangements and comforting the bereaved to what embalming is all about. Music for the last day was "That's Life" as sung by Frank Sinatra. This record explains the need to continue living and what this person would do if life were not worthwhile. The class listened, evaluated, and generalized about all the music studied for the past three days. Students listened to and discussed a story titled "The Man Who Gave Himself Away," by Gordon Sheppard. This beautiful story tells about an old man who gives himself back to nature when he finds out that he is near death.

The last activity for the session was a questionnaire. The pupils were asked if this three-day unit on death education had been worthwhile. Their written comments revealed a variety of reactions. Two children said "It was worthwhile, but too brief." Two others said, "It wasn't worthwhile because the subject shouldn't be studied now." Two others wrote, "Yes and no, because it made us feel sad, but again it wasn't really that bad." The rest of the children thought it was a good idea. Their comments included: "It was worth the time to study about death because you can understand a death in the family." "We should know how to take it [death]." "I found out about writing a will." "I know how to control myself." "We can understand life to enjoy life while we can." And, "Now we're not afraid of dying as much as we were."

After teaching this experimental three-day unit on death, I personally feel that the children benefited. Consultation with parents, support from fellow teachers, encouragement from the administration, and the cooperation from 26 special fifth-grade children all contributed to a successful teaching/learning experience.

JAMES M. MUELLER, JR. (Millersville State College Chapter) is a fifth-grade teacher in the Buchanan Elementary School, Lancaster, Pa.

Death and Dying in Three Days?[27]

by Jayne Freeman

Death education, certainly, says Ms. Freeman, but really now. . . .

In opposing Mueller's particular approach to death education, I am not trying to say that we should avoid all discussion of death with children. There is no doubt that our society takes an ostrich approach to the subject. We don't discuss it, we don't explain it, and we hope it will just go away even though we know it won't. We don't even use the word "die." People "depart" or "pass away." As a rule, children are not taken to funerals. Often they are not even told when someone dies. Or

27 Ibid., p. 118. Reprinted from *Phi Delta Kappan*. Copyright© 1978, Phi Delta Kappan, Inc.

they are told in euphemisms: "Grandpa has gone away to heaven."

Avoiding reality is unhealthy, and I believe that combating it through education is a worthwhile idea. However, I object to the overwhelming way in which Mueller attempted to teach his young students all about death in three short days.

Moreover, I am concerned about his shotgun approach to the subject. When I was a student teacher in the sixties, it was popular to attempt to integrate basic skills into the subject being studied. It seems to me that Mueller has embraced this integration far too enthusiastically. I question the educational necessity of fifth-graders' being able to spell such words as "morgue" and "mortician." Research on mummies, pyres, cryonics, etc., seems more grisly than enlightening, and the activity in which students listed all the ways to die struck me as being very likely to frighten students of this age. The understanding of death, and of one's own mortality in particular, requires a certain level of emotional and mental maturity, and I question whether fifth-graders

have reached that level—or should be forced to try. The mental picture I have of 10-year-olds measuring themselves and/or each other for coffins frightens even me, and I have witnessed several deaths.

Many of the subjects Mueller offers for classroom discussion seem beyond the knowledge and maturity level of the students. "Which is better, burial or cremation?" is a question with both religious and sociological implications, and it's pretty heavy material for fifth-graders to handle. At best, the class discussions must have been shallow; at worst, upsetting to the students.

A few months ago the local papers in my community carried these headlines: "School District Settles Lawsuit Out of Court." My district paid several thousand dollars to the parents of a 13-year-old girl who was under a psychiatrist's care after attending a summer-school class on death and dying. The parents brought suit on the grounds that they had not signed the permission slip that the teacher had issued to class members, had not authorized their child's attendance in the class, and in particular had not authorized the viewing, in an unexpurgated edition, of the film *Helter Skelter*, which seems to have been the culminating experience for their daughter, crystallizing her fear of death into an obsession.

A teacher planning a unit on death and dying should realize that he is dealing with controversial material and take certain precautions to protect himself and his students. He should discuss the proposed class with the principal or curriculum consultant, who may have a feel for the possible community reactions. He might also plan a parents' meeting to explain the goals and activities of the class and to solicit parental input as to course content. Finally, for the protection of all, the teacher should require a permission slip from each participant's parents. Parents will know better than the teacher whether or not their child has the emotional maturity to handle the subject matter. Some parents may prefer to deal with this subject in the home rather than have it explained in detail at school. Mueller did not discuss how he handled school and community relations, except for his refer-

ence in the final paragraph to "consultation . . . encouragement . . . support." I wish he had shared his planning for teaching controversial material in more detail.

A number of Mueller's class activities would be valuable for children of this age, if not crowded into such an intensive study period. Over a longer time span—a semester or even a school year—students could probably gain valuable insights from such activities as the filmstrip viewings and discussions, the song analysis, the creative writing assignments, the role playing. I like the idea of approaching the concept through literature, as Mueller did with "The Man Who Gave Himself Away." There are also children's books that deal with death. Such books as *Grandma Didn't Wave Back* could be read to the class. Followed by a class discussion, they can clarify feelings and prepare children to accept the inevitable loss of loved ones through death.

There should also be time in the course of a school year to deal with the subject in a spontaneous manner, building upon common and familiar experiences in the children's own lives, such as the loss of a pet or of a grandparent. Children need to acquire an acceptance of the inevitability of death and of their own mortality, but I do not believe they can acquire such mature insights in three short days. Or even three short years. When children are only 10, schools should focus more directly on acceptance of the loss of loved ones than on one's own certain mortality. Mueller fails to accommodate his concepts and material to the maturity level of the student.

Let's introduce the concepts at this age and develop them more fully later, perhaps in high school.

_____

JAYNE FREEMAN (Portland Oregon Chapter) teaches at the Seth Lewelling Elementary School in Milwaukie, Ore. A mother of seven children, she has taught in every elementary grade except second. Her articles have appeared in a number of professional and popular journals, and she serves as a Kappan editorial consultant.

Some of Jayne Freeman's concerns are also shared by mental health specialists. The possibility of psychological harm resulting from death education is high. Studies conducted on grade ten students by Case Western Reserve University researchers have this to report:

One of the main goals of these modules was to have students understand and, therefore, fear death less. These two modules did not meet this goal. The students participating in these modules increased their fear of death and dying scores as measured by the Collet-Lester Fear of Death Scale. This was true of an overall measure (the total score) and more defined measures of death of others, dying of others, and dying of self. The students, in general, were more fearful of death and dying of self than death and dying of others, which, given the nature of adolescence, was not surprising. This study replicated the results of Mueller. She found that upon completion of a death education unit, eighth grade adolescents scored higher than a control group on a measure of fear of death.[28]

28 Lawrence A. Bailis and William R. Kennedy, "Effects of a Death Education Program upon Secondary School Students," *The Journal of Educational Research*, vol. 71, no. 2 (November/December 1977), p. 66.

If this is the effect on students of fourteen and fifteen years, how much greater the risk for ten-year-olds? Although it would be farthest from the intention of many who are involved in teaching death education, it has been suggested that consciousness-raising courses should also be taught concerning the right to suicide.

In *Common Sense Suicide: The Final Right*, the author points to the Japanese attitude toward suicide as a model to be followed. "Japanese suicides alone . . . could supply a wealth of study material for a consciousness-raising course on suicide."[29] While the author addresses herself primarily to suicide among older adults, and is not advocating youth suicide, she recognizes:

> Make old-age suicide acceptable to one generation of children and the attitude is reversed. First thing you know, kids will be wondering not why we do, but why we *don't*.

> Of course it is not that easy, but it may be much easier than anyone would have thought a decade or two ago. Attitudes toward almost everything have changed drastically; why not toward suicide?[30]

The author recommends

> a linking of suicide prevention and suicide facilitation probably through existing or similar suicide prevention centers. . . . One can imagine that an elderly person planning a rational suicide would be willing to take "time out" to talk with a younger person who showed suicidal tendencies. Whether or not such talks would be beneficial is a decision for members of the staff familiar with each individual situation.[31]

But on what basis does such a center or the MVE teacher who elects to "discuss" this topic, attempt to "prevent" or "facilitate" suicide? Nobel Laureate, Dr. Max Delbruck

29 Doris Portwood, *Common-Sense Suicide: The Final Right* (New York: Dodd, Mead & Co., 1978), p. 90. Reprinted by permission of Dodd, Mead & Company, Inc. Copyright© 1978 by Doris Portwood.
30 Ibid., p. 96.
31 Ibid., p. 98.

firmly places suicide education in the same category as offering birth control information:

> A person should be given instruction in the techniques of control over his or her own death, as we are now given information in the techniques of birth control. Society must have free access to information about forms of suicide that are not repulsive.[32]

No one would disagree with the fact that we live in a society where both adults and youth are having trouble coping with life. Rates of suicide—especially among children and youth—are escalating by leaps and bounds. The causes are sometimes baffling. However, courses which focus on death and suicide education, such as the ones described, are causing many to ask whether a correlation exists between what is being offered in this section of the moral values cafeteria and the statistics on suicide which are skyrocketing in this age group.

PROFESSIONAL TRAINING

Carrying the analogy of the self-serve cafeteria one step further, leads us to inquire how those who are in charge of the cafeteria decide what content should be offered, for which ages, with what objectives and nutritional value. What is the training of those working in the cafeteria: Are they equipped to do this work? Are they supervised? Is the sky the limit in terms of menu preparation and experimentation, or are there specifically defined ingredients which must be included in order to meet certain criteria and standards?

When we examined the three most popular approaches to MVE, it was clear that MVE educators are by no means agreed on the answers to these fundamental questions. Indeed, there is not even much agreement as to what values education really is, let alone how a truly "values-educated individual" might be described.

If we found that the adult encounter groups and the sensitivity sessions of the sixties were often conducted by

32 Max Delbruck, "Education for Suicide," *Prism*, (Journal of the American Medical Association), vol. 2, no. 11 (November 1974) p. 19.

people ill equipped to handle the complexity of emotions set free, we should surely consider similar hazards involved in teaching many facets of MVE. Some educators are very aware of these hazards and are offering similar remarks to those made by Dr. Sobol, Superintendent of the Scarsdale Schools, when he addressed fellow educators at a Moral Education Conference meeting in Scarsdale, New York:

1. Are you teaching values . . . ? If so, *what* values and whose values are they, and who told you to teach them to our children?

2. If you are not teaching values, why aren't you? Don't we all believe in the same fundamental values in this society—honesty, decency, respect for life? Do you really mean that one person's view of such matters is as good as another's? In emphasizing your "process of valuing" apart from values and your "structures of moral reasoning" apart from content, aren't you teaching a moral relativism? And again, by what authority do you do so?

3. Who are you to teach moral development anyway? Are you all at Stage Six? Are you the models of morality that I would select for my children? And even if you are "good" people (on my terms), how do I know that you really know what you're doing? And who is supervising?

4. As you proceed with your dilemmas and your discussions, are you really helping children to become more moral, or are you simply teaching them to be more glib? I know that your purpose is not to make children behave better but to enhance their development from one moral stage to the next, and I know that some studies have shown that principled moral choices are more likely to be made in behavior where principled moral reasoning is a precondition. But we also know that principled moral reasoning, while it may be a necessary, is surely not a sufficient condition for principled moral behavior. Are we simply teaching children how to talk the game?

The Self-Serve Cafeteria

5. Finally, how do you know that the theory on which
    you base your work is wholly correct?[33]

Many teachers are exceedingly concerned about these
very questions. To be a moral educator in the modes now
recommended has not, after all, been either suggested or
required in the past and, therefore, has not been considered
a specific part of teacher training. Now, regardless of the
fact that their specialty has always been teaching kindergarten; or all subjects to grade 4s or 6s, or History in senior
high, or English and Social Studies to grades 8-10, teachers
are under considerable official pressure—and in some states
legislative ruling—to integrate values education into their
curriculum area(s). Typically, lists of recommended MVE
books, films and tapes are circulated to them and they are
encouraged to press forward regardless of the well known
fact that,

> [i]n the academic world at present ... there is a con-
> siderable amount of controversy over the nature of
> morality and over the criteria for deciding moral issues.
> It is difficult to see then how academics can agree
> upon what form moral education should take.[34]

Despite this, and because many educators consider MVE
highly important, teachers are encouraged to "tackle it,"
despite their lack of training, and to "learn by doing." For
example, a Teachers' Federation booklet on *Values Education* simply advises:

> Until some clear consensus is reached, however,
> among scholars, it is necessary for teachers to produce
> their own synthesis, drawing from the several schools
> of thought, to develop an individual approach that is
> suitable both for themselves and their students.[35]

33 Dr. Thomas Sobol, "A Word to the Wise," Moral Education Confer-
    ence, Heathcote Elementary School, Scarsdale, N.Y., 30 April 1978.
    Reprinted in *Moral Education Forum*, vol. III, no. 3 (June 1978), p. 12.
34 Clive Beck et al., eds., *Moral Education: Interdisciplinary Approaches*,
    p. 11. Reprinted by permission of University of Toronto Press and
    Paulist Press. Copyright© University of Toronto Press, 1971.
35 S. Barrs et al., *Values Education: A Resource Booklet*, p. 6.

And going further, "It is hoped that after a time teachers would supplement the materials with their own or become completely independent of them."[36] Thus, many consultants in MVE are encouraging a situation in which each teacher ultimately designs and implements his or her own materials.

There is some value in this attitude. Like most other professionals, particularly those who have chosen to work with people, many teachers are not happy to have their creative abilities confined to a set curriculum or even to a set approach to instruction. They consider that such restriction makes them technicians, rather than professionals. They want latitude to create their own forms and their own manner of packaging instruction. This is not difficult to understand. At the same time, other teachers realize that the role of the moral educator is fraught with questions too complex to be simply dropped in their individual laps. As one Curriculum Supervisor of a large school board said, as he resigned his post to protest the feasibility of teachers responsibly implementing official department of education directives on MVE: "The greatest problem ... is that the department assumes that every teacher has a research assistant, a large library, one lesson to prepare a day at most, and the skill, time and talent to develop his own course as well as teach it."[37]

In an effort to learn the views of various educators about their responsibility in MVE, one jurisdiction undertook a survey of over 10,000 teachers, 650 administrators and 550 teacher educators. They reported:

(a) The *TEACHERS'* greatest concern is their role and the parents' role in moral education. The teachers' main fear is that of *indoctrination*; one-half of them see it as a "conflict between teacher and parent values." They asked this question: "Who has the ultimate responsibility and how much should we as teachers accept?"

The teachers see a large number of their own group as having little moral integrity. Few choose

36 Clive Beck, Appendix F, *The Moral Education Project (Year 3)*, (Spiral Bound Edition), p. 8.
37 Quoted in the *Edmonton Report*, 5 January 1976, p. 18.

to take leadership in moral education, and they are fearful about being explicit about their own personal values; yet they wish the students to see them as they are. Many teachers also condemn the students as having little morality and tie this in with the parents' values rather than society, the media, or their peers. While admitting their own need for training in moral education, the teachers felt that the parents too would benefit from such a training.

(b) *ADMINISTRATORS* see their main thrust in moral education as its *implementation* in the schools, "to help the students develop a personal value system."

(c) *TEACHER EDUCATORS* are primarily interested in the "urgency to" "get off our asses" and "provide *strategies* in the field and in training," "to produce skills in the area of valuing" such as "role-taking, clarifying, discussion, and decision-making." They want to "spread the word" so that students may be able to "articulate" and be comfortable with their own values.[38]

A MIXED BAG

From the consumers' point of view, the present system provides little accountability. Because MVE is such a mixed bag of so many conflicting approaches, and because it actively encourages the teachers to do their own personal synthesizing and creating in the classroom, its implementation is as wide and diverse as the particular views of each teacher concerned. These views affect the topics the teachers choose to discuss with particular age groups, the objectives they may have in such discussion, and how they will guide, or not guide, the session. For without standards and approved materials in MVE, the process of discussion itself

38 Clive Beck, "Determination of Curriculum Formats, Teaching Techniques, and Study Materials That Are Effective in Teacher Education," *The Moral Education Project (Year 4): Annual Report 1975/76*, pp. 6-7. For the full report of this survey, see Susan Pagliuso, "Survey of Ontario Teachers, Administrators, and Teacher Educators," Appendix A. pp. 29-80.

becomes both the means and the end. The use of the process at any time and the manner of its use depend almost wholly on what the individual conducting the session chooses to bring to that process.

As emphasized earlier, one of the most serious problems in MVE is that the overabundance of materials available makes it practically impossible for teachers who are already heavily committed in other areas to scrutinize both the appropriateness of MVE materials, and the underlying philosophies they actually represent. Moreover, while educational journals may print many useful and enlightening critiques of MVE materials, most of these, unfortunately, are both written and read chiefly by academics. Meanwhile, classroom materials continue to be used by teachers who have too little time or, in their own view, too little training or experience in MVE to question its approaches or "the experts."

Furthermore, when they are given "Recommended MVE Resource Materials" in a state or local school board curriculum guide, teachers logically assume that these materials have, indeed, been carefully reviewed and approved. In many instances, teachers know that Values Education Committees have been meeting for many months to study these documents before they recommend them to teachers. If there are exercises, philosophies or methods which the "authorities" question, teachers naturally expect that these qualifications and cautionary notes will be cited in the hand-out. Very often, as documented in chapter 7, this is not the case. This means, for example, that it is entirely possible for a teacher to pick up the popular *Values Clarification: A Handbook* and choose to do the "Cave-In Simulation" or the "Obituary," simply "because it is there," and because it is among officially recommended materials.

A BASIC PARADOX

Not only do "authorities" disagree as to appropriate content for values education, but they are also divided as to how much and what kind of training is adequate for teaching MVE. American educational analyst, Douglas Superka, who undertook an extensive study of MVE models, contends:

> [There is] a vital need for experienced, qualified and committed persons to work with teachers and students on a long-term, in-depth basis in establishing, maintaining and improving values education programs. One- two- or even five-day workshops are insufficient. These persons must be willing to work throughout the year for several years in order to help teachers on a concrete, realistic basis to develop the approaches and valuing activities most suited to their instructional styles and needs.[39]

Yet Superka does not examine the type of "experience" or "commitment" or "qualifications" which would accredit a person to be such a trainer of teachers.

We are overlooking a very basic paradox in our current approach to teacher training in MVE. On the one hand, teachers are being expected and required to help students develop a more analytical and thoughtful approach to ethics and morals. At the same time, in their preparation for this endeavor, teachers are rarely exposed to even the most basic fundamentals of philosophy or the philosophic endeavor. Consequently, through no fault of theirs, in teaching MVE, their ability to appreciate or practice the rigors of logic; to understand the categorical distinction between a moral principle and an extenuating circumstance; to analyse or question the philosophic assumptions underlying various theoretical approaches to MVE, or to engage in or foster the moral dialectic, is severely limited and limiting to both themselves and their students.

The examination of ethics and morals is, of course, primarily grounded in the study of philosophy. Yet with a few notable exceptions, psychology and sociology figure as the most prominent and primary reference points of teacher training in MVE. This observation is not intended in any way to depreciate or exclude the vital contributions of these two disciplines. It is, however, to suggest strongly that without a grounding in the basics of philosophic rigor, teachers and teacher-educators overlook an essential prerequisite to conducting responsible moral value inquiry.

---

39 D. Superka et al., *Values Education Sourcebook*, p. 250.

That there is little co-opting of professors of philosophy to Faculties and Colleges of Education and MVE in-service training programs is a critical loss. Additional consideration of professional training will be raised in chapter 10.

A "HOW TO" FOR TEACHERS

It is obvious by now that it is not only students who stand in the midst of a self-serve moral values cafeteria. Teachers too are faced with competing "dishes" for their choosing. In 1978, it was estimated that over 200,000 teachers and other counsellors had been trained in Values Clarification workshops, and over 750 had been trained in Kohlberg's method in one center alone.[40] Often, commitment to their particular "choice" takes on the nature of a "mission" and the question arises as to how to market it to others standing in the cafeteria.

In order to appreciate more fully all that is caught up in this issue, for both teachers and students, let's look at one of many approaches to introducing values education that has been put forward to teachers. In an article in the *Journal of Teacher Education*, entitled "How Teachers Can Innovate and Still Keep Their Jobs," the author encourages teachers to become "change agents" through, for example, conducting "simulation games [and] human relations training."[41] At the same time, Palmatier cautions teachers to "carefully plan strategies for meeting the inevitable resistance from colleagues, administrators, and their own students."[42] He offers ten guidelines from which to choose, "depending upon how extensively one wishes to deviate from current practices and the degree of impact planned on the total school."[43]

- Keep the door closed. . . . The successful teacher. . . innovates quietly and without fanfare. . . .

---

40 See Introduction to "Moral Education and Secular Humanism," *The Humanist*, (November/December 1978), p. 7. The article first appeared in *The Humanist*, and is reprinted by permission.

41 Larry L. Palmatier, "How Teachers Can Innovate and Still Keep Their Jobs," *Journal of Teacher Education*, vol. XXVI, no. 1 (Spring 1975), p. 60.

42 Ibid., p. 60.

43 Ibid.

- Use a special vocabulary. . . . Avoid "change," "fun," "friendly," "excitement," "new," "enjoyment," "kids," "sensitivity," "students' rights," "students' choice," "future." Publicly stress instead "mastering basics," "students' responsibility," "hard work," "respect," "traditional values," "proven," "discipline," and "results."

- Enlist the students in your game plan. . . . Make a rule and gain students' agreement that they will not ask other teachers why they do not do what you are doing. Comparisons like this will make other teachers uncomfortable and bring down their wrath upon you and your program.

- Carry a book around. . . . Often potential blockers will give you more latitude to operate if you appear to know what you are doing, and especially if you can provide a rationale and program description from one or more authors.[44]

But not all teachers buy the "game plans" recommended to them by colleagues, or the MVE "package" which is officially prescribed. In 1968, teachers in Alberta, Canada were instructed by their provincial Department of Education to make Values Clarification the basis for value inquiry in the Social Studies curriculum. The Raths' book, *Values and Teaching* (see chapter 2) was recommended as the text of choice, and teachers were advised, "The process by which a student arrives at his values is more important than the value position he obtains."[45]

Seven years later, an extensive study was conducted in order to determine the success of the program. It was discovered that 32 per cent of the teachers had rejected this orientation to values education. In a section of the report entitled, "A Concluding Thought," the team of educators retained to conduct the survey charged that at least part of the blame for the program's failure lay in the fact that the

---

44 Ibid., p. 61.
45 *Responding to Change*, Alberta Department of Education (Edmonton: 1974), p. 64.

teachers whose convictions did not fit into the Values Clarification approach of the program had sabotaged it.

Throughout this inquiry, one very troublesome issue
has returned to us over and over again. This is the
matter of *teacher selection.*

It now appears abundantly clear to us that no depth of
scholarship, no technical excellence, no classroom
expertise will serve the needs of the new ... program
unless the personality and the disposition of the
teacher are supportive of its intents.

About one-third of our teachers reject the inquiry and
valuing orientations, and less than one-fifth actively
promote them. Effective programs of teacher education may do much to change these ratios. It is clear,
however, that many candidates for teacher education
enter professional programs with attitudes and philosophies and convictions (variously derived from the
home, the church or the community) which are partly
or wholly antagonistic to student prerogatives of open
inquiry and valuing. In many cases these characteristics
are so firmly ingrained that no amount of study
(disciplinary or interdisciplinary) and no amount of
liberalizing experience (professional or other) will
dispose them towards other than establishment kinds
of thinking and acting in the classroom.

Is this not a kind of sabotage?

... Given the fact of our pluralistic society and a ...
program that purports to accommodate a plurality of
positions and values, is it reasonable to leave the
implementation of that program in the hands of
teachers who, themselves, cannot tolerate pluralism?[46]

Is it just possible that it was not "pluralism" that those
teachers could not tolerate, but rather the prospect of
teaching valuing as a process in which any and every value
conclusion is accepted as equally valid?

46 *The Social Studies in Alberta—1975: A Report of an Assessment,* L. W.
    Downey Research Associates Ltd. (Edmonton: 1975), p. 12.

If parents can be labelled, so also can teachers. Some are asking if the Values Clarification "disposition" toward "choosing freely," the acceptance of all moral positions as equally valid: the self-serve cafeteria, may become a basic standard for screening teachers of moral values education in North America? Some teachers consider their jobs to be in jeopardy if they refuse to follow the directives of their official guidelines. It begins to look as if certain approaches to MVE have developed into a human rights issue not only for children, but also for teachers. Is this the educational system we choose?

7

But Not In
Our State!

Once again U.S. citizens have "voted" in favor of moral education. The 1981 Gallup Poll on the Public Attitude toward the Public Schools listed six major educational objectives [and] asked respondents whether they felt high schools devoted too much, too little or the right amount of attention to each area. Of the six, "Developing students' moral and ethical character" received the highest number of votes for "Not Enough Attention"—62%. On another question, "Would you favor or oppose instruction in the schools that would deal with values and ethical behavior?" 70% said Yes [in favor], 17% said No [opposed] and 13% had no opinion.[1]

Were those "in favor" aware of the range of current MVE approaches they were endorsing? For it has been evident from examining these approaches that what is considered "moral" or "ethical;" what is defined as "instruction" and by what methodology that instruction will be given to youth, stand in current practice as essentially open questions. Few respondents to the Gallup Poll would realize that for more

---

1 "The Leading Edge," *Ethics in Education*, Vol. 1, No. 4, November 1981, p. 1.

than fifteen years, U.S. academics and educators have been engaged in heated controversy amongst themselves over what values education strategies should or should not be used with students. A conservative estimate of U.S. books and articles published in the past decade would run over 1000.

However, as we noted earlier, because this material circulates chiefly in educational circles, the public, for the most part has been singularly uninformed about the values education movement, to say nothing of the controversy which surrounds it at its source. Only in 1981 did one government official concede that "the criticisms of the various approaches and their philosophies has been essentially an 'in house' affair."[2] In that United States taxpayers have been paying for implementation of the new values education since the 1960s, it is essential that they be party to the controversy. That is the purpose of this book. As our children are the consumers, it is vital that every citizen has the information necessary to participate in what is easily one of the most crucial issues shaping the nation's legal, economic and social future.

All of us want to believe that the survival dilemmas, the group "therapy," the invasion of student privacy, are simply among officially recommended materials, but are not actually being used in our classrooms. I too wanted to comfort myself with this hope. For one thing, to think otherwise appears to border on the sensational, to which many of us have a knee-jerk reaction. However, one only has to read teachers' own accounts of the materials they are using, to realize that—with the best intentions—the above activities, and variations on them, have been in use for nearly a generation of children. Moreover, these activities are integrated into all subjects of the curriculum, so that they may constitute a part of any class from kindergarten to grade 12 at any time.

The following account is written by a teacher, Susan Pagliuso, who is auditing another teacher's integrated Literature and Values course for grade 12 students.

2 Donald M. Santor, Review of books, *Canadian Materials*, Vol. IX, No. 3, 1981, p. 168.

A Problem With Values Discussion

During a discussion of the poem, *"My Last Duchess,"* a fundamental problem emerged about the view that a values component of an English class means simply raising and discussing values issues. This problem will become clear as we discuss the poem, the students' response, and the teacher's and class's response to the students. Here is the poem:

My Last Duchess

That's my last Duchess painted on the wall,
Looking as if she were alive. I call
That piece a wonder now: Fra Randolf's hands
Worked busily a day, and there she stands.
Will't please you sit and look at her? I said
'Fra Pandolf' [sic] by design, for never read
Strangers like you that pictured countenance,
The depth and passion of its earnest glance,
But to myself they turned (since none puts by
The curtain I have drawn for you, but I)
And seemed as they would ask me, if they durst,
How such a glance came there; so, not the first
Are you to turn and ask thus. Sir, 'twas not
Her husband's presence only, called that spot
Of joy into the Duchess' cheek: perhaps
Fra Pandolf [sic] chanced to say "Her mantle laps
Over my lady's wrist too much," or "Paint
Must never hope to reproduce the faint
Half-flush that dies along her throat:" such stuff
Was courtesy, she thought, and cause enough
For calling up that spot of joy. She had
A heart—how shall I say?—too soon made glad,
Too easily impressed; she liked whate'er
She looked on, and her looks went everywhere.
Sir, 'twas all one! My favour at her breast,
The dropping of the daylight in the West,
The bough of cherries some officious fool
Broke in the orchard for her, the white mule
She rode with round the terrace—all and each
Would draw from her alike the approving speech,

Or blush, at least. She thanked men,—good! but
    thanked
Somehow—I know not how—as if she ranked
My gift of a nine-hundred-years-old name
With anybody's gift. Who'd stoop to blame
This sort of trifling? Even had you skill
In speech—(which I have not)—to make your will
Quite clear to such an one, and say, "Just this
Or that in you disgusts me; here you miss,
Or there exceed the mark"—and if she let
Herself be lessoned so, nor plainly set
Her wits to yours, forsooth, and made excuse,
-E'en then would be some stooping; and I choose
Never to stoop. Oh sir she smiled, no doubt,
Whene'er I passed her; but who passed without
Much the same smile? This grew; I gave
    commands;
Then all smiles stopped together. There she stands
As if alive. Will't please you rise? We'll meet
The company below, then. I repeat,
The Count your master's known munificence
Is ample warrant that no just pretence
Of mine for dowry will be disallowed;
Though his fair daughter's self, as I avowed
At starting, is my object. Nay, we'll go
Together down, sir. Notice Neptune, though,
Taming a sea-horse, though a rarity,
Which Claus of Innsbruck cast in bronze for me!

                                    Robert Browning

Pagliuso continues:

There are several value issues which this poem raises,
the most important being murder. The teacher asked
the class whether they thought it was OK for the Duke
to have [got] rid of (either killed or locked up in a
nunnery) his *latest* wife (there had been others before
her). Two of the fifteen students thought it was OK in
this case! The rest of the class did not think it was OK.
The two students were given the freedom to respond
with and continue to hold the attitude that murder in

this situation is justifiable. The rest of the class freely chose the attitude that murder in this situation was *not* justifiable.

If we stop the action at this point:

some students: murder is justifiable
other students: murder is not justifiable

we see a crossroads here for the teacher. The teacher can choose from several alternatives:

A: ignore the two students' response
B: express a reaction of disapproval (approval) and drop it
C: bring out the two sides and debate it, leaving the direction of resolution purely up to the students, remain neutral
D: encourage debate *from* a stated and accepted value position, in this case that murder is wrong
E: simply state that murder is wrong and go on.

In this case the teacher chose B and so did the students: there was an immediate response of incredulity and disagreement to these two students by the teacher and the rest of the class. However neither teacher nor students felt responsible to find out why these students held this view, or to debate the issue.[3]

Pagliuso points out the dangerous notion of "free" choice and license which this exercise projects to youth:

[In our system] we believe that students should be free to choose whatever values they want to—and that teachers should be neutral. We may not like what students choose, but we basically are not responsible to confront the values of a person. We feel, however, much more responsible [about] the *behavior* of people. If someone kills another out of jealousy we call

3 Susan Pagliuso, "The First Questions to Ask about Values Education: Case Study: Grade 12: Integrated Literature and Values Course," Appendix 6, Clive Beck, *The Moral Education Project (Year 5): Final Report 1976/77*, (Spiral Bound Edition), pp. 5-7.

that murder, and immediately take action. But, if a student THINKS it is OK to kill someone out of jealousy, we say that student is free to think what he wants. Is this a correct notion of freedom and responsibility? For where are the seeds of the actual murder if not in thought? Is it actually possible for the educational system and the teacher to take a stand that one view is just as acceptable as another?[4]

IS IT JUST ACADEMIC?

But, we may ask, "Isn't this all academic?" To what extent do such class discussions, about murder for example, make any real impression on students' actual behavior? On November 3, 1981, at Milpitas High School in California sixteen-year-old Anthony Broussard, bragging about having killed his former girl friend, fourteen-year-old Marcy Conrad, offered to show her strangled body to over a dozen of his classmates. Thirteen students saw the body of the murdered girl, but it was finally an auto worker who reported the murder to the police. Broussard was arrested almost forty-eight hours after police said the girl died. Milpitas Police Sergeant Ron Icely described the thirteen students as:

> cold and callous about the incident.

> "Their prime objective was to cover up their friend. . . . They showed no remorse at all for the girl. These kids got their priorities mixed up. I just couldn't believe it."

> . . . [The] Sergeant said one student covered the body with leaves so it could not be seen from the road, and others threw rocks at it.

> . . . "This kind of thing could happen on any campus," said [school principal] Mr. Perotti. He called it a reflection of a larger social problem.[5]

Perhaps classroom discussions about murder are actually *too* "academic." Or is it that the Life Raft scenario and

---

4 Ibid., p. 7.
5 " 'Messed up priorities' cited in coverup of girl's murder," *The Globe and Mail*, Toronto, November 26, 1981, p. T2, AP, Milpitas, California.

other MVE activities like it, where the least "worthy" class-mate is voted to die, has, for some students, become integrated into their view of life and their approach to people?

Only a month earlier, the *New York Times*[6] had run the following piece. Across the nation—regardless of race, color, financial status, political, religious or non-religious convictions—people are asking the same questions as New York Police Commissioner, Robert McGuire. And they are coming to the same conclusions.

"... 14 and 15 year-old kids who have no sense of what human life is worth, that it's precious...."

"... who have a look in their eyes that says, 'your life isn't worth anything to me...'"

"... Something is happening to kids across the board...."

"... Is there a commitment by government and community leaders to do something about it? The answer is no."

But government and community leaders would counter that something *is* being done and, among other programs, many would point to moral values education programs in our schools. Quite logically, they assume that these have been put in place to reflect a positive re-instatement of such time-proven values as honesty and human compassion. But looking behind the enticing label to some of the actual exercises children are being given in their classrooms—and hearing students talk about them—throws considerable light and suggests directions to take in pursuing the objective which Commissioner McGuire defined for all of us: "I would try to understand [why there are fourteen- and fifteen-year-old kids who have no sense of what human life is worth]. I would try to figure it out."

Not so strangely, the same month that the *New York Times* printed, "The violent kids who pull the wings off

6 Sydney Schanberg, "The violent kids who pull the wings off people," *The New York Times*, October 3, 1981, p. 27. Copyright © 1981, The New York Times Co. Reprinted by Permission.

The violent kids who pull the wings off people

BY SYDNEY SCHANBERG
New York Times Service

NEW YORK — THERE MAY be no new words or phrases to describe the awesome crime in New York City or the frightening fact that more and more is being committed by children, but it is obvious that if we do not address it with at least as much energy as we devote to acquiring a new TV set, things are going to get worse.

Police Commissioner Robert McGuire, a caring man of many sensitivities, talked about youth crime in his office. Here are some of the things he said:

"There's no question that so much of the crime now has to do with kids. Not just quality-of-life crime like senseless vandalism, ripping up park benches, but serious, violent crime. It has become a fact in this city that older people are afraid of kids.

"Sometimes I ask myself, 'Are we being hysterical? Wasn't there crime before? Are we getting old and old-fashioned?' No. This isn't the same. The statistics are three, four, five times what they were 20 years ago. And the pathology is much worse.

"The kids who prey on people have a look in their eyes that says 'your life isn't worth anything to me.' Whether they injure you is irrelevant to them. Random. Gratuitous. Like pulling wings off butterflies, only the butterflies are people.

"None of our discussions at the governmental level ever get to the question of 14- and 15-year-old kids who have no sense of what human life is worth, that it's precious."

If you were God for one day, he was asked, and could do what you thought was most important, what would it be?

"I would try to understand it. I would try to figure it out. What are the dynamics? It can't be just poverty. That's a factor, but there must be so many others. The poor live cheek by jowl with those who have more. Television gives them instant communication about the good things in life — and about violence.

"What about mal-education? No parental control? Moral breakdown? No respect for authority?

"There's been Vietnam, Watergate, pornography, divorce, no one goes to church any more. And then we expect kids to be God-fearing. I'm not trying to be self-righteous, but you are reaping what you're sowing.

"Is there a commitment by government and community leaders to do something about it? The answer is no.

"If I were God? Sure, I'd want to provide all the infrastructure — counselling, remedial reading, full employment. But would this do it?

"At what age do you have to try to save the child? By 10, his character is by and large formed. If he's stabbing someone at 10, it's probably too late.

"People say it's racial, because those in the subculture, at the bottom of the economic ladder, are mostly minorities. Yes, blacks and Hispanics are committing most of the violent crime. But that's too simplistic.

"What about kids from the same, poor, black family? One becomes a violent, career criminal. But the other goes through the system — school, college, the rest — and comes out OK.

"And there are a lot of white kids in trouble. Something is happening to kids across the board. You may not be as afraid of the white street kids in Yorkville, but they can take your wings off as quickly as anyone.

"A reporter said to me, 'Hey, there's a lot of crime. You're the Commissioner. What are you doing about it?' Look, there has to be self-enforcement. Like the income tax laws. We have limited police. People have to share responsibility. If the social contract is breaking apart, then all the police can do is conduct a holding action.

"Everything always works its way back to the things people don't want to face, don't want to talk about — morality, application of values, anything other than their obsession with instant gratification.

"What does it mean down the road? If people in New York City will no longer have a sense of their own safety . . . then what's the next step? Is that an acceptable society?

"I'm a liberal but, down the road, if I have to admit the police can't protect people, will the hard-liners be proved right? Will we need a more oppressive and repressive society? Will we have to bring in the National Guard for emergency patrols? How far behind, then, would the army be and the Joint Chiefs of Staff?

"Unless we come up with better responses, what's ahead is going to be worse than what we have now."

people," (October 1981), *The Sunshine News*, a sizeable monthly newspaper which circulates to 125,000 high school students across Canada, ran an article entitled, "I want to live! Sorry, you don't qualify." It described students' opinions of MVE survival exercises. Of the Fall-Out Shelter (cited in full in chapter 2, page 38) Ann LeBlanc said, it was "pretty good. We were told there was no right or wrong, although I got frustrated when I was making decisions between life and death."[7] Allison McColl of Monarch Park Secondary School talked about being given the Cave-In Simulation (cited in full in chapter 2, page 39). As the reader will recall, this is an exercise which involves digging out of a cave where the class is trapped. Each child lobbies his or her classmates to be chosen for the front of the line rather than the back which means much less chance of survival. Upon hearing each other's reasons, each member of the class is required to rate the worth of every other classmate. Thereby the group determines the value of each person and the order in which their life should be saved. Then the students line up in this order to file out.

> "It was really sick," says Allison, "sort of like playing God. You had to sell yourself to save your life. Most of us thought it was really bad."

> Joyce nods in agreement, adding: "What if you were the one chosen to be at the end of the line? Everybody took it as a joke, but I don't think they should be doing it anyway. It's pretty negative."[8]

Clearly, there is a stage some children go through in which they "take it as a joke" to do things like pull the wings off butterflies, "just to see what will happen." Normally, they grow out of this rather quickly. They come to feel an identity with other living creatures and realize that it is cruel to inflict abject torture on another just to see what their reaction will be. They will tell you that this is inhuman.

Yet in many classrooms across North America, in promoting self worth to the extent of deciding which classmates

---

7 David Hayes, "I want to live! Sorry, you don't qualify," *The Sunshine News*, October, 1981, p. 7.
8 Ibid.

will die, by majority vote, we run every risk of formalizing the desensitization and dehumanization of those very youth. So very ironically, and certainly unwittingly, could it be that in our ignorance or our dismissal of these and similar MVE materials and their affects, that we: parents, teachers, principals, administrators—all of us—are in danger of clipping the wings of *children* even before they have had a chance to try them out?

Is it so surprising that some kids "have a look in their eyes that says, 'your life isn't worth anything to me:' " that violence and crime among youth are escalating at such a pace? When Commissioner McGuire observes, "something is happening to kids across the board," it would be much too simplistic to reduce the complex factors involved to the problematic nature of values education in schools. By the same token, this influence cannot be discounted. As McGuire concludes, after having considered a number of other factors, "Everything always works its way back to the things people don't want to face, don't want to talk about—morality, application of values. . . ."

GETTING DOWN TO EVERYDAY BASICS

Susan Pagliuso, the teacher we quoted earlier who described the teacher's open-ended handling of the issue of murder, contends that unless—individually and collectively—we attempt to identify and accept some value standards, the resolution of each and every value question will always be open-ended. Applying this to the school situation, she asks, "What happens when something dishonest occurs?" She illustrates this with two examples which she has observed and which she considers to be common:

Example 1. In a public school a teacher walked into the staff room and told how he had caught some kids swearing, and had, of course, scolded them for it. The teacher told the story as a funny incident and obviously did not disapprove of swearing.

Example 2. In a high school the staff room is out of the main stream of student traffic so that few

students are around. Each morning the
students are required to stand for the
national anthem and stop talking. Teachers
in the staff room ignore it, teachers in sight
of students quietly stand.

How many of us as parents and teachers unwittingly allow
ourselves to fall into similar kinds of situations? Pagliuso
continues:

These two examples of dishonest behavior—double
standard—could easily be confronted *if the value of
honesty was actually being worked out in our everyday
lives.* But obviously this is not happening.

In order to have more than supermarket values we
have to do *work* on *values;* work must be done to

1. make clear what values we accept as a group

2. personally accept these values

3. study these values (IN THEORY) continuously
   (weekly!) with those people with whom we live and
   work

4. apply these values to everyday situations; that is
   apply the theory. Debate and discuss, work them
   out, [come to a] resolution

5. confront situations and attitudes counter to the
   values.

Is this necessary values work to be done with students,
but not teachers? Illogical. Teachers in a school must
work things out together so that students don't become hopelessly confused by as many different perspectives as they have teachers.[9]

Pagliuso points out:

We can talk about principles relatively easily and
smoothly. But when those principles/values are part of
people's everyday life (like honesty) discussion of them

9 Susan Pagliuso, "The First Questions to Ask about Values Education,"
   Clive Beck, *The Moral Education Project (Year 5): Final Report 1976/77,*
   (Spiral Bound Edition), p. 10.

produces CONFLICT. Conflict is an inevitable part of the process of working out values in everyday life. But we can't end the process in a state of conflict. The conflict can be resolved *IF* we have an accepted set of group values; we can use them as standards. These are the *theoretical principles* of the group. Hence the process goes on: everyday practical issues—conflict—theoretical base—resolution and repeats itself. Without the practical issues/conflict we end up with fuzzy, liberal thinking; without the theoretical base/resolution, we end up with supermarket values.

... Recalling our grade 12 English class we see that on this issue (murder) the two students were *not* confronted with the fact that [the law and official educational objectives] do not accept murder as justifiable. This grade 12 English teacher *and* the students (with up to 13 years experience in [our] schools) did not feel it their *PLACE* to *CONFRONT* these two students on this issue.

But whose role should it be? Just teachers'? Or just judges'? Or just policemen['s]? How can we function from common goals with the support of only a few? We must become much clearer about what we expect teachers to do about values. "Do something" is not enough of a mandate.

So we see that the original question of this research: "How can values be integrated into a grade 12 English program?" rests upon more fundamental questions about our [larger] value system: How clear are we about the values we hold together? Do we personally accept any values in common with others? Do we want to work out these values in practical situations? Do we feel responsible for confrontation on these values? It is only AFTER these questions are answered that it will really make sense to talk about programs of values education in English programs. Until we tackle these fundamental questions our values programs will be no better than advertising for different brands of values in your values supermarket.[10]

10 Ibid., pp. 11-13.

Pagliuso reflects the concerns of many, pointing out that people recognize the need to "do something" in the crucial area of moral values but, so far, have been unable to confront the fundamental questions. Thus it can be seen that official but ambiguous education directives throw the door open and leave it open for programs of open-ended content and process.

THE COST OF POLITICAL CONFUSION

There is no question that values education has the potential to make a positive contribution in schools. Equally, it is not a matter of conjecture that critical problems exist in the practice of values education in North American school systems. Not the least of these problems is the plethora of memoranda, directives, guidelines and recommended resource materials which issue from as many levels of officialdom and the fact that they are often contradictory.

In order to appreciate the ad hoc and highly confused process in which MVE operates it is necessary to look in some detail at one educational jurisdiction and identify the competing forces at work within it. Only then does one recognize that it is not only the content of MVE programs which is left open-ended, but also its political administration. On the rationale that one may be inclined to look more objectively at a situation beyond one's own borders, we will briefly take Ontario, Canada as a case study. Those who have made themselves familiar with the case of MVE in their own state will recognize how typical Ontario is. Those who do not know their local situation, may, in looking at Ontario, be less tempted to dismiss the issue in the United States as simply peculiar to Ohio, Virginia or New York.

If we place the law (in this case, the Ontario Education Act) side by side with the materials which have been recommended by the highest level of government authority in education (in this case, the Ontario Ministry of Education), we are struck by fundamental discrepancies and contradictions. For example, typical of numerous state laws, Section 229 1 (c) of the Education Act states:

It is the duty of a teacher to inculcate by precept and

example . . . the highest regard for truth, justice, loyalty, love of country, humanity, benevolence. . . .[11]

At the same time, the Values Clarification, Kohlberg and Beck models which figure most prominently in the government recommended materials,[12] assure us that their brands of MVE will *not* involve the inculcation of moral precepts, nor will teachers necessarily support certain precepts by their own example. Indeed these approaches are rooted in the firm contention that to teach moral precepts is to deal in indoctrination and totalitarianism. For example, a basic tenet of Values Clarification requires that whatever values a student adopts, be they ". . . intolerance or thievery . . . . Our position is that we respect his right to decide upon that value."[13] Specifically, one of the latest government Guidelines for Intermediates describes *Values Clarification: A Handbook of Practical Strategies for Teachers and Students* as having "seventy strategies that can be used at any grade level [7 to 10]."[14] This is the book—extremely popular throughout North America—which recommends, among less traumatic exercises, write your own Obituary, the Fall-Out Shelter and the Cave-In Simulation, the latter two having been discussed earlier in this chapter. It is difficult to comprehend government assessment of such strategies as "use[ful] at any [intermediate] grade level." It is equally difficult to understand what has been their unqualified recommendation of MVE approaches which are in direct conflict with the Education Act.

Predictably, with the government financing MVE projects since the late 1960s and urging school boards to integrate this focus into all subjects of the curriculum from kindergarten to grade 12, as one school board member put it, "We've had the directive . . . it isn't a matter of *whether* we'll be doing the new MVE—it's only a matter of how."

11 The Education Act, Statutes of Ontario 1974, Chapter 109, Section 229 1(c).
12 See, for example, "Resources," *Guidance: Curriculum Guideline for the Intermediate Division*, Ontario Ministry of Education (Toronto: 1978), pp. 17-18.
13 L. Raths et al., *Values and Teaching*, 1st ed., p. 227.
14 *Guidance: Curriculum Guideline for the Intermediate Division*, Ontario Ministry of Education (Toronto: 1978), p. 18.

Typical of many government policies, on the matter of "how," the Ontario Ministry has issued sufficiently global statements that they have been described as "systematically ambiguous, thus having the virtue of being politically defensible from a variety of incompatible points of view."[15] A report prepared by the largest school board in Ontario clearly reflects the simultaneous owning and disowning of jurisdictional responsibility. It states:

The Minister issues guidelines, rather than detailed courses of study. He believes that "to be effective, curriculum must be closely related to the characteristics and needs of the particular pupils for whom it is planned. Thus, while the Ministry articulates broad goals, it is the responsibility of the local school boards—through their supervisory officials—to formulate local programs that are within the rationale of the provincial policy and at the same time reflect local needs and priorities. . . ."[16]

We feel that the Board must first acquaint the public with the fact that the Minister of Education has the authority to set curriculum policy and then endorse his policy concerning Values Education. By thus informing the public of the constraints within which the Board must operate in formulating its own policy of Values Education, the Board can focus future debates on the topic on those aspects in which the Board's policy differs from the Minister's.

The Board may decide that there are values, other than those which the Minister specifies . . . which should be included in its Values Education Program. The Board should then identify these values.[17]

At the same time, the report reminds us that: "It is the individual teacher's responsibility, as the Minister states, to

15 A. Wesley Cragg, "Moral Education in the Schools," *Canadian Journal of Education*, Vol. 4. No. 1, (1979), p. 29.

16 *Values Education: A Report Prepared for the Values Committee of the Toronto Board of Education* (Toronto: 1977), pp. 31-32.

17 Ibid., p. 33.

'select strategies, resources and activities appropriate to the needs of the individual children.' "[18]

AND IN THE CLASSROOM . . .

Which are teachers to follow, and which are parents to understand are being followed: the law (the Education Act); or materials recommended on government guidelines; or those of teachers' unions; or board policy statements (if, in fact, they exist) and suggested resources; or, as has been recommended, a teacher's decision to become completely independent of [others' materials][19] and create his or her own? In fact, most school boards operate without specified or monitored policies: their teachers—genuinely concerned to "do something" in this important area from kindergarten to senior high—are experimenting without a curriculum, with little or no training, without supervision or even approval of the content, methods or techniques applied in their classrooms. Understandably enough, the range of approaches is numerous: from the useful and helpful to the potentially very damaging. This means that not only is the credibility gap enormous, but as has been raised by teachers themselves, so is the accountability gap.

The fact that these gaps are not only structurally built into our systems, but are very much a part of classroom application of values education day by day, is typified in the following. It is a report of a P.T.A. meeting at which a government education official, the Superintendent of Curriculum of the local school board and the author were invited to speak.

> [The three speakers] agreed that we could not subscribe to Situation Ethics, Moral Relativism. We agreed that survival exercises and superficial problem-solving dilemmas, class voting strategies which ask children such questions as "Hands up, those who would rather have different parents?"[20] have no place in the classroom.

---

18 Ibid., pp. 35-36.
19 Clive Beck, Appendix F, *The Moral Education Project* (Year 3), (Spiral Bound Edition), p. 8.
20 S. Simon et al., *Values Clarification: A Handbook*, 1st ed., pp. 46.

... The Superintendent [assured the meeting] that these activities ... were not, in fact, happening under his board. And I have no doubt he thought and believed this to be true. Then in the discussion period, one after another parent rose to document different facts. One woman said that her child in grade 6 had been given the Life Raft; another that she had seen a questionnaire to be filled in by her eleven-year-old son, asking: "What bothers you most about your mother; your father; your brother and sister ...?" Another said her daughter in the local high school had been given a class survival exercise, and so on.

Superintendent: "Well ... the problem is that there are a thousand teachers out there, and they can and do decide what materials they'll use."

Audience: "Has the Board or the Administrative staff, then, no control over what happens in the classroom?

Superintendent: "Well, if you have a concern, and if some of these strategies are being used with which you disagree, and certainly with which we all disagree, you should go to your local principal and discuss it."

Audience: "That's like closing the barn door after the horse is out! Students have already *had* the exercise! Do we really have to wait until they've had it and then go to the principal and complain ...?" One woman asked why materials were being recommended by the Ministry and by School Boards which included these kinds of exercises and the philosophy of Situation Ethics. She asked, "What is this School Board and the Ministry going to do to ensure that in fact these will not continue to be implemented in the classroom?"[21]

Her question was not answered, but the message came through quite clearly. In point of fact, the onus is placed on individual parents to question first of all their children as to classroom activities they are being given; then sort through,

21 K. Gow, "The Emergent Reality," *Colloquium '81 Proceedings*, Ontario Institute for Studies in Education, (Toronto), January 9, 1981, pp. 108-109.

and follow up the pedagogical and administrative confusion which surrounds the politics of such MVE practice on their children—all of this, often "after the fact." This situation is all the more ludicrous when one considers that millions of taxpayers' dollars and far more importantly, students' and families' lives are caught up in implementation of this clearly unaccountable morass.

It is my conviction that the confusion and inconsistencies in the stances cited above do not stem from a consciously devised plan to contravene education laws, or are the result of lack of good intentions. I believe that departments of education and local Boards are seriously committed to the moral development of our students. Rather, it has been because of a concern not to offend anyone by being in any way doctrinaire that we have adopted MVE approaches at the other extreme: moral relativism and individual utilitarianism. These approaches, of course, can be just as doctrinaire in their own perspectives. The missing factor has been the lack of in-depth examination of these approaches and the underlying philosophies they promote. The packages were offered for sale in a ready market, and we have been buying them with too little analysis: without looking beneath the natural appeal of the label, and without studying the specific ingredients. At the very least, we need to identify which aspects we can support and utilize with benefit, and which we cannot.

This message is reaching an increasing number of citizens who are recognizing that the vulnerability and possible exploitation of their children is on the line. In April 1981, twelve years after the initiation of values education by the government, the Minister of Education issued a memo to elementary and secondary principals of all public, separate (Roman Catholic) and independent schools in Ontario:

> The Ministry has been receiving an increasing number of complaints from parents and other members of the public concerning certain classroom activities involving the making of moral decisions by students. The Ministry is concerned about activities, games, and values exercises which may involve an invasion of the students' personal and family privacy, which may be seen

as emotionally manipulative in certain circumstances, or which are conducive to moral relativism. . . .

The Ministry is committed to the concept of moral values education which respects the privacy of the individual, which recognizes the traditional values of our society, and encourages the development of responsible citizenship.[22]

This memo is a forthright acknowledgement of existing problems in the practice of MVE and offers a useful vehicle for more honest communication among principals, teachers and parents. But, as everywhere, the "concern" expressed on a government memo will remain "on paper" unless it actually carries legal "clout" as to monitoring policies and penalties for infringement.

Significantly, and typical of many U.S. jurisdictions, the very issue of whether parents have in fact, any legal authority to challenge their school board with respect to MVE curriculum was taken before the Ontario Supreme Court.[23]

BUT WE HAVE U.S. LAWS WHICH PROTECT US!

How many Americans are aware that since 1974, Section 439(a) of the (federal) General Education Act which relates to "protection of pupil rights" has been in place and is available for their use?

"439(a) All instructional material, including teachers' manuals, films, tapes or other supplementary instructional material which will be used in connection with any research or experimentation program or project shall be available for inspection by the parents or guardians of the children engaged in such program or project. For the purpose of this section "research or

22 The Hon. Dr. Bette Stephenson, "Re Privacy of Students and Values Education," Memorandum to Directors of Education, Principals of Schools, Office of the Minister [of Education], Government of Ontario, April 2, 1980-81:28.

23 See "B. Hewitt, M. Launchbery and W. Gowanlock, personally and on behalf of the members of the Simcoe Taxpayers Researching Education vs The Simcoe County Board of Education." Court ruling in favor of parents' rights, by Madame Justice Van Camp, Supreme Court of Ontario, released October 27, 1981.

experimentation program or project" means any program or project in any applicable program designed to explore or develop new or unproven teaching methods or techniques.[24]

Clearly, moral values education programs qualify as "designed to explore or develop new teaching methods and techniques." That these methods and techniques are also largely "unproven" is evident in conflicting research findings to date.[25] Yet from the minimal use which has been made of this law, it would appear that few citizens are aware of its existence. This is probably because, in the main, the public either does not know about the values education movement, or is unaware that it has potentially negative aspects. Whatever the reason, few parents, since 1974, have asked to review MVE instructional materials, teachers' manuals, films, or other supplementary instructional materials which are being used on their children. Few are aware that such research, experimentation programs or projects are integrated into regular curriculum subjects from kindergarten to grade 12 and in this way are often not designated or referred to as "new" programs (see pages 191-192). Yet how exceedingly "new" the MVE objectives, methods and techniques actually are becomes obvious when one reviews the directives circulated to educators. Curriculum Director Robert Dorion quotes a National Education Association directive which is entitled, *Education for the '70s and Beyond:*

> "Schools will become clinics whose purpose is to provide individualized, psychosocial treatment for the student, and teachers must become psychosocial therapists."[26]

Dorion speaks about the implementation of this directive:

> In the State of Maine today [February 1980], more and more schools are using psychological techniques such

24 (20 U.S.C. 1232h) Enacted August 21, 1974, P.L. 93-380 sec. 514 (a), 88 Stat. 574 (General Education Provisions Act).
25 D. Superka et al., Values Education Sourcebook, p. IX.
26 Robert P. Dorion, "Direction of Education," *Bangor Daily News*, February 11, 1980, p. 13.

as "Glasser's therapy programs," "values clarification
. . . ." Teachers' workshops buzz with talk of neurosis,
resistance, maladjustment, attitudinal change. After
these workshops, teachers go blithely into the classroom as "psychotherapists," arrange children in what
is known as a Magic Circle and set up situations where
all youngsters will reveal intimate feelings about themselves, their siblings, their parents and their peers.[27]

Few people would question the concept of the "whole
child" and the need for a teacher to relate to a student, not
only as a Math pupil, or an English pupil, but also as a
thinking, feeling, acting individual with his or her own special attributes—and the need to discover these and be
proud of them. But for the school to engage in systematically probing the psyches of students to test them out and
apply "treatment" is, in fact, against federal law.

Are many Americans aware that on November 2, 1978,
the Hatch Amendment was signed by the president of the
United States and passed into federal law? The following
subsection was added to Section 439 of the General Education Provisions Act which relates to "protection of pupil
rights."

(b) No student shall be required, as part of any applicable program, to submit to psychiatric examination, testing, or treatment, or psychological examination, testing, or treatment, in which the
primary purpose is to reveal information concerning:

(1) political affiliations;
(2) mental and psychological problems potentially embarrassing to the student or his
family;
(3) sex behavior and attitudes;
(4) illegal, anti-social, self-incriminating and
demeaning behavior;
(5) critical appraisals of other individuals with
whom respondents have close family relationships;

27 Ibid.

(6) legally recognized privileged and analogous relationships, such as those of lawyers, physicians and ministers; or

(7) income (other than that required by law to determine eligibility for participation in a program or for receiving financial assistance under such program), without the prior consent of the student (if the student is an adult or emancipated minor), or in the case of unemancipated minor, without the prior written consent of the parent.[28]

If a school or board which is receiving federal funding contravenes this law, their funding can be withdrawn. Again, from the minimal use which has been made of this law, it seems that few citizens are aware of its existence. In fact one might question how many *teachers* have been made party to the facts of Section 439 (a) and (b). Perhaps in many cases they may not have been advised of such legislation or its implications.

In Maine, Commissioner of Education, H.S. Millett Jr., informed all superintendents, and elementary and secondary school principals. Reactions, as reported in the *Maine Sunday Telegram* were various:

Mollie Reynolds, state director of curriculum . . . said the "Magic Circle" group discussion is based on the Glasser method of behavior modification which attempts to "get children involved with their own feelings and the feelings of others."

She said it would be difficult now for schools to use the Magic Circle if groups of parents objected to its use. . . .

Roger Goodson, director of the School Health Education Project at the University of Maine at Farmington, said the Hatch Amendment could cause difficulty for schools and other agencies conducting surveys as a tool for developing health programs—or any cur-

28 Public Law: 95-561, 92 Stat 2143 (1978).

Who is Monitoring the Laws?

riculum—especially those dealing with sex education. . . .

Dr. Peter Greer, assistant superintendent of Portland Schools said, "All schools must take the time, now, to concern themselves (with the new law) because parents are rightfully finding out what their rights are and asking more and tougher questions."[29]

For example, in one area, a program "which demonstrated new 'classroom management' techniques was redesigned after parents complained that advanced methods of behavior modification are really mind-altering or mind-management tools."[30]

Thus, if not in theory, in actual practice, once again it is evident that major responsibility for supervision and administration of such educational laws, as the above, rests with parents. The onus is on them to protest such "testing" and to ask to review instructional manuals, films and other supplementary teaching tools. Otherwise—in the face of government-funded programs and official materials which recommend activities which directly contravene the Hatch Amendment—contentious values education activities of the type we have been examining, can continue unchallenged in any classroom.

USING THE LAW

A California citizen pursued the implications of the 1978 Hatch Agreement for her state. After due processing of letters, the California Department of Education officials indicated that, in fact, Education Code, Article 4, Section 60650 Personal Beliefs had been law in the state since April 30, 1977. It holds:

"No test, questionnaire, survey, or examination containing any questions about the pupil's personal beliefs or practices in sex, family life, morality and religion, or any questions about his parents' or guardians' beliefs

29 Maryline White, "Law gives new rights to parents and pupils," *Maine Sunday Telegram*, May 6, 1979, p. 3-4.
30 Ibid.

and practices in sex, family life, morality and religion, shall be administered to any pupil in kindergarten or grade 1 through grade 12, inclusive, unless the parent or guardian of the pupil is notified in writing that such test, questionnaire, survey, or examination is to be administered and the parent or guardian of the pupil gives written permission for the pupil to take such test, questionnaire, survey, or examination."[31]

One would expect, as with the federal laws we discussed (Section 439 (a) and (b)), that once passed, they would be implemented. As we have noted, however, it is entirely possible that the law may only be respected and applied to the extent that the community requires that it be respected and enforced. The above-mentioned California individual, who belongs and contributes materials to family organizations, describes a series of events which are repeated in varying forms across the continent.

Sometime after [notification of the existence of the California Code], I received a call from a friend ... who told me about a survival game which her son had refused to take [as part of a final test in English Composition] ... the Bomb Shelter. [When the parent and I took a copy of the game and the Education Code 60650], to the principal of the high school, he decided this student could take another test but refused to notify the other parents about their rights to object or agree to the survival game/bomb shelter testing. There was no indication from this principal that in future he would uphold the law which states that "prior parental notification" be given and parental approval or disapproval be obtained.

Many months after the above incident, the newly appointed high school District Superintendent was contacted and told that survival games were being given in his district as a "mandatory requirement for advancement in school" [i.e. test final in English Com-

---

31 California State Law: Education Code 60650 "Personal beliefs." Article 4 was enacted by Stats 1976, C1010 2 operative April 30, 1977.

position]. I then quoted E.C. 60650.... He has since
taken positive action and on November 14, 1980 a
memorandum from the district office was forwarded
to all high school principals in his district and the principals have notified all parents about Education Code
60650.[32]

Importantly, assurance was given by the District Superintendent, in writing, that distribution of information to parents in regard to Education Code 60650 will be provided on
a regular basis as part of the yearly mailout to parents. It is a
legal fact that teachers must notify parents in writing before
a "test, questionnaire, survey, or examination containing
any questions about the pupil's [or parents' or guardians']
personal beliefs or practices in sex, family life, morality and
religion ..." is given, and, significantly, the teacher must
receive in return, written permission from the parent or
guardian in order to administer it. However, it would appear
that it falls to parents to monitor the law.

It must be asked: how many citizens in other states have
pursued the implications of the Hatch Act for their state or
have questioned whether state legislation exists relative to
"personal beliefs" or "protection of pupil (or parent)
rights?" How many would discover, as in California, that a
law of critical relevance to MVE had been on the books for
a number of years? A simple letter to the Attorney General
in every state would provide the answer to this question.
That is where the individual in California began her inquiry.

Moreover, if there are loopholes in existing legislation,
for example relative to the Hatch Act—loose definitions of
"primary purpose" and what constitutes "test;" or if, as we
noted earlier, there are no mandatory policies for monitoring a particular law, or penalties for contravening it, then
these inequities must also be brought before the judiciary.

If it is true, as politicians have stated, that every letter
received from a constituent represents many times the
number which are unwritten, then surely politicians at various levels in the educational system including federal, state

32 Documentation available from Valuing Strategies Research Advocates,
Box 43-148, Pt. Hueneme, CA, 93043.

and local leaders of political parties, need to hear from the citizens they represent. It is essential to be familiar with existing laws pertaining to MVE; to make use of them and to create them where controls do not exist. If, in fact, so much of the responsibility for enactment of the law is left to actual consumers—who are, in this case, too young to undertake that task for themselves—then, all the more reason that this task must not be relinquished.

BUT NOT AT *OUR* SCHOOL!

We are all familiar with the unprecedented rate of removal of children from public schools to independent schools. As in the public system, many parents assume that "moral values education" implies the support of time-honored moral principles and can, therefore, only constitute a positive influence. Also, if the question of MVE is even considered, the assumption is—and often validly so—that the independent school will not have bought any of the "packages" without thoroughly screening their ingredients. Consequently, parents whose children are in independent or sectarian schools rarely ask teachers or principals to go into any detail regarding MVE content or strategies. These parents should know that a spokesperson for the U.S. National Association of Independent Schools names values education as "probably the hottest issue in private education today."[33]

The following letter to the editor, written by a sectarian school parent will alarm many readers:

> I notice your article on Values Education (Register, Nov. 28, 1981), said nothing about these materials being presented in [sectarian] schools. I know you must surely be aware this is not an accurate picture and pointing a finger at only the public school system is unfair as well as untrue.
>
> Maybe my experience will help you to realize this. . . . While in Grade 4 (age 9) my daughter was separated with her class into groups of eight students and took

33 Georgia Dullea, "Prep Schools Explore Ethics," *The New York Times*, 4 May 1975, Section 13, p. 26.

part in the two most offensive exercises—the life raft and the cave-in. I was shocked to find that her group was the only group out of four that solved the life raft problem by having the strongest swimmers take turns swimming along with the raft, therefore avoiding throwing someone overboard to die.

These children were made to feel that this was not a solution that was acceptable because they were asked to choose whom they would throw over, not whether they would.

I complained to the teacher and was told "not to be so upset, it was only a hypothetical problem."

I complained to the principal and he told me that "these exercises weren't harmful, they were stimulating."

I complained to the parish priest and was told that educational programs being removed was a political problem and that he could not and would not get involved.

I complained to the [sectarian] school [officials] and they treated me like a crazy person. "How could [I] say teaching moral values was wrong?"[34]

While the above will alarm many readers, it will strike a strangely familiar note with many other parents whose children are in independent schools, sectarian or non-sectarian.

"He's not a *bad* kid, but he's clammed up. Something is happening in school, and I can't seem to reach him. The most he ever says is "you have your values. I have mine."

"Yesterday my 8-year-old came home with a gold bracelet she found on the gym floor at school. When I asked her about taking it to the principal's office, she said their class had taken a vote and decided, "You find it: you keep it."

34 "Catholic schools must share the blame, reader believes," *The Catholic Register*, (Toronto) December 12, 1981, p. 4.

"One day Gail said, "At least I wasn't the one thrown out of the raft." Everything is so different in school these days . . . I didn't even ask her what she meant. . . .

THE GALLUP POLL RE-VISITED

We inquired earlier whether the 70% of Gallup Poll respondents who "voted" in favor of "instruction in schools that would deal with value and ethical behavior" had any notion of the range of MVE approaches they were endorsing under this label. Indeed it is virtually impossible in our super-specialized society to even attempt to evaluate the "small print" on every issue. Given the fact that most of us are already over-involved with other pressing issues and concerns, we—educators, parents, citizens in general—may be tempted to do one of the following:

- We can elect to dismiss the issue. Despite the documentation, and without researching our own district or state, we can convince ourselves that it is not happening in *our* area.

- We can discount the efforts of both educators and parents in a number of states to establish and put "teeth" into school board and legislative processes as "over-reaction."

- We can, in effect, pigeon-hole this entire matter into yet another example of the "Far Left" against the "Far Right," and, because many of us have a knee-jerk reaction to such extremes, we can satisfy ourselves that "rational moderates" have no place in this issue.

If we choose any of these ways: if we choose not to do our "homework:" if, for whatever reason, we designate this as a matter for "others," we run the risk of setting this generation of youth and others to follow, adrift on an ocean without shores, "just to see what will happen." Are we willing to take such a risk?

8

Another Doctrine?

Obviously, the overriding concern in our public educational system is that moral education should not favor any particular religious point of view. To that end, moral values education programs have been developed which appear, on the face of things, to be devoid of religious bias and even of moralistic bias, and thus to qualify admirably as nonsectarian and nondoctrinaire. But is this true? With exceptions we noted earlier, the explicit and inescapable message and dogma of many current MVE programs is, as Rhodes scholar, T.W. Harpur, points out:

> Provided that they are not malicious, anybody's values are as good as anybody else's. In other words, everything, good, bad, better, best is relative. There are no moral absolutes.... Man and his needs, his pleasures and fulfillments become the criteria of good and evil.[1]

This is not a neutral position. This is the doctrine of Sovereign Man: situation ethics; moral and cultural relativism. Have we recognized the implications of the fact that many of the most widely recommended materials in MVE reflect this doctrine? There is every indication that we have not succeeded in eliminating doctrinal bias from the curricula at all, but are simply trading former models for indoctrination in the ideology of Sovereign Man and moral relativism.

1 T.W. Harpur, "You Can't Teach Right and Wrong without Standards," *The Toronto Star*, 11 February 1978, p. G5.

In order to look at the implications of this "trade," let's look at what we can conclude thus far about moral values education. Whether we use the term "world view" or "life stance," the fact remains that all moral values education is based on one of two underlying philosophies. Each of these philosophies excludes the other:

1. There are core moral precepts.
2. There are no core moral precepts.

In fact, it would be accurate to say that all world systems of morality take one or other of these two positions. For they represent two opposite views about the nature of morality.

Many people have assumed that the logical solution to the problems of teaching morality in a pluralistic society is simply to lay out the beliefs of both positions in self-serve-cafeteria style and to encourage the students to choose their own values. This method, they claim, gets students talking about moral value issues, yet does not require the school to take a particular position about moral precepts. People who opt for this solution argue that to place both views before students is to reflect the real world. On the other hand, to present only one view or the other is to be guilty of indoctrination. Further, they argue, both philosophies can and should be advanced simultaneously in MVE programs in order to increase students' understanding of others and tolerance for others' viewpoints. This strikes a sympathetic note for many of us and might appear, on the face of it, to close the issue.

BRINGING IT DOWN TO CASES

But we must bring this pluralistic philosophy down to actual cases, such as, the issues of stealing, cheating, and lying that confront every student during the educational process. Of course, there are many issues which can be appropriately debated in the classroom and which may remain unresolved there. Capital punishment is one example. Few would argue that a school as such should take a definite position on one side or the other of this issue. A thoughtful, responsibly handled debate with students of appropriate age and teachers participating could provide a constructive and valuable educational experience. But for teachers to teach or even imply indirectly that such issues as stealing, cheating, and lying are *fundamentally* negotiable—fundamentally a question of individual opinion—is another matter. That is the policy with which I take issue: the blanket application of the so-called neutral, "pluralistic" approach to MVE.

We need to examine carefully the possibility of presenting both positions noted earlier: there are core moral precepts or, conversely, there are no moral precepts. Moreover, we need to make this examination by means of a logical, consistent, and morally tenable discussion. What actually happens in a classroom when the teacher tries to apply what has been called a "pluralistic" approach to cheating, for example? Is it, in fact, logically possible to simultaneously present these two positions, or does it simply create irreconcilable confusion? Let's consider again an example we looked at in another context in chapter 2. It is a classroom discussion about cheating, which is recommended in *Values and Teaching* as being exemplary.

Teacher: So some of you think it is best to be honest on tests, is that right? (Some heads nod affirmatively.) And some of you think dishonesty is all right? (A few hesitant and slight nods.) And I guess some of you are not certain. (Heads nod.) Well, are there any other choices or is it just a matter of dishonesty versus honesty?

Sam: You could be honest some of the time and dishonest some of the time.

Teacher: Does that sound like a possible choice class? (Heads nod.) Any other alternatives to choose from?

Tracy: You could be honest in some situations and not in others. For example, I am not honest when a friend asks about an ugly dress, at least sometimes. (Laughter.)

Teacher: Is that a possible choice, class? (Heads nod again.) Any other alternatives?

Sam: It seems to me that you have to be all one way or all the other.

Teacher: Just a minute, Sam. As usual we are first looking for the alternatives that there are in the issue. Later we'll try to look at any choice that you may have selected. Any other alternatives, class? (No response.) Well, then, let's list the four possibilities that we have on the board and I'm going to ask that each of you do two things for yourself: (1) see if you can identify any other choices in this issue of honesty and dishonesty, and, (2) consider the consequences of each alternative and see which ones you prefer. Later, we will have buzz groups in which you can discuss this and see if you are able to make a choice and if you want to make your choice part of your actual behavior. This is something you must do for yourself.

Ginger: Does that mean that we can decide for ourselves whether we should be honest on tests here?

Teacher: No, that means that you can decide on the value. I personally value honesty; and although you may choose to be dishonest, I shall insist that we be honest on our tests here. In other areas of your life, you may have more freedom to be dishonest, but one can't do anything any time, and in this class I shall expect honesty on tests.

Ginger: But then how can we decide for ourselves? Aren't you telling us what to value?

Sam: Sure, you're telling us what we should do and believe in.

Teacher: Not exactly. I don't mean to tell you what you should value. That's up to you. But I do mean that in this class, not elsewhere necessarily, you have to be honest on tests or suffer certain consequences. I merely mean that I cannot give tests without the rule of honesty. All of you who choose dishonesty as a value may not practice it here, that's all I'm saying. Further questions anyone?

Thus in this discussion a teacher who is concerned that students develop an intelligent and viable relationship with their worlds, that is, develop clear values, (1) helps them to examine alternatives and consequences in issues, (2) does not tell them, directly or indirectly, what is "right" for all persons and for all times, (3) is candid about his own values *but insists that they not be blindly adopted by others, (4) sometimes limits behavior that he considers ill advised but never limits the right to believe or the right to behave differently in other circumstances, and (5) points to the importance of the individual making his own choices and considering the implications for his own life.*[2]

Clearly this discussion does not support the view that honesty is a core moral precept—that is, that honesty has inherent goodness. It reduces honesty to a question of individual choice: of "see[ing] which [alternatives] you prefer." In this particular situation, the teacher demands from the students a specific type of behavior. At the same time, he stresses individual autonomy as the most important factor in making a decision about cheating. He does not undertake or encourage a reasoned analysis or examination of the concept of honesty so that students might systematically explore it. His solution for the students in his summary statement is situational pragmatism: each individual should value whatever he or she prefers, but be aware of possible consequences. Yet the students' choice of individual values is arbitrarily subjected to behavioral practice chosen by the teacher.

WE CAN'T HAVE IT BOTH WAYS

What is overlooked in the argument for a "pluralistic" approach to MVE is the fact that the very decision *not* to take a position on certain objective moral principles *is* in effect to take a specific philosophic position. A school which adopts an "open" stance on all moral values is really adopting a philosophy of subjective, moral relativism, whether it explicitly acknowledges that this is its position or not. That adopting this "open" policy to moral precepts automatically reflects the philosophy of total moral relativism—and does not, therefore, represent true "pluralism" at all—is a fact which many who genuinely wish to practice the ethical pluralism of our day have not yet grasped. Table 4 offers a working model for analysis and comparison of the two positions, and suggests a guide for clarifying the

2 L. Raths et al., *Values and Teaching*, 1st ed., pp. 114-115.

Table 4. Moral Education in a Pluralistic Society

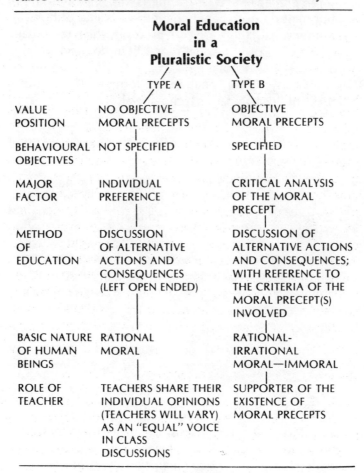

	Moral Education in a Pluralistic Society	
	TYPE A	TYPE B
VALUE POSITION	NO OBJECTIVE MORAL PRECEPTS	OBJECTIVE MORAL PRECEPTS
BEHAVIOURAL OBJECTIVES	NOT SPECIFIED	SPECIFIED
MAJOR FACTOR	INDIVIDUAL PREFERENCE	CRITICAL ANALYSIS OF THE MORAL PRECEPT
METHOD OF EDUCATION	DISCUSSION OF ALTERNATIVE ACTIONS AND CONSEQUENCES (LEFT OPEN ENDED)	DISCUSSION OF ALTERNATIVE ACTIONS AND CONSEQUENCES; WITH REFERENCE TO THE CRITERIA OF THE MORAL PRECEPT(S) INVOLVED
BASIC NATURE OF HUMAN BEINGS	RATIONAL MORAL	RATIONAL-IRRATIONAL MORAL—IMMORAL
ROLE OF TEACHER	TEACHERS SHARE THEIR INDIVIDUAL OPINIONS (TEACHERS WILL VARY) AS AN "EQUAL" VOICE IN CLASS DISCUSSIONS	SUPPORTER OF THE EXISTENCE OF MORAL PRECEPTS

differences which exist among the three MVE approaches we have discussed, and others which we have not considered.

- In Type A MVE, the value position recognizes no objective moral precepts.

- In Type B MVE the value position accepts that such precepts: stealing, cheating, and lying, for example, are wrong. Extenuating circumstances in which another moral precept such as saving a life becomes more important do not change the intrinsic value of honesty. In other words, there are core precepts which must make up the basis of individual moral behavior and a viable society. This concept is *not accepted as an unquestioned given*: it is critically analyzed in terms of its historical, legal, philosophical, psycho-social, and ontological components.

Typically, Type A and Type B MVE systems have different objectives concerning behavior.

- Type A MVE emphasizes the individual's needs and wants. It considers how each situation may or may not fit into these needs and wants, and then chooses behavior accordingly.

- Type B assumes the existence of certain core moral principles and the need to use this base in order to examine particular situations, and then chooses behavior accordingly.

In their teaching methodologies, both Type A and Type B encourage discussion of moral issues and the range of alternatives and consequences involved. However—

- Type A handles the question of morality as basically subjective and therefore open-ended.

- Type B, in the final analysis, evaluates the alternatives and their consequences relative to the basic precept(s) involved. *This does not mean that Type B method is authoritarian and requires acceptance or conformity to a particular precept*. In the end, students under either method will make their own decisions. The difference lies in the base from which each type conducts its analysis.

The presuppositions concerning the basic nature of human beings are fundamentally different in Type A and Type B approaches. Understanding this central difference clarifies much of the whole issue.

- Type A MVE operates on the assumption that human

beings are rational and moral by nature. This means that each person is capable of being his or her own moralist and judge of his or her own behavior. A law unto himself or herself, the individual will almost inevitably and automatically choose the rational and the good.

- Type B MVE operates on the assumption that human beings are, by nature, rational/irrational and moral/immoral. Left entirely to their own devices, individuals will not always choose the rational and the good. It is as a person examines the rationale and various values and behavioral components of objective moral precepts and finds an opportunity to identify with moral realities beyond his or her own subjective creation, that the truly authentic individual may evolve.

It follows logically, then, that the role of the teacher will vary in each type.

- The Type A MVE teacher is to present his or her opinions—(teachers will vary)—on any moral issue as an equal voice in class discussion.

- In Type B, where, for example, such actions as stealing, cheating, and lying are at issue, the teacher supports the existence of core moral precepts as realities necessary to a viable society and fulfillment of the self.

It becomes obvious that to advance these two philosophies in the same MVE program is impossible from both a logical and a practical point of view. They represent totally opposing views concerning the nature of morality; they represent subjective as opposed to objective truth. But let it be restated: to opt for Type B MVE is *not* to opt for an authoritarian teaching methodology which requires compliant acceptance—to, for example, the moral precept of honesty—with no questions asked. It encourages open discussion of alternatives to honesty and realistically examines their consequences, and even the seeming lack of consequences in some instances. Type B MVE operates on the knowledge that students will make their own decisions about honesty, in any event. The difference lies in the base from which the analysis of the issue of honesty is conducted.

("Honesty has intrinsic value" or "honesty has no intrinsic value.")

To approach the discussion of lying, cheating, stealing, and murder via Type A MVE is, in my view, patently irresponsible. Such an approach also represents a false impression of legal reality. It is alien to our concept and practice of jurisprudence which is based, essentially, on the recognition of objective values, and not on individuals' momentary preferences or choices.

THE COST

In case we are unaware of just how devastating this can be to a civilization, Walter Lippmann points out, in *The Public Philosophy*, just how high the stakes are:

> If what is good, what is right, what is true, is only what the individual "chooses" to "invent," then we are outside the traditions of civility. . . . There is left no ground for accommodation among the varieties of men; nor is there in this proclamation of anarchy a will to find an accommodation.[3]

Lippman gives an account of our tacit withdrawal from a commitment to objective moral precepts and how we have sold out the traditions of civility.

> . . . the liberal democracies of the West became the first great society to treat as a private concern the formative beliefs that shape the character of its citizens[4] . . . . It became the rule that ideas and principles are private—with only subjective relevance and significance. . . . All that has to do with what man is and should be, or how he should hold himself in the scheme of things, what are his rightful ends and the legitimate means, became private and subjective and publicly unaccountable.[5]

> . . . This has brought about a radical change in the

3 Walter Lippmann, *Essays in the Public Philosophy* (Boston: Little, Brown and Co., 1955), p. 176.
4 Ibid., p. 100.
5 Ibid., p. 99.

meaning of freedom. Originally it was founded on the postulate that there was a universal order on which all reasonable men were agreed: within that public agreement on the fundamentals and on the ultimates, it was safe to permit and it would be desirable to encourage, dissent and dispute. But within the disappearance of the public philosophy—and of a consensus on the first and last things—there was opened up a great vacuum in the public mind. . . .[6]

But there are strings attached to accepting the view that there are objective moral precepts. There are costs involved.

Morality always involves a sentiment of submission, a sense of service and obligation. In other words, it demands the recognition of an authoritative norm, be it secular or religious. The terms submission, service and obligation are all antithetical to the contemporary concept of freedom.[7]

THE "TRADE"

Pursuing this contemporary concept of freedom has brought about our almost frenetic obsession with "autonomy"—translated to mean the search for and assertion of the authentic self, the Sovereign Man, answerable to no one but himself. In its November/December 1978 issue, *The Humanist* published a symposium on "Moral Education and Secular Humanism" which brings to light another aspect of the opposing ideologies of Type A and Type B MVE. The editor introduces the topic by commenting that there has been "vigorous opposition" to school MVE programs on the basis that

"secular humanism" is being introduced and that this constitutes a violation of the separation of church and state. . . .

In spite of strong opposition, moral-education and

6 Ibid., p. 100.
7 Duncan Williams, *Trousered Apes* (New Rochelle, N.Y.: Arlington House, 1972), p. 108.

values-clarification programs are making rapid progress in school curricula.[8]

What is at issue here is the question of simply having traded former approaches to morality for the doctrine of moral relativism, situation ethics.

The Humanist Manifesto II, published in *The Humanist* in 1973, is rooted in situation ethics. It actively and explicitly denies the validity of religions:

> ... traditional dogmatic or authoritarian religions that place revelation, God, ritual, or creed above human needs and experience do a disservice to the human species[9] ... humanists still believe that traditional theism, especially faith in the prayer-hearing God, assumed to love and care for persons, to hear and understand their prayers and to be able to do something about them, is an unproved and outmoded faith[10] ... we can discover no divine purpose or providence for the human species. ...[11]

> We affirm that moral values derive their source from human experience. Ethics is *autonomous* and *situational*, needing no theological or ideological sanction.[12]

The Supreme Court of the United States has declared, in the Schempp case for example, that belief in this dogmatic creed and its assertions concerning the nature of Truth constitutes "a 'religion of secularism' in the sense of affirmatively opposing or sharing hostility to religion thus preferring those who believe in no religion over those who do believe."[13]

---

8 Introduction to "Moral Education and Secular Humanism," *The Humanist* (November/December 1978), p. 7. This article first appeared in *The Humanist*, and is reprinted by permission. See also Larry Schmidt, "The 'New Religion' in Public Schools," *School Guidance Worker*, vol. 34, no. 3, pp. 36-38.

9 "Humanist Manifesto II," *The Humanist*, vol. XXXIII, no. 5 (September/October 1973), p. 5. This article first appeared in *The Humanist*, and is reprinted by permission.

10 Ibid., p. 4.

11 Ibid., p. 6

12 Ibid.

13 School District of Abington, Tp., Pa. v. *Schempp*, [1963] 83 S. Ct. at 1573, 374 U.S. 203.

William B. Ball, a leading constitutional attorney, who has traced the development of the meaning of religion in American constitutional law documents that it is

> belief—not body, creed or cult which appears to be the essence of "religion;" [that Torcaso versus Watkins renders] it quite clear that for the court, theistic belief is but one sort of religion and that non-theistic belief may qualify as "religion" . . . [and that] "belief" refers to some sort of universal view of life, of the world of mankind. . . .[14]

So widespread is the opposition to the teaching of Secular Humanism in American schools and so strong the opposition to federal government support for education projects involving Secular Humanism, that the issue was brought before the U.S. House of Representatives. As a result, the Conlan Amendment to the Higher Education Amendments of 1976 was passed. The Amendment stated:

> No grant, contract or support is authorized . . . for any educational program, curriculum research and development, administrator-teacher orientation, or any project involving one or more students or teacher-administrators involving any aspect of the religion of secular humanism.[15]

The Conlan Amendment passed in the House by a vote of 222 to 174.[16] After considerable lobbying by officers of the American Humanist Association, it was dropped from the final version signed by the president.[17]

In "Answering the Critics" in *The Humanist*, Robert Hall makes a distinction between "secular" and "secularistic" humanism, arguing that "secularistic humanism" is the phi-

---

14 William B. Ball, "Implications of Supreme Court Decisions for Contemporary Church-State Problems," *The Catholic World* (August 1963), pp. 6-7.
15 For the debate on this amendment, see the *Congressional Record*, 12 May 1976, pp. H4317-H4319.
16 *Congressional Record*, 12 May 1976, pp. H4318-H4319.
17 See *Education Amendments Conference Report*, 94th Congress, 2nd Session, Report no. 94-1701, 27 September 1976, p. 211.

losophy which holds clearly antireligious convictions.[18] Unfortunately, however, Hall does not actually define "secular humanism" nor does he refer specifically to the Humanist Manifesto II which might have clarified many still unanswered questions. In fact, several of those appointed to the symposium to respond to the relation between secular humanism and moral education actually avoid or skirt the issue.

Certainly the term, *secular humanism*, with or without the "istic" is one which incorporates a broad range of attitudes, beliefs and life-stances. This is why, labels aside—for they tend to evoke confusion, denial, emotion, much heat and little light—a central question still remains. In our quest to disestablish any particular religious view in the public educational system, are we simply trading in one set of ideological labels for another and, at the same time, disestablishing the view that there are objective moral precepts? For in striving to create an educational system which will meet the pluralism of our day, we appear to operate as if we believed the following equations were true:

1. To teach that core moral precepts exist is:

   • to teeter on the brink of promoting a religious view;
   • to engage in authoritarian indoctrination.

2. To teach that core moral precepts do not exist is:

   • to dissociate education from any religious view;
   • to be consistent with a pluralistic society.

But it becomes plain that these equations suffer both in the validity of their facts and in their logic.

1. "Religious views" (according to the U.S. Supreme Court) may or may not incorporate belief in objective, core moral precepts. (For example, although the "religion of secularism" is based on the belief that ethics are autonomous and situational, it must still be defined as a religion.)

18 See Robert Hall, "Moral Education Today: Progress, Prospects, and Problems of a Field Come of Age," *The Humanist*, (November/December 1978), pp. 8-9. This article first appeared in *The Humanist*, and is reprinted by permission.

2. Authoritarian indoctrination is a method of teaching which can be used just as forcefully to promote the view that there are no core moral precepts as to promote the view that there are.[19]

In fact, it turns out that in the equations formulated above, we are not comparing entities of the same order. Because we have failed to think through these equations, MVE approaches which support the view that there are no core moral precepts continue to be promoted as the hallmarks of a tolerant, progressive, pluralistic society, instead of being recognized as virtual indoctrination in that particular dogma and ideology.

UNIVERSAL VALUES

But this is scarcely the first time that a society has questioned the existence of universal or core principles of morality. In his study of civilizations—including the Ancient Egyptian, Old Norse, Ancient Jewish, Babylonian, North American Indian, Hindu, Ancient Chinese, Roman, Christian, Greek, Australian Aboriginal, Anglo-Saxon, Stoic, and Ancient Indian civilizations—C.S. Lewis identifies eight objectives values which they all held in common. Lewis refers to these as the *Tao*, or

> the doctrine of objective value, the belief that certain attitudes are really true and others really false to the kind of thing the universe is and the kind of thing we are....[20] Only the *Tao* provides a common human law of action which can over-arch rulers and ruled alike. A dogmatic belief in objective value is necessary to the very idea of a rule which is not tyranny or an obedience which is not slavery.[21]

19 For a distinction between "education" and "indoctrination," see J. Coombs, "Concerning the Nature of Moral Competence," *The Teaching of Values in Canadian Education*, Canadian Society for the Study of Education, vol. 2 (Edmonton: 1975), pp. 7-8.
20 C.S. Lewis, *The Abolition of Man* (London: Geoffrey Bles, Centenary Press, 1947), p. 17. Lewis's term, the *Tao*, should not be confused with the religion Taoism. Reprinted by permission of Wm. Collins.
21 Ibid., p. 50.

The eight objective values these civilizations have held in common are listed below and described in more detail in appendix II:

    I. The Law of General Beneficence
   II. The Law of Special Beneficence
  III. Duties to Parents, Elders, Ancestors
  IV. Duties to Children and Posterity
   V. The Law of Justice
  VI. The Law of Good Faith and Veracity
 VII. The Law of Good Mercy
VIII. The Law of Magnanimity.[22]

Lewis makes it clear:

> I may add that though I myself am a Theist, and indeed a Christian, I am not here attempting any indirect argument for Theism. I am simply urging that if we are to have values at all we must accept the ultimate platitudes of Practical Reason as having absolute validity: that any attempt, having become skeptical about these, to introduce value lower down on some supposedly more "realistic" basis is doomed.[23]

The anthropological studies of the late Clyde Kluckhohn of Harvard University are concerned with the same phenomenon:

> Standards and values are not completely relative to the cultures from which they derive. Some values are as much givens in human life as the fact that bodies of certain densities fall under specified conditions. These are founded, in part, upon the fundamental biological similarities of all human beings. They arise also out of the circumstance that human existence is invariably a social existence. . . .[24] The very fact that all cultures have had their categorical imperatives that went be-

22 Ibid., pp. 56-64.
23 Ibid., pp. 36-37.
24 Clyde Kluckhohn, "Values and Value-Orientations in the Theory of Action," *Toward a General Theory of Action*, eds. Talcott Parsons and Edward A. Shils (New York: Harper and Row, 1962), p. 418.

yond mere survival and immediate pleasure is one of vast significance.[25]

Thus, we are faced with the fundamental question: Is the "authentic self" discoverable within humanity's subjective view of values—"there are no core moral precepts" (Type A MVE), or is the self, paradoxically, discoverable when it recognizes and becomes identified with objective values—"there are core moral precepts" (Type B MVE)?

THE DECISION

Perhaps Type B MVE could be taught responsibly by focusing on the moral imperatives which both ancient and modern civilizations, secular and religious, have held in common, and which Lewis refers to as the *Tao*. This would give students the opportunity to consider what history tells us about the very survival of civilizations relative to the nature of their morality and to assess this morality relative to the heritage we all share. An intelligent and reasonable analysis of the components of morality requires the understanding of those precepts which have stood the test of civility. Consequently, the objectives and strategies for Type B MVE would be worked out using these objective moral precepts, and current issues would be approached in classroom sessions from this basis. (See the model outlined in table 4.)

On the other hand, Type A moral education, which effectively dispenses with the past as mere "tradition," fails to present to its students for their consideration the best human values, insights, skills, and ways of acting which previous centuries and civilizations have recorded.[26] MVE which is silent or indifferent about history places in the hand of each student a blank sheet entitled, "Your Moral Heritage." There is no need for the student to go beyond his or her own experience or environment in order to apply

25 Ibid., p. 419.
26 See Paul F. Schumann, "History and Geography Should Be Scrapped," *Educational Leadership*, vol. 37, no. 4 (January 1980), pp. 342 and 364. For more on the necessity of the school nourishing three basic reference points for life—history, present reality, and imagination—see J.R. Wilkes, "Narcissism or Truth at the Crossroads," *Canada's Mental Health*, vol. 27, no. 3 (September 1979), pp. 16-18.

the ultimate test for value. Lacking an objective focus, the imagination is stunted: potential for moral vision becomes thwarted and turned in upon itself. "What works for you" becomes the prime focus, rather than the discovery of what is objectively or intrinsically good. Accordingly, the objectives and strategies for Type A MVE are developed from the basic concept that there are no core moral precepts and its classroom sessions would follow the Type A model outlined in table 4.

The most intelligent way to assess any particular MVE materials personally is to examine its author's materials and stated philosophy of life so carefully that the objectives of its content and the existence or nonexistence of its moral precepts will become clear. Only by doing this is it possible to judge whether MVE material can be used responsibly and whether it meets the regulations of the school education act of each jurisdiction. Only so is it possible to determine whether such material supports the hidden curriculum of moral relativism or individual utilitarianism or any other "ism" or "istic," which would qualify it as Type A MVE.

If this is a pluralistic society and a democracy, then those who do not favor the "trade" for Type A moral values education in our schools will have to make themselves heard. Much as we may dislike the idea of making waves, we ought to assess how important this issue is to us, not only as individual educators and parents, but as citizens of a nation whose main resource is its youth. This is particularly crucial, considering the fact that MVE is not a single course from which a parent or student may request exemption, but is being advanced as an integral part of all subjects in curricula at all age levels. We have more than enough evidence that in the United States, MVE is indeed "one of the most ... explosive developments in education."[27] Yet we observe that federal and state laws which provide controls on the practice of MVE are scarcely used. A nation-wide study of MVE in Canada is exceedingly relevant:

Public sentiment concerning the role of schools in values and moral education is strikingly confused and

27 D. Superka et al., *Values Education Sourcebook*, p. ix.

sometimes surprisingly apathetic . . . many of the public are curiously silent or perhaps indifferent about what schools should do about values and morality.[28]

Much of this stems from the fact that for the most part, the issue of values education and the fundamental questions it raises have not been aired. Essentially those fundamental questions factor down to one's concept of freedom. Presumably most of us desire, as the American founding fathers put it, "life, liberty, and the pursuit of happiness." But our definitions of these terms differ. It follows, therefore, that we will differ in our choice of the means by which to achieve these objectives.

- "Life" can be defined as the intrinsic value of all human life, or as my own life above all others.
- "Liberty" can be freedom from tyranny—including the tyranny of self—or it can be licence to pursue one's own wants.
- "Happiness" can be creative interdependence for and with others, or it can be rank hedonism.

"Thinking for oneself" in a given situation can be based on recognition of the existence of objective moral principles or on total moral relativism. Depending on our perspective, we will see our objectives in MVE to be the encouragement of a responsible conscience and a responsive will, or we will consider that the vagaries of each situation and individual preference of the moment are the major components of decision making.

Do we agree that in the United States schools should be undertaking moral values education to the extent and depth which is being recommended and currently practiced in many areas? This is the first question, to which many are answering, "No." At the same time, if we believe that, handled at a more responsible level, MVE can be an important part of our schools' curriculum, then surely we should attempt to make the administrators of our educational systems realize that Type A and Type B approaches are totally

---

28 Don Cochrane and David Williams, "The Stances of Provincial Ministries of Education," *Canadian Journal of Education*, p. 12.

opposed ... in their fundamental value positions, their behavioral objectives, the factors which they consider to be of central importance, their methods of teaching, their assumptions concerning the basic nature of human beings and the role of the teacher. Further, they will recognize that to advance Type A and Type B approaches in the same MVE program is both logically and pragmatically unrealistic. Such recognition will open up this crucial issue to honest and long-overdue action. Most important of all, it will modify the system in which moral values education presently operates—and in most cases is encouraged to operate—as a law unto itself, which is accountable to no one.

9

Who Will Control
the System?

At the center of much of the MVE controversy is the question of who will control the educational systems. This issue is both a legal and a political question. School boards, parents, students, administrators, teachers' unions, principals, teachers, federal and state departments of education: each makes a legitimate case for some measure of authority over the goals and processes of education.

LABELLING

One of the major weaknesses of educational systems is lack of involvement and communication even at the basic level. Jerrold Coombs of the Association for Values Education Research comments:

> I do not mean to imply that teachers should be the final arbiters of educational goals ... my own view is that, in the final analysis, the authority for such decisions should rest with the community served by the educational institution. But, the community, aside from a few vocal minority groups, does not make clear in any detail what it expects of the schools. This means

that, like it or not, teachers must make decisions about goals.[1]

Coombs' point is a good one. How many of us, as consumers, make clear what we expect of the schools? And, as a corollary, if and when a school does get feedback from its community, how does it determine to what extent that praise or criticism is representative of the community? Do school officials sometimes have a very human tendency to interpret positive feedback as representative of the majority of the community and to assume that negative feedback comes from a few highly unrepresentative (or even unbalanced) individuals or a small, usually right-wing, minority group? The temptation to accept these notions as true is very compelling. And, in some instances, there is just cause. In fact, only extensive involvement of the majority in the community will ever provide the necessary data to answer such a question accurately.

If this labelling process exists—even to a degree—it can serve to prevent many moderates from getting involved, except on a "praise" basis. Parents fear—with good reason in some instances—that their child will be labelled too. Rather than risk this, a higher percentage of parents than ever before are registering their criticism by quietly withdrawing their children to enrol them in independent schools. There is, of course, no guarantee that the same "labelling" process may not be operative there also. The process can, in fact, operate as a very effective hidden factor in communications between home and school. Effective, that is, in terms of reducing the need for trouble shooting by the school, but ineffective in establishing genuine supportive relationships between home and school.

In fact, many people contend that a crisis of authority and confidence now exists between parents and professional helpers. People are becoming increasingly concerned about the extent to which average parents are in fact "qualified" to make the best decisions about their own children.

The fact is, the "therapeutic view of the world" has

1 Jerrold R. Coombs, "Objectives of Values Analysis," *Values Education: Rationale, Strategies, and Procedures*, pp. 4–5. Used with permission.

become big business. Young parents are becoming more and more convinced that they are not equipped to look after their own children. They have been conditioned to seek outside help from professional helpers. One young mother I know told me that she was more than satisfied with the day-care arrangements she had made for her young daughter because she was convinced that the "instructors" were more intelligent than she was. They had higher IQs, she said. What was incredible about this was that the child was only 5 months old.[2]

During a Parent Education Week, a high-ranking government educational official was quoted as saying, "Schools have a community responsibility to help improve the quality of parenting."[3] What she and others appear to be proposing is that the school-community support system can and should work both ways. Constructive criticism and constructive, as opposed to empty, praise should flow in both directions.

THE LAST WORD

Not everyone will agree with this reciprocal model when it comes to the moral education of children. "When you come right down to the crunch," some will ask, "Are teachers any more qualified to teach children about moral values than parents? And especially without parental collaboration and consent on specifics?"

But educators point to what many identify as a problem of epidemic proportions: many parents do not discuss the question of moral values with their children. "How many parents really care?" teachers ask. "How many really know how to talk to their kids?" So it is out of this basically well-intentioned and often valid context that schools have ventured into the field of MVE. The school is seen as the last bastion of communication between adults and children.

---

2 S. Williams, "Me: A Magnificent Obsession," *Toronto Life* (December 1977), p. 69.
3 "Child Care Revolution Triggers a Search for New Parent Skills," *The Toronto Star*, 18 September 1978, p. C1.

Moreover, some educators insist that the school should be free to conduct this communication as they see fit. On a radio phone-in show directed in part to this issue, a teacher protested that it is no more appropriate for parents to challenge teachers on their choice of classroom materials in the area of values than it is for patients to challenge a doctor on the treatment he or she has prescribed for them. Teachers are professionals, the caller contended, and should not be told how to do their jobs.[4]

His statement points up an interesting and crucial distinction. While parents are expected to support the wide-open scrutiny by their children of whatever value topics, from whatever point of view (moral, immoral, or amoral), and at whatever age the teacher chooses, that same parent should not be expected or perhaps even allowed to exercise a similar scrutiny of the values education curriculum. In terms of advocating "Openness to the Validity of All Opinions," this argument is internally inconsistent.

Conversely, on the basis of having been through the system themselves, some parents may assume that they are experts, having little time for the insights and perceptions of the "new" MVE educators. But this does not eliminate the need to free up parental access to classroom materials so that at least the opportunity for forthright discussion is created and offered openly.

In an article in *The Public Interest*, the authors draw attention to the contradictory way in which Sidney Simon's philosophy of "liberation" operates when it is opposed:

> In defense of his [Values Clarification] methods against what he regards as powerful dogmatic and political traditions of indoctrination, Simon sometimes disparages his opponents in authoritarian terms, thus avoiding the need to consider the merits or shortcomings of their arguments. For example, when the school district in Great Neck, New York, cut from its budget funds for [Simon to train] teachers in Values Clarification,

Simon was quoted as saying, "An orthodox Jewish right-wing group got hold of it and just raised hell."[5]

Unfortunately, too many parents have asked whether the new openness to the validity of all opinions applies only to students and not to their parents. They have wondered this as they have been either implicitly or explicitly discouraged from examining controversial classroom materials. How would any parent react if they heard that their child's teacher had said, "Don't discuss this with your parents—they're not there yet."[6]

One would hope that this does not happen frequently, but the fact that it is documented in various briefs and letters to the editor is alarming. This is why many parents are apt to react when it is suggested to them—again either specifically or by implication—that the parent-teacher relationship all comes down to parents' "trust of the teacher." It is interesting that the caller on the phone-in show pushed this point even further: "Parents who question the 'morality' of certain materials and want them excluded from required curriculum are the ones who do not trust the integrity of their own children."[7] Another reason is often implied, either directly or by inference: such parents are not confident about their own parenting. Such is the name calling and bitterness that can surround the question of control of curriculum content.

AVENUES FOR COMMUNICATION

Certainly there is a difference between overprotection of children by spoonfeeding them moral values, and thrusting them headlong into the midst of the self-serve cafeteria. In

5 William J. Bennett and Edwin J. Delattre, "Moral Education in the Schools," *The Public Interest* (Winter 1978), fn. p. 84. Reprinted with permission of the authors from *The Public Interest*. Copyright© 1979 by National Affairs, Inc. Great Neck incident also reported in *Kohlberg and Simon: An Exchange of Opinion*, available from the National Humanistic Education Center, 110 Spring St., Saratoga Springs, New York 12866.
6 K. Gow, "What Every Parent Should Know," *The Canadian*, 21 May 1977, p. 8.
7 CBC, *Radio Noon*, 14 June 1978.

any case, it is clear that open avenues for communication between parents and the educational system are essential. These points need to be considered within the context of the following account, in which T.P. Millar, a Vancouver doctor, describes a situation in his community and his attempts to draw it to the attention of people at several levels of educational authority.

The following grade eleven English assignment appeared in my community recently.

The children were to read the following anecdote and give their opinion about the rights and wrongs of the various behaviors involved.

Here is the anecdote, exactly as given:

The Story of Hector and Isobel[8]

Isobel and Hector live on two separate islands. They have known each other ever since they were children and as they grew into their teens they started to date each other. Neither of them dated anyone else. Now they are both away at university—different universities. It's June and they are both returning to the islands for the summer. Both are really excited about getting back home and seeing each other again, but when they get back, they discover the bridge that joins the two islands has been destroyed by a storm.

Isobel is wandering around her island, wondering what to do, and really feeling forlorn when she runs into Fritz. Fritz lives in a small cabin at the south end of the island, reads a lot and is really a bit of a hermit. Isobel tells her story to Fritz and says, "What shall I do?" and Fritz says, "I really can't tell you. It's your decision, Isobel."

So Isobel goes away, still feeling depressed and meets Sinbad. Sinbad has a sailboat. He's somewhat of a playboy and he tells Isobel that he will take her to the island where

---

8 This is a variation of Strategy Number 50, entitled "Alligator River," in S. Simon et al., *Values Clarification: A Handbook*, pp. 290-294.

Hector is, but there's an "if" in his offer. Isobel has to agree to spend the night with Sinbad first.

Isobel wanders around for several more hours, agonizing over what to do, and she finally decides. She goes to Sinbad and tells him that she's willing to sleep with him, and in the morning he sails her over to the island where Hector is.

Isobel rushes to find Hector and everything is wonderful. They are both really glad to see each other and feel very close. Everything feels just like it used to be. After a couple of hours, during which they have been together in a sunny meadow, Isobel, who is feeling guilty about Sinbad, "confesses" what happened.

Hector is furious. He tells her she has ruined their relationship, that things can never be the same between them again. He is really enraged and when she tries to talk to him, he pushes her aside and storms off. While Isobel is lying on the grass, weeping, up comes Butch. He asks her why she is crying and when she tells him the story, he rushes off, finds Hector and gives him a good thrashing.

Dr. Millar comments:

> This assignment, it seems to me, raises some quite important questions, such as: What has this got to do with the teaching of English? Can anything be learned about chastity, or restraint, or tolerance, or truth, from studying the actions of such trivial characters? What is the "teaching" purpose behind this *moral dilemma* anecdote...?

> There is [also] the one about the wagon train going West with the band of settlers hiding from marauding Indians. A mother is faced with the choice of suffocating her infant son to prevent him crying out or allowing him to live and all of the settlers to be killed by the Indians. There is the torture anecdote. Your wife and children are being held prisoner in an unknown place and a time bomb is set to go off in half an hour. You have the man who hid them, but he refuses to tell you where they are. The only way you can find out is to torture the man. What will you do...?

Millar explains:

> Since I feel *moral dilemma anecdotes* communicate values alien to those taught in my home and are exceeding of the educator's mandate, I wrote my school principal to request the termination of this teaching.
>
> The principal told me this was part of the Grade Eleven English Curriculum as laid down by the Department of Education in Victoria, and referred me to the Superintendent. I contacted the Superintendent, who indicated that this was an enthusiasm of this particular teacher, but when I pointed out that this was contrary to the law, he too told me this was part of the Grade Eleven English Curriculum emanating from Victoria. He told me that he was powerless to alter this, and I should pursue my concerns at other levels of educational authority. . . .[9]

Dr. Millar goes on to explain that he is "not prepared to accept that this is simply part of Grade Eleven English."[10] He refers to Mr. Jim MacFarlane, a past president of the British Columbia Teachers' Federation, who describes similar use of moral dilemmas in his Grade Ten Social Studies class.

> As a classroom teacher I always have attempted to develop as the paramount thing in young people an ability for critical thought. I used to make up philosophical problems in Grade 10 social studies—problems of human conflict.
>
> I'd ask them: "How would you respond if your friend were dangling at the end of a rope and you were holding him but only one of you could survive? What would you do? Cut him loose? Or what would you do if the only way to get information to save a life was to torture somebody?"
>
> These little moral problems had no answer—I wasn't

9 T.P. Millar, "Moral Indoctrination in the Classroom," paper presented at an Educational Forum at West Vancouver Secondary School, Vancouver (November 1978), pp. 2-6.
10 T.P. Millar, "Moral Indoctrination in the Classroom," p. 6.

looking for the answer. My students used to get frustrated and would ask: "What is the answer?" I'd say there is none—and that's for you to worry about.[11]

Mr. MacFarlane was perhaps simply reiterating the directive to teachers in Robert Hawley's book, *Values Exploration Through Role Playing:*

When the teacher views his or her role as a facilitator, a coordinator, and a provider of learning experiences, then the question of "what to do when things go wrong" becomes one for the whole class to share in; it is no longer a burden for the teacher alone.[12]

Having introduced and promoted the exercise, can this possibly be construed as responsible MVE?

"A MACHIAVELLIAN APPROACH:" A CONSTITUTIONAL ISSUE

Before we dismiss this whole issue as simply incredible and "certainly not happening under our school board," the following incident should be considered. In May 1977, a seminar was conducted by the leader of a values education project, funded by government for the purpose of introducing and establishing MVE in a given area. In speaking about involving the community in discussion of values education program in the schools, the leader was asked,

"But what if the community objects to values education in their school?"

"Well then," he said, "you take a Machiavellian approach. You call it 'life skills' and you do it anyway. You do not ask the Board for their approval. You simply work it into the existing courses."

Before anyone condemns this particular individual too harshly, it is important to realize that he was only reiterating

---

11 Neale Adams, "Why Teachers Move toward Militancy," *The Vancouver Sun*, 3 July 1975, p. 6.
12 Robert C. Hawley, *Value Exploration through Role Playing* (New York: Hart Publishing Co., 1975), p. 150. Reprinted by permission of A & W Publishers, Inc.© 1975 Hart Publishing Company,

a firmly entrenched and widely accepted goal among many values educators—that is, the autonomy of the child. We have mentioned Kohlberg's statement earlier, but it is important enough to state again:

> The constitutional issue arises from the point of view of the child's parent, who can object to the teaching of values other than the parent's own. Respect for the parent's rights is not respect for child's autonomy, a more legitimate concern.[13]

Sidney Simon's approach to community knowledge and involvement is similar. In an article by Farnum Gray, Simon explains that by simply closing their classroom doors teachers have succeeded in accomplishing what they believe in. Referring to his teaching position at Temple University, Simon advises:

> "I always bootlegged the values stuff under other titles. I was assigned to teach Social Studies in the Elementary School, and I taught values clarification. I was assigned Current Trends in American Education, and I taught *my* trend."

Gray concludes:

> Simon's closed-door policy brought teaching success without controversy.[14]

The above statements from leading proponents of each of the three major MVE approaches we have studied give some indication of the importance of realizing that each of these approaches must be understood as a social movement or a mission. Rather than encouraging genuine two-way communication, they are taking another approach to en-

---

13 L. Kohlberg, "Stages of Moral Development as a Basis for Moral Education," *Moral Education: Interdisciplinary Approaches*, p. 72. Reprinted by permission of University of Toronto Press and Paulist Press. Copyright© University of Toronto Press, 1971.
14 Farnum Gray, "Doing Something about Values," *Learning* (December 1972). Also available from the National Humanistic Center, 110 Spring Street, Saratoga Springs, New York 12866. Excerpt reprinted by permission of *Learning*, the Magazine for Creative Teaching. Copyright© 1972 by Education Today Company, Inc.

suring that their mission is accomplished. For, to their disciples, the end justifies any means which may be necessary to spread their particular message. In fact, this very rationale may be the most dangerous of all aspects of the MVE approaches we have looked at. It exploits the vulnerability of children by violating their right to privacy and their right to protection from abuse by administrative authority.

CONFRONTATION

The following example of official withdrawal of material in one area of the curriculum and subsequent reinstatement of it in another is not atypical. In Saskatchewan, Canada, Sidney Simon's book, *Values Clarification: A Handbook*, was prominently featured as recommended resource material in a wide-ranging number of courses. However, due to a groundswell of public opinion against this and other books, the Saskatchewan Department of Education issued revised guidelines. In the June 1978 issue of *Chronicle*, its official journal of record, the department formally directed that among other books, Simon's *Values Clarification: A Handbook* "be struck from the Division I & II Health Curriculum Guide."[15]

New Guidelines Issued for Health and Family Life Education

The attention of teachers, administrators, and school boards is drawn to the following clarification and expansion of the guidelines contained in the Division I & II Health Curriculum Guide.

- The family life education part of the health program may only be taught with the concurrence of the school board.

- Parents of Division I & II students must be informed

---

15 Division I—Year II—Mental Health (p. 48). Drug Education (p. 49); Division II—Year I—Family Life (p. 82), Division II—Year II—Mental Health (p. 94), Family Life (p. 101); and Division II—Year III—Fitness, Care of the Body and Dental Health (p. 105), Mental Health (p. 118), Drug Education (p. 122), Family Life (p. 124).

of the nature of the family life education program and must have an opportunity to discuss the content of the course and the resource materials to be used.

- The school board is to confirm the content of the course and the resource material to be used.

- Resource material for teacher use is not to be made available in the classroom nor placed in the school resource center.

In order to emphasize the intent of these guidelines and to prevent possible misunderstandings regarding the listing of teacher resource material in the curriculum guide, the Department of Education *formally directs* that the following teacher reference citations be struck from the Division I & II Health Curriculum Guide.

Burt and Meeks, *Education for Sexuality.*
Burn, *Better Than the Birds, Smarter Than the Bees.*
Hofstein and Bauer, *The Human Story: Facts on Birth, Growth and Reproduction.*
Pomeroy, *Boys and Sex.*
Pomeroy, *Girls and Sex.*
Readers Digest, Life Values Series: *Perspectives on Sex and Sexuality* and *Perspectives on Love, Morals and Sexuality.*
Simon, *Values Clarification: A Handbook of Practical Strategies for Teachers and Students.*

Teachers should find sufficient background material in the remaining teacher reference books listed in the curriculum guides.[16]

However, anyone in Saskatchewan who has made a point of monitoring officially recommended resources will have noted that despite this 1978 directive regarding the Health curriculum, by September 1979, the department of education was once more recommending Simon's *Values Clarifi-*

16 *Chronicle*, The Saskatchewan Department of Education, no. 78-004 (Regina: 19 July 1978), p. 3.

cation: A Handbook, on their *Career Education, Activities: Teacher Handbook for Kindergarten: Division I and II,* and enthusiastically describing it as: "An excellent set of strategies for student use. Offers a variety of techniques and topics, and sample lessons for all age groups. Can be easily used and/or modified to suit specific needs."[17]

In the United States, this same book was one among several introduced in Congress as "an example of the decadent and immoral approaches being used in schools."[18] Lawsuits, as we have noted in chapters 6, 7, 8 and on page 201, are not in the least uncommon. In 1977, in the article, "Mind Bending in the Schools Stirs Growing Protest," *U.S. News and World Report* revealed:

> Public outcries over attempts to shape students reached a peak in the 1975-76 school year with violent demonstrations in Kanawka County, W. Va.
>
> Many parents there and elsewhere claimed that new textbooks which exposed children to foul language, violence and unusual sexual customs of other cultures trampled on their families' moral and religious views.[19]

But to conclude that the center of the controversy revolves around a handful of particular books would be to fail utterly to recognize the range and magnitude of the new MVE as a major movement. As the internationally renowned social scientist, Amitai Etzioni, reiterates in the *Chicago Tribune:* "The hottest new item in post-Watergate curricula is 'moral education'.... But moral education means different things to different people...."[20]

As in most movements, the MVE leaders are not unaware that their message and their methods are highly contentious. Howard Kirschenbaum lists eight ways "[to] Deal With

17 *Career Education, Activities: A Teacher Handbook for Kindergarten: Division I and II,* The Saskatchewan Department of Education (Regina: September 1979), p. 153.
18 H. Kirschenbaum, *Advanced Values Clarification,* p. 151.
19 *U.S. News and World Report* (Washington), 4 July 1977, p. 44. Copyright© U.S. News and World Report.
20 Amitai Etzioni, "Education in Morality Poses Ethical Dilemma in Schools," *The Chicago Tribune,* 13 October 1976.

Those Parents Who Oppose Value Clarification."[21] And in their chapter on "Personal-Growth Activities for Teachers," Hawley, Simon, and Britton suggest that teachers prepare for trouble by practicing the following exercises amongst themselves.

1. Brainstorm possible responses to each of the following charges:

   (a) You are accused of amateur psychologizing. As a teacher unqualified to meddle with the adolescent psyche, your assignments are reckless.

   (b) You are charged with using the young as guinea pigs for inadequately tested and potentially dangerous materials.

   (c) You are accused of using English class for fun and games.

   (d) You are poking into the private affairs of the young—into areas heretofore reserved for the family and/or the church.

   (e) You are undermining real education by giving the young the impression that the titilation of some superficial psychological tactics is as worthy as the enduring satisfaction afforded by the mastery of an academic discipline.

   (f) You are encouraging intensive self-examination in an age group already nearly paralyzed by self-consciousness and self-doubt.

2. Role Play: You are summoned to court to answer one of the six charges listed above. You are questioned by one of the groups listed below.

   (a) Three traditional teachers (good ones) who are scandalized by your program.

   (b) Three parents who have asked for a conference.

   (c) The principal, assistant principal, and English department chairman (until now a supporter of experimentation).

3. List additional charges that one might encounter as

21 H. Kirschenbaum, *Advanced Values Clarification*, p. 54.

a result of using these materials, and brainstorm appropriate defenses.[22]

There is no doubt that proponents of these MVE approaches see the need to prepare themselves for confrontation. For all that departments of education advise that school boards and schools should respect the opinions of parents in the immediate community, teachers are being cast in the role of social engineers by many MVE authors who know that much of their material will pit the school against the home and catch the child in the crossfire. I do not believe that most teachers deliberately set out to do this at all. Many, however, feel they have a mission, and it is particularly when their concept of mission differs from that of the parents that close collaboration becomes crucial.

But close collaboration is impossible when those parents who are informed at all about the moral value content in, for example, Family Life Education, receive such vague information, that they learn virtually nothing. As one mother related: "I was told that the course for our daughter in Grade 8 would cover basic approaches to understanding human sexuality as an integral part of human development. What she got was a course on the use of contraceptives."[23] Surely there is no area which requires more collaboration between home and school than moral values education, since it carries the highest potential for pulling students between home and the open-ended values which many MVE approaches promote. In a discussion about the availability of information about MVE, one full-time co-ordinator was asked:

"Why couldn't details of MVE resource materials be shared with all parents so that those who wish to discuss this further with the school or precede or follow up these same topics with their children at home could do so?"

22 R. Hawley, S. Simon, and D.D. Britton, *Composition for Personal Growth* (New York: Hart Publishing Co. Inc., 1973), pp. 169-170. Reprinted by permission of A & W Publishers, Inc.© 1973 by Hart Publishing Company, Inc.

23 K. Gow, "What Every Parent Should Know," *The Canadian*, 21 May 1977, p. 8.

"Oh, I don't think the kids would like us to do that,"
she replied.

Her response is puzzling, particularly in view of the fact that
most schools would see the need for better communication
between students and parents. At the same time, all of us
who have been involved in teaching or counselling youth
know well the temptation to see oneself as "the only person
(or at least one of the few) that the child can talk to." This is
personally gratifying and is often the element which keeps
school personnel committed to their jobs, despite high
levels of frustration with administrative hierarchies. Confid-
ing in teachers is also a vital support to many students. But
we also know that in many cases, a student's problem can
be made worse if he or she perceives—whether this is
explicitly stated or not—that "We're with you ... we (at
school) understand you better than your parents ... we're
on your side. . . ."

One of the unpopular but important questions which
needs to be considered is whether some MVE programs
inadvertently or otherwise use the "generation gap" between parents and their children as a rationale for virtually
excluding parents from information, in-put, and involvement relating to the education of their children. Or are
they—and if not, can they—become actively instrumental
in helping to bridge that gap between student and home by
involving parents whenever and wherever they can?

WHAT'S ON RECORD?

A very important aspect of this question—also a constitutional issue—is the type and quality of the data placed in a
child's school record and the accessibility to parents of this
record. Professor Edward Humphreys, undertook a nation-
wide study of school record-keeping practices in Canada. A
review of this study reports:

Chaotic record keeping is the chief protection students
and their parents have from the misuse of student
records ... information in the records was not "statis-
tically reliable" and often out-dated and in many prov-

inces there is no legislation governing its collection or use.[24]

Dr. Humphreys found more than 600 different kinds of data recorded—ranging from students' religious practices, "comments on citizenship" and "trustworthiness" to information about parents such as their "lineage" and "racial origin."[25] According to one government education official, the record can contain "any other information that teachers may wish to place in the record folder."[26] Given the importance which has been accorded to values education in many schools, it would be quite feasible for a student's file to contain excerpts from his or her Politics or Religion diary,[27] self-written Obituary,[28] or answer to "would [you] like to have different parents?"[29] There is every evidence of the same situation in the U.S.[30]

MVE exercises are not introduced to students as "tests," are not conducted by trained psychologists, and may, therefore, not be formally classified as "psychological testing." Students and parents would find it alarming, therefore, that their private lives—as revealed by the student in MVE sessions from kindergarten forward—may be reported in such detail by virtual novices in the field of psycho-social diagnosis.[31]

In some jurisdictions, parents and students over 18 may challenge the accuracy of a student's record, bringing in a psychiatrist or other appropriate professional of their own choosing to refute the judgments recorded in the docu-

24 Howard Fluxgold, "Chaos Guards Student Files, Study Reports," *The Globe and Mail* (Toronto), 18 October 1979, p. 4.
25 Ibid.
26 Ibid.
27 S. Simon et al., *Values Clarification: A Handbook*, rev. ed., p. 390. Copyright© 1972, A & W Publishers, Inc. Copyright© 1978, Hart Publishing Company, Inc. Reprinted by permission of A & W Publishers, Inc.
28 Ibid., pp. 311-313.
29 Ibid., 1st ed., p. 4.
30 See for example, Leonard S. Kenworthy, *Social Studies for the Seventies*, Ginn & Co., Waltham, Mass., 1969, p. 254.
31 In some jurisdictions, particular protest has been raised in relation to the evaluations involved in Early Identification Programs which begin with four- to five-year-olds.

ment. In other jurisdictions, however, not only has this pro-
vision not been written into legislation, but even initial
access to the child's file can be virtually closed to the family.
Thus, for any student, it is possible that a form of "values-
labelling" can begin. Because of the teacher's understandable lack of expertise in this area, comments—which may
or may not be accurate—may continue to influence the
way in which that child is perceived by every succeeding
reader of that record for the remainder of his or her school
year and beyond.

> Mr. Humphreys contends that with the increasing use
> of computerized record-keeping and the use of the
> social insurance number to identify students, there is
> great potential for abuse.

> "The development of a comprehensive school record
> is bound to attract the attention of those who require
> information for the sorting and sifting that character-
> izes North American society.... The temptation exists
> to employ the records that have been collected over a
> number of years to supplement the investigations of
> [... various levels of government] and possibly even
> private investigation agencies," he writes in his study.[32]

Groups who are aware of these dangers have been lobbying against such practices as a gross invasion of the child's
privacy and an unwarranted extension of the school's mandate. Schools counter that they are simply attempting to
evaluate children's moral and social adjustment as part of
their overall development, that they are attempting to
detect problems which are still at an early, more treatable
stage. Can anyone argue against the preventive treatment
of problems? Of course not. However, there are important
questions which must be raised once more:

- Can the MVE exercises we have examined be fairly classified as "preventive?"

- To what degree is it the role of the school to undertake

---

32 Howard Fluxgold, "Chaos Guards Student Files, Study Reports," *The
   Globe and Mail* (Toronto), 18 October 1979, p. 4.

such "evaluations" by teachers untrained in this area—however well-intentioned they may be?

- Are there valid reasons why parental consent should not be obtained regarding the specific content of these moral and social assessment exercises?

- Are there valid reasons why parents should not be consulted and informed in detail about all the reports in their child's record?

WHO HAS THE RIGHT?

Another whole aspect of this question of communication—control of classroom materials, and community in-put centers around the issue of assigning certain English books as required curriculum. William French, a book critic, maintains that school boards should not have the right to intervene. Referring to one school board's decision to eliminate certain books listed as compulsory reading, he argues:

> . . . No one questioned the board's power to make the decision and enforce it. Does the board—and the other school boards around the country that are trying to drag us back into the Victoria[n] era—have the legal right to remove books from high school English courses and school libraries? The assumption is that they have, but perhaps it's time to challenge that view, particularly in light of a current court case in California.

> A school board in the northern part of California recently ordered five novels by Richard Brautigan removed from the curriculum, on the grounds of alleged obscenity. As a result, the board is being sued by the American Civil Liberties Union, two teachers and three students at Anderson Union High School in Shasta County, and Brautigan's publisher, Seymour Lawrence Inc. The lawsuit charges violations of the First Amendment, which guarantees freedom of speech and freedom of the press.[33]

33 William French, "Heated Response to Problem of Censorship in High Schools," The Globe and Mail (Toronto), 14 November 1978, p. 17.

Predictably, there was considerable community reaction to French's article through letters to the editor. The majority of printed responses maintained that as elected representatives of the taxpayers, school boards do have the prerogative to intervene.

There seems to be some suggestion that the freedoms to write and publish guaranteed by the First Amendment have to be matched by an obligation to buy. The school board's reaction has in no way restricted the rights of the author or publisher, nor, of course has it prevented teachers, students or others from studying books in question anywhere except in schools or courses in question. How this conflicts with freedom of speech or freedom of the press is hard to see.

W. James Mizen,
Toronto[34]

... Surely all educators and parents know that it is improper and ridiculous to forbid a student in the senior grades to read certain books. But it is equally improper to *force* him to read certain books.

Helga D. Stewart,
Peterborough[35]

... Authors and publishers who have a vested interest in selling their books should not subject boards of education to legal harassment in the event that some books are found unsuitable for school use.

John Boyce,
Toronto[36]

The following is an interesting comment on the effect of outside groups attempting to exercise control over the educational system:

---

34 Letters to the Editor, *The Globe and Mail* (Toronto), 23 November 1978, p. 6.
35 Ibid.
36 Letters to the Editor, *The Globe and Mail* (Toronto), 28 November 1978, p. 6.

Where outsiders have been involved, as when the Writer's Union sent a delegation to Huron County in June to defend the books under attack, they have succeeded only in swelling the ranks of the local opposition. (Concerned Citizens [in Huron County] was formed in July as a direct result of what was interpreted as an invasion of alien elements with no stake in the community and an obvious vested interest in promoting books . . . .)[37]

There are other dimensions to this question of intervention in the school system by outside organizations. While many of these groups may be considered to be acting in the best interests of the students, others, which have not cleared their mandate with educational officials, may still use the school as a captive audience. This occurred in 1977 when one city's Public Health Department instructed their public health nurses, who are paid by the city, but who are located and practice in the schools, to conduct a Birth Control Week in the high schools. This caused considerable administrative furor, as the program was planned and implemented without consulting or asking the permission of the school board involved or even, in some cases, the principals of the high schools involved.[38]

In fact, the gamut of federal-state-provincial-municipal interaction, as it involves education, brings up a host of new problems concerning the matter of control. In Canada, despite the fact that education is under provincial jurisdiction, the federal department, Health and Welfare Canada materials have been used by teachers with or without authorization from their provincial educational authority or local school board. One sex education kit issued by Health and Welfare Canada offended many people by presenting what they felt was a not-so-hidden message about pregnancy and child-birth to children and youth. The section entitled "Medical Risks" [of abortion] points out that "pregnancy will mean certain medical problems, abortion

37 Paul Stuewe, "Better Dead Than Read?" Books in Canada, vol. 7, no. 8 (October 1978), p. 6.
38 See Alden Baker, "Dozen High Schools Reject Birth Control Week," The Globe and Mail (Toronto), 12 February 1977, pp. 1-2.

may mean others. However early abortion will be less risky than full-term pregnancy."[39]

In the United States, of course, education comes under federal jurisdiction. Despite present administration goals to place more control locally, the fact that at a number of levels, unelected bureaucrats, rather than local elected officials, appear to control policies and procedures, is also generating heated controversy. An article entitled " 'Mind Bending' in the Schools Stirs Growing Protests" documents the conflicting messages conveyed by opponents and supporters of the free enterprise system "and a host of environmental and consumer-education programs" who are competing to sell their "wares" to youth. The article cites the examples of "one business-funded group, the Education Research Council of America [which] claims to reach 22 million of the nation's 49 million school children with its curriculum."[40]

LIP-SERVICE

It becomes obvious that the question of jurisdictional rights and discretionary powers within the educational system extend far beyond parents, teachers, and their local school board. Beyond making motherhood statements about the importance of community involvement, are educational authorities really committed to involving local interest groups in actual decision making? This important question was considered in the United States, at the National Education Association's meeting in February 1979, in one of the sessions called "Curriculum: Shall Professional or Community Standards Prevail?"[41] By the same token, the 1982 theme of the 4-day conference of the Educational Division of the Society for the Study of Social Problems asks, "Autonomy and Technique: How far may we go before profes-

---

39 "Birth Control and Abortion," Booklet no. 4 in *Sex Education* (kit), produced and distributed by the Family Planning Division, Health and Welfare Canada (Ottawa: 1976), p. 24.

40 " 'Mind Bending' in the Schools Stirs Growing Protest," *U.S. News and World Report*, p. 44. Copyright© U.S. News and World Report.

41 See Official Conference Program, *National Education Association Meeting*, Mayflower Hotel, Washington, D.C., 24 February 1979.

sional solutions for all problems will begin to diminish human life?"[42]

That this question of relationships between educators and the community would often appear to be almost adversarial in nature was again evident when the Organization for Economic Cooperation and Development sent six international specialists to study educational practices and policies in Canada. Among their findings they reported:

> The question is not whether more or less decentralization means more or less democratization, but: how can it be arranged that open decision-making and execution of affairs in the educational realm be brought about in a democratic manner. . . ?

> The attitude of the . . . authorities to the interest groups seems to the Examiners to be strangely ambivalent . . . [they] usually took a rather negative position, whenever the Examiners suggested that it would help if the interest groups had a stronger and more secure role in the process of educational decision-making.[43]

It might seem only logical for values educators to whom this statement applies to "take a Machiavellian approach" to MVE decision making and "do it anyway." Such educators are part of a movement which so firmly believes in this particular form of moral education for children that they will teach it whether or not parents agree to it. Its purpose is just that important in their eyes.

This stand, of course, is in direct opposition to the United Nations Universal Declaration of Human Rights, which states that "parents have a prior right to choose the kind of education that shall be given to their children."[44] This is why some people are claiming that moral values education is a major civil rights issue. It is certainly more than a parental issue. It is the nation's issue. There is every possibility that tomorrow your child, or my child, or any American child

---

42 Educational Problems Division Newsletter, *Society For The Study of Social Problems*, No. 1, Fall 1981, p. 1.
43 *Reviews of National Policies for Education: Canada*, Organization for Economic Cooperation and Development (Paris: 1976), p. 78.
44 United Nations Universal Declaration of Human Rights, Section 26 (3).

may be taken through a values education exercise. There is no way of guessing whether it will be concerned with stealing, with a drowning man, with the validity of parental rules, with the "life raft," or writing one's own obituary. Nor has one any way of knowing—unless one knows the teacher very well—which of the MVE approaches he or she may choose to adopt in dealing with the topic.

POSSIBLE REMEDIES

There are several possible responses from school boards to the situation:

- School boards could, as some have in the United States, ban values education—with or without issuing direct statements or offering definitive guidelines for future policy.
- Others have formulated specific directives for existing MVE programs and are prepared to monitor their contents, while still others have issued only the most general motherhood statements.
- Some boards have the question of MVE under current review, and are inviting—or not inviting—continuing input from various sectors of their constituency.
- Others view values education less as a Board concern than as a matter for individual principals and schools to decide and act upon. As one trustee points out, "Trustees know what the issue is but are politically afraid of it."[45]
- Still others have not considered the question at all.

The same range of knowledge or lack of knowledge about this issue *as an issue* and the same range of involvement or lack of involvement holds true for principals, teachers' federations and for home-and-school associations. Yet, unless studies of MVE materials and definitive policies concerning them can be produced by educational system/community teams, much of the material in present use will cause increasing numbers of children to become more confused and directionless than ever in this important area of education.

45 Arnold E. Hancock, "A Trustee's View," *Religious Education*, vol. LXXIII, no. 2 (March/April 1978), p. 167.

Recognizing these dangers, it is useful to review the way in which one Board worked toward the formulation of a policy on MVE. These "Statements of Policy Related to Certain Areas of Curriculum" were adopted in July 1976 by the Board of Education of Frederick County, Maryland for implementation in all Frederick County schools. A closer look at these policy statements will help bring our discussion into focus.

PREFACE

Many promising and innovative practices and highly commendable instructional strategies are used daily within the schools in Frederick County. The Board of Education wishes to acknowledge the contributions of the sincerely dedicated teachers within the system and to commend them for the consistency of quality reflected in their performance.

In occasional instances, certain educational practices and curriculum materials are brought to our attention that cause concern to members of the Board of Education, the professional staff, students, and parents.

In an effort to assure that the best interests of students are met, it is important that these issues are addressed. It is for this reason and to clarify the Board's position in reference to some highly sensitive areas that this policy statement has been prepared. This policy has been adopted as the result of interaction and consensus between Board members and the Central Office Staff. Information related to these policies and the policy statements follow:

HUMANISM

. . .

Policy

Humanism as is related to the religious or irreligious life is the area of concern. Judaism and Christianity are built on absolute standards such as the Ten Commandments. Secular humanism is defined as a religion that denies the existence of God and bestows that role

to the individual. It grants maximum individual autonomy and implies the right to make life and death
decisions.

Any persuasion of humanism that promotes a religious
or irreligious belief is in violation of the constitutional
separation of church and state. As a result, such per-
suasive techniques are not legitimate areas of curriculum in the Frederick County School System.

VALUES AND VALUING

. . .
Policy

Valuing, value clarification, and moral education will
not be taught in the Frederick County School System
as courses in and of themselves or through a series of
contrived situations without specific approval by the
Board of Education. Contrived techniques should not
be used for the indoctrination of values or to bring
about social change or to explore social structures and
inner conflicts that constitute an invasion of privacy.
Valuing, as it naturally emerges in valid instructional
settings, will be considered as appropriate and useful
teaching strategy.

SITUATION ETHICS

. . .
Policy

The consideration of situations and circumstances that
arise in curricular areas that cause students to engage
in problem-solving activities and make resultant decisions, some of which have moral and social implications, must be handled wisely and judiciously. Issues
that invade one's privacy or cause emotional trauma
must be avoided.

Situation ethics, in the precisely defined religious sense,
is not appropriate to public school use and is strictly
prohibited.

GROUP COUNSELING

. . .
Policy

Group counseling when conducted by carefully selected and trained personnel and strictly monitored by qualified consultants will be offered to certain students who have obtained written parental consent. Every caution should be exercised so that this program does not infringe on regular instructional activities.

The Board of education directs program supervisors, directors and principals to remain alert to possible irregularities and invasions of privacy and to take immediate corrective action.

GROUP THERAPY

. . .
Policy

Group therapy, involving staged encounters which are used to break down behaviors and defenses so that more effective reactions can be constructed by a carefully designed management program, will be excluded from all curricular areas.

SURVIVAL GAMES

. . .
Policy

The maturity level of public school students is such that these games would be of little benefit and could cause undue emotional stress and as such are invalid techniques to use in the instructional program.

SENSITIVITY TRAINING

. . .
Policy

Sensitivity training which involves encounter groups and in-depth analysis of personal feelings shall not be practiced in the public schools in Frederick County.

PROGRAMS OF A SENSITIVE AND
CONTROVERSIAL NATURE

Background

Some programs of a sensitive and controversial nature are included in public schools without adequate examination by the various segments of the professional staff or the knowledge of the Frederick County Board of Education, and other interested parties. It is our belief that this practice is not in keeping with the best educational procedures which should be followed in the Frederick County Public Schools.

Policy

Programs of a sensitive nature likely to generate legitimate public concerns should be screened by the appropriate subject area supervisor or director. It is the responsibility of the supervisor to determine the necessity of involving the Curriculum Committee of the Board of Education in judging the suitability of the material before approval is given.[46]

These policies—scarcely to be considered as extreme or reactionary in any way—were adopted because of several significant factors:

Many dedicated teachers had expressed alarm at the increased use of experimental psychological techniques such as values clarification in the classrooms. Using a "low-key," person-to-person approach, concerned citizens informed their school board members of the problems and urged consideration of a comprehensive policy to protect First Amendment rights. The successful adoption of the guidelines was in large part due to the exceptional leadership of the school-board president ... a retired high-school English teacher.[47]

---

46 *A Statement of Policy Related to Certain Areas of Curriculum*, The Board of Education of Frederick County (Frederick, Maryland: 1976), pp. 1-7. (Adopted July 7, 1976.)

47 Onalee McGraw, *Secular Humanism and the Schools*, The Heritage Foundation (Washington, D.C.: 1976), p. 13.

Clearly, it was because of pressure from various sectors that reasoned examination of materials and formulation of policies was carried out. This is important. Too often, concerns relating to the educational system are left unheeded because of ineffective communication and buck passing. Can we identify rules of thumb which could be of help?[48] When asked what communication strategies are most effective, authorities stress:

1. Concerns should be well documented;
2. Whether the form of communication is verbal or written, concerns and progress, or lack of progress, should be recorded from the outset *in writing*: for example, "Yesterday, we discussed the question of . . . and agreed that I would be responsible for . . . and that your Committee would undertake . . .;"
3. Whenever possible, assign and try for agreement on specific dates for response and/or action;
4. Copies of each phase of correspondence should be sent to the full range of educational authorities who are even potentially implicated in the issue: for example, teacher, principal, (the board of directors, in the case of independent schools), trustees, Parents' Association, district superintendent, state and federal officials and administrators. Where appropriate, the Attorney General may be asked to examine material to establish the legality of its use vis-a-vis the Education Act of that jurisdiction;

In these ways a particular concern is noted at various levels and this facilitates communication and response. As in several of the cases that we discussed earlier, many issues appear to fall between specific areas of responsibility within the system. This being so, a multi-faceted approach to making concerns known must be adopted;

5. Through the press, education of the public about these concerns can also facilitate response and action.

---

48 For further suggestions on steps in communication which "look to mutual respect rather than either parental or institutional domination," see Blair Shaw, *The Parents' School Book* (Oakville, Ontario: Graphic Arts Press Inc., 1978), p. 52 and following.

At the end of this chapter a more extensive set of recommendations is offered as a guideline for the involvement of the parent or professional educator, as an individual or part of a group.

JURISDICTIONAL AUTHORITY REVISITED

The question of jurisdictional authority is, in many cases, highly ambiguous. To what degrees decision making about MVE policy, standards, and approval of materials should be shared among federal, state, school/district and local school board; to what extent parent and community in-put and feedback is fundamental to an accountable system—are issues which need to be continuously in the forefront of planning and implementation.

It is not difficult to understand why responsibilities for MVE are owned and disowned in a way which often makes little other than political sense.[49] Unless there are questions from concerned educators and the community about specific MVE materials in use, it is standard policy that principals, school boards, and state and provincial departments of education make few moves to monitor the classroom situation. This is not a reflection on teachers, many of whom, as the above report points out,

> ... in attempting [under official directives] to include Values Education in their courses of study ... will understandably feel personally and professionally under a certain degree of pressure.[50]

The situation does, however, lead to questioning the accountability of our education system itself. Beyond general statements of intent, the way in which these areas of responsibility are specifically defined and programs are actually carried out depends largely on the strength of educator and community concern and in-put.

Few individuals, I suppose, whatever their role or function

49 See Don Cochrane and David Williams, "The Stances of Provincial Ministries of Education," *Canadian Journal of Education*, p. 9.
50 *Values Education: A Report Prepared for the Values Committee of the Toronto Board of Education*, pp. 39-40.

in the education of youth, will consider that the policies drawn up and adopted by the Frederick County Board are extreme. But many will wonder if such action is necessary, especially in their own area. For few of us have time for—or really enjoy—the planning and organizing required to become involved to this degree in the educational system.

Yet, until teachers' unions, principals' associations, school board members and parents' associations, government officials and citizens in general commit themselves to becoming knowledgeable about and involved in the evaluation of MVE programs by studying materials and registering their considered opinions, we will scarcely be justified in complaining that the educational system is unresponsive and irresponsible. Teachers, parents, principals, and trustees could instigate discussions to define the elements of values education which are relevant to their particular community. Co-operation in this area could help significantly to end the polarization which has developed between a dissatisfied public and increasingly frustrated members of the teaching profession. Federal and state departments of education and local school boards would gain credibility by organizing and supporting the efforts of such groups of educators and citizens. Unless such teams commit themselves to the task of studying and approving *specific* MVE materials and formulating *explicit* policies, we will continue to have no definite figures that show where the citizens and taxpayers stand on this issue. The very problems which values educators want to think they are solving, will be aggravated. School board member Johns, whose board was unable for several years to solve a polarization between parents' rights and teachers' rights, offers his recommendations:

> We suggest a search for a practical way where decisions on ideological-cultural conflicts are not handed down by elected officials, but worked out on a contract basis between persons of self-respect who are committed to the democratic society. This must be actual participation in the power structure of the educational system and not political busywork handed out by the politician who keeps real authority in his own hands. Yet there must be enough public or government authority lying

behind the local committees to keep them together while agreements are hammered out and properly supervised. There may be a role for professional mediators when polarization occurs as it has in [our] county between parent and teacher rights. Let the parents and teachers feel that they have an input and a veto, and much of the anger should subside.[51]

PARENT IN-PUT

The idea of recommending community in-put is anything but new. In actual practice, such in-put can range from an isolated patronizing gesture to firmly entrenched continuing involvement. In his paper, "Values Education and the Role of the Community," John Ross, who has been engaged in establishing values education programs, identifies the "community in-put phase" as being the one in which the goals of MVE are defined. Then he suggests:

> The priority sets of goals identified in the community in-put phase would be fed back into the school system to be made operational by educators as intended outcomes for students and to develop appropriate instructional strategies, learning materials and assessment tools. These tasks are properly the responsibility of professional educators—parents and lay persons would typically not have the time, inclination or expertise to act upon them.[52]

Ross does not suggest that the educators reconvene the community in-put group to discuss the actual approval of these "strategies," "materials," and "tools" which have since been devised. Yet in MVE, this is where the crunch comes. Undoubtedly, community in-put into the aims and goals of

---

51 E. Johns, "Values Education: A Critical Reflection," *The Ecumenical Study Commission Newsletter*, vol. 1, no. 3, (1978), p. 8.

52 John A. Ross, "Values Education and the Role of the Community," *Religious Education*, p. 180. Quoted from the March/April 1978 issue of the journal, *Religious Education*, by permission of the publisher, The Religious Education Association, 409 Prospect Street, New Haven, CT 06510.

MVE is useful and important. But statements at this level often remain general, noncontentious, motherhood-type statements. To agree on the goal of "helping students to develop a sense of their own self-worth" is one thing. To assign the Life Raft exercise or the Cave-in Simulation or to ask students to write their own obituaries as a means of achieving this goal, is another. To "aid students in developing decision-making skills" is an acceptable enough goal. To rate various types of stealing and be encouraged to choose freely one's own preference is a questionable strategy at best.

It is true that in most areas of the curriculum, the community does not expect to be closely involved in reviewing strategies, materials, and tools. This process is, appropriately, left in the capable hands of professional educators. However, the field of moral values education is a unique area. Because of the newness and lack of consensus regarding both content and process, many educators find themselves wanting to help youngsters, but clearly realizing the potential dangers of MVE. As a result, some teachers are, themselves, asking, Can teachers fairly be considered "professional" in the area of selecting, approving, and even creating their own values education tools and strategies? Given the general lack of training and experience available in teaching MVE, we can readily ask: Are teachers any more qualified than parents to select, approve, and apply moral value strategies (especially if there has been no collaboration or consent on specifics)?

It was in recognition of this very question of control over MVE content that federal laws such as Section 439 (a) and (b) and state laws such as the California Code, Section 60650 were enacted and have been in place for several years. However, as noted in chapter 7, minimal use of these laws or reference to them has been made. Yet MVE, as we have seen, is not just one more subject among many. It is put forward as the means of providing moral perspective for all courses on the curriculum. It constitutes, therefore, a most vital and far-reaching issue—an issue which many of us are not facing.

If we will not face it, it will be because of our collective inertia. We are all human. We may be—

- The disinterested parent, or the concerned parent who chooses not to "ask questions" which might reflect negatively on his or her child;
- The concerned but immobile educator who fears the consequences of speaking outside the official body of the teachers' union;
- The overburdened principal who lets things ride rather than inquiring as to what his or her teachers are promoting in MVE sessions;
- The creative producer or administrative promoter of MVE material who believes that to be "progressive" is to discard history;
- The conscientious school board member or community leader who confuses "leading" with following trends;
- The committed politician at any level, who is aware of the inherent contradictions among education acts, recommended department of education materials, Board policies and school implementation, but who, when the crunch comes, is more concerned with keeping things quiet than with taking a stand.

We all know the high percentage of the tax dollar which goes to finance education. In 1977, one school board mounted a five-week-long phone-in campaign in a concerted effort to encourage feedback from the community on matters of educational concern. The Board considered this in-put so important that they spent $5000 on the campaign. It was publicized in local newspapers, on radio and on television. At the end of the five weeks, there had been 85 responses from a population of 500,000.[53] Virtually all elected officials in education have, at one point or another, stated plainly that they want and expect to hear from the community. That includes not just parents, but educators and citizens in general. The ball is in our court.

Surely the issue should not be *who* should control the educational system, but rather *how* all groups concerned

53 "Transcripts of the Telephone and T.V. Tapes," Appendix C, *A Compilation of Reactions to the Green Paper on "The Goals of Education,"* Department of Educational Research and Development, North York Board of Education (North York: February 1978).

can collaborate to develop a more open and accountable system of moral education in our schools. These groups should include representatives from federal and state departments of education, school boards, district administrators, principals, teachers, and parents. As one teacher asked, "How much do we all care anyway?"

RECOMMENDATIONS

A guideline for action on the part of the parent and the professional educator, as an individual or member of a group. For more complete subject references, refer to Index, pages 249-256.

1. Assess knowledge of MVE as an issue, 22-23, 215-216, or Apathy toward it, 163, 180-181, on the part of one or more of: self, 226; community, 142, 154, 226; school, 159, 161-162, 190-191; school board, 202, 212; state/federal officials, 23, 159, 160.

2. Review MVE materials re their underlying philosophic assumptions—see Philosophic Assumptions in Index, and 139-140, 168-172; for accountability re contradiction between Education Laws and officially recommended classroom materials, 40, 147-150, 158-160, 190; for contradiction/discrepancy between Education Laws/policies and use of materials in classroom, 110, 150-152, 156-160, 193-195, 205.

3. Specifically define problem/objective, 225-226. (For example, if there has been a problem in communication, 184-187, parental review/consent re classroom materials 153-160, 197-198, this may be the objective, 160-161, 227.) The goal may be short/long term (phased); limited/far-reaching; to be achieved individually/collectively.

3A. If the objective is to be achieved collectively, seek to co-opt a representative committee to form the basic work group. Choose representation relevant to the nature of the problem and goal, not "in-grown" in the sense of limited perspective, 23, 97, 224-225, 236.

4. Re-define the objectives and goals even more specifically.

5. Research in depth
   • Federal/State Education Acts, 153-154, 155-156, 158-159 (e.g. write State Attorney-General re existing State legislation related to MVE, 160)
   • Federal/State department of education, teachers' unions' policy statements, guides, recommended classroom materials, 40, 154, 158-160, 222

- School board policy statements, if any, 206, 222, and recommended resource materials and bibliographies. (Do they provide general motherhood-type statements, or do they specify particular areas for caution and limitation? 207-210.)
- Local school(s) MVE policy, if any, and classroom implementation of MVE materials. Do teachers select and design their own? 17-18, 126-127. Are they required to teach new MVE models despite their misgivings? 132-134. How would Dr. Sobol's questions be answered? 123-126.

6. Establish with community-educator teams, 213-214,
    - accountable system for monitoring implementation of existing legislation concerning MVE: see Index re Legislation, lack of monitoring
    - where required, lobby for "teeth" in existing legislation, 160 (for reference, see footnote 32)
    - where required, lobby for new legislation (for reference, see Oklahoma Parents Consent bill, in October 1981 issue of *Family Protection Report*, 721 Second St. N.E., Washington, D.C. 20002).

7. Establish or re-clarify with community-educator teams, 213-214, specific policy for reviewing all MVE materials based on
    - the underlying assumptions of the approach(es) being used: see analytic model, 168-172
    - the identification of certain "timeless moral principles" which the history of civilizations has produced, 177-179, as criteria for MVE acceptable to all, 222

These community-educator teams will have various ranges of representation and, depending on the levels and objectives concerned, will be standing committees or ad hoc (i.e. project centered) in nature. Community in-put will not be relegated to the initial "goal-setting" phase of MVE planning, 214-215, but will constitute permanent, on-going review and approval of policy, classroom materials and strategies, 214-215.

8. Seek to re-direct emphasis on teacher training in MVE, 130-131, 228-237.

9. Communications with related individuals and groups may utilize strategies for collaboration identified on page 211.

NOTE: Fundamental to the foregoing is that, irrespective of committees, there should be full access to MVE materials (either proposed or in use) to the community and to all levels of the educational system, immediately upon their request (contrast Federal Education Law, 153-154 with "Constitutional issue," 191-193).

10

So What's It
Worth?

We are all victims of the art and science of packaging. Some years ago, *The Hidden Persuaders* taught us a great deal about why we buy what we buy without checking the ingredients and the safety factors.

There are several packages of MVE on the market, and I have briefly outlined the three which are most widely recommended and utilized in schools in the United States. As stated at the beginning, when a buyer is considering any package for consumption, he or she necessarily focuses on the more controversial aspects of the package: so in this book. At the same time, I have not suggested that any of the models is without its positive contribution to the field of values education. For all its attention to the problematic aspects of these three models, this book is intended to be constructive and to urge that we press forward to find ways in which we may all build upon the efforts of the authors of MVE materials.

Most emphatically, I am not against teaching moral values in schools. It is an important part of education:

> The most important thing about any society is the kind of people it produces. The gross national product, the size of its military establishment, its artistic creativity, its

place in the power firmament, even its political institutions, are ultimately less important than the quality of the human beings who emerge from its culture. More than by any other factor, that quality is determined by the moral and ethical principles honored by its people.

If this reasoning is sound, a further conclusion follows. If schools ignore or give minimal attention to transmitting the best of our moral and ethical heritage to the young, they are failing in their foremost responsibility.[1]

As I pointed out earlier, my own notion of responsible MVE is not the pious recital of lists of virtues and sanctimonious nodding of heads about rules to match. To reduce values education to mere rule giving and to define morality as obedient conformity, rather than compassionate and reasoned commitment, is to retard students' growth and development in moral sensitivity and to reduce their ability to think intelligently for themselves.

MVE PACKAGES

There are several general points about MVE which deserve particular emphasis.

1. It seems ironic that those who are so strongly opposed—and rightly so—to indoctrinating children with rigid rules, and to preventing or discouraging them from thinking for themselves, are so often the same people who fail to perceive any middle road between those practices and a totally open treatment of moral values, which explicitly or implicitly teaches children that one view is as good as another. This latter totally open-ended approach to values education does not foster genuine autonomy of the individual: it simply presents the doctrine of moral relativism ("Good" is what is good for me) under the guise of autonomy:

Autonomy is not threatened by membership in a community that nurtures [sensitivity to moral concerns

---

1 Reo M. Christenson, "McGuffey's Ghost and Moral Education Today," *Phi Delta Kappan* (June 1977), p. 737. Reprinted from *Phi Delta Kappan*. Copyright© 1977, Phi Delta Kappa, Inc.

and which cares about acting in conscientious and rightful ways]. . . . It is threatened when a community is itself absolutist, indifferent to evidence, and committed to the idea that reasonable people of goodwill can never disagree. If all participation in a community of moral agents, and all learning in such a community, threatened autonomy, then autonomy would have to flourish only in ignorance, solitude, and capriciousness. Everyone would be forced to create the world and morality for himself. This is not autonomy, but the moral vacuum. As Professor Hall observes, "In no other field of education do we expect young people to re-invent the subject from their own experience, and there is no reason why we should insist on this in moral education." As C.S. Lewis rightly observed, open-mindedness is not empty-headedness.[2]

2. The modern world is complex and confusing, and clearly requires tremendous skill in decision making and the resolution of value conflicts. Such skill does not come automatically: it develops as it is consciously pursued and nurtured in a supportive environment. There is, however, an inherent fallacy in emphasizing moral dilemmas and skills of problem solving and decision making as the primary components of morality and, therefore, of values education:

> The problem of moral education is not so much teaching children how to make moral decisions, as giving them the background out of which the demands that decisions be made arise. . . . The adult of good moral character must indeed be able to handle difficult situations as they arise, and to reason about problems unforseeable by his parents; but to reason well he must already be an adult of good moral character: loyal, just, sensitive to suffering, and the rest. Every-thing is not up for grabs! Unless he has these qualities, moral dilemmas will not arise for him. Unless he has a

2 Edwin J. Delattre, "The Straightjacket and the Vacuum in Moral Education," *The Humanist*, vol. XXXVIII, no. 6 (November/December 1978), p. 20. This article first appeared in *The Humanist*, and is reprinted by permission.

well-formed character his prescriptions for himself and others are not likely to be morally acceptable.[3]

3. Gradually, there are coming forward a number of critical thinkers in MVE who are looking to the fact that there must be a middle road[4] between confining students either to the straightjacket of totalitarianism or to the moral vacuum of relativism;[5] that there are "timeless principles of moral behavior[6] . . . [which] can be [defined and] treated in such a way as to win the almost unanimous approval of concerned parents—liberal and conservative, religious and irreligious alike."[7] A case in point, Talawanda School Board near Oxford, Ohio held public hearings on this very issue. Without serious objection from anyone in its widely diverse population, including a homogeneous university community, the Board adopted a list of twenty-one values and attitudes as their guidelines for MVE. The list—though exceedingly different in style—is not unlike the *Tao*. It includes: "telling the truth especially when it hurts to do so;" "treating others as we would wish to be treated;" "self-discipline, defined as the strength to do what we know we ought to do when we would rather not;" and so on.[8] Encouraging open discussion of these attitudes and principles and welcoming dissent, Reo Christenson, a professor of political science at Miami University in Ohio, asks:

3 E. Pincoffs, "Quandary Ethics," *Mind* (October 1971), pp. 566-567. For further discussion on this point, see A.I. Melden, *Rights and Persons* (Los Angeles: University of California Press, 1977)—especially the Introduction, pp. 1-31.

4 See "Moral Education: An Emerging Consensus," *Phi Delta Kappan*, Vol. 62, No. 7, March 1981, pp. 479-493.

5 See Edwin J. Delattre, "The Straightjacket and the Vacuum in Moral Education," *The Humanist* (November/December 1978). This article first appeared in *The Humanist*, and is reprinted by permission.

6 Reo M. Christenson, "McGuffey's Ghost and Moral Education Today," *Phi Delta Kappan* (June 1977), p. 739. Reprinted from *Phi Delta Kappan*. Copyright© 1977, Phi Delta Kappa, Inc.

7 Ibid., p. 738. In answer to requests, Christenson's article suggests relevant books for student groups studying the themes suggested in this article.

8 Reo M. Christenson, "Clarifying 'Values Clarification' for the Innocent," *Christianity Today*, April 10, 1981, p. 503.

Would straightforward instruction by the schools in this area stunt students' capacity to think for themselves and encourage a rote response to moral issues? Nonsense. There is no evidence whatever that parents who do a good job of moral education in the home produce young people with a shrunken, enfeebled ability to think creatively about moral questions. What sensible instruction does do is make people more morally sensitive and concerned, more thoughtful, more prone to explore the bases, ramifications, and applications of moral principles.[9]

Taking part in *The Humanist* Symposium, Robert Hall is ready to admit:

Actually, the atmosphere that seems most conducive to the development of effective moral orientation is one in which some definite value perspectives are presented. There is a realm of commonly held social values in our society, and teaching young people to understand it is actually a way of helping them attain autonomy.[10]

But having said this, Hall immediately backs off:

There is an important but subtle difference, however, between *teaching values*, such as justice, honesty, or benevolence, in the sense of promoting or inculcating values, and *teaching about values* in the sense of helping young people to appreciate the fact that certain values are commonly held in the society in which they live.[11]

Keep in mind that Hall is objecting to the teaching of the values of justice, honesty, and benevolence! Ryan's response to Hall is very direct:

9 Reo M. Christenson, "McGuffey's Ghost and Moral Education Today," *Phi Delta Kappan* (June 1977), p. 739. Reprinted from *Phi Delta Kappan*. Copyright© 1977, Phi Delta Kappa, Inc.
10 Robert Hall, "Moral Education Today: Progress, Prospects, and Problems of a Field Come of Age," *The Humanist* (November/December 1978), p. 12. This article first appeared in *The Humanist* and is reprinted by permission.
11 Ibid.

We seem to be afraid of doing something strong. We seem too unsure of ourselves as a society to challenge our young . . . we avoid calling on [them] even in the name of sheer human decency, to "love thy neighbor" and to give of one's time and goods to the poor. And so our "program of moral education" will be something abstract and sterile that does not penetrate into the being of our children. It will not reach the nerve center of their lives where the strong emotions and yearnings to reach out to others reside. Apparently we do not want to get them excited about that in the same way they can get excited about sports or their social lives. We do not want a program of values and moral education to have that kind of flesh and blood. Why not? Well, we are told that in our pluralistic society, with many religious and ethnic groups, we have no unanimously prescribed values or morality. From this we are to believe that a moral education program that attempts to instill courage in the young or gives them opportunities to be of real service to the poor or to the elderly, or that teaches them how to cooperate toward common goals, would not be well received.[12]

Just how reactionary this and similar views are considered to be by many MVE proponents is reflected in Hall's final word to his colleagues in MVE, whom he describes as:

moving much further toward a more forceful approach to moral education than ever before. In fact, they seem openly and unashamedly to flirt with indoctrination, at times accepting it in ways that would scandalize the readers of this journal were they not committed to the creative potential of intellectual flirtation.[13]

If to give responsible support to the precepts of justice, honesty, and benevolence is to "openly and unashamedly

12 Kevin Ryan, "Is It Going to Be Just a Word Game?" *The Humanist* (November/December 1978), p. 21. This article first appeared in *The Humanist*, and is reprinted by permission.
13 Robert Hall, "Indoctrination Revisited," *The Humanist* (November/December 1978), p. 23. This article first appeared in *The Humanist*, and is reprinted by permission.

flirt with indoctrination," I can only suggest: ask any Jews, Moslems, Christians, Atheists and Agnostics whether they wish their children to operate from the premise that stealing is wrong, or whether they wish them taught that the "right" and "wrong" of stealing always depends on the situation, the people involved, and their own preferences and inclinations. To listen to their answer is to realize that their response is not a matter of ethnic, religious, or non-religious bias. They share a common belief that there are core moral precepts, and that these should form the basis for critical analysis of situations and behavior. The extreme extenuating circumstance does not change the value of the precept.

4. The degree to which most of us are aware of the extent and influence of these "flirtations" with MVE in our schools varies greatly. As we saw earlier, Values Clarifications is the most popular of the MVE approaches. Over half a million copies of *Values Clarification: A Handbook* are in circulation. This is one of the two texts chiefly quoted in chapter 2, and was among several books introduced in the United States Congress as "an example of the decadent and immoral approaches"[14] being used in schools. Yet as the editors of the *Moral Education Forum* point out: "[It] continues to draw heavy criticism and despite less than convincing rebuttal, the movement's momentum continues unaffected. Such a phenomenon raises interesting questions of its own."[15]

To realize that nearly fifty books and over two hundred articles were published in 1977 alone is to have some idea of the phenomenal growth of the entire field of moral values education. Yet, "in the midst of this frantic, wide-ranging activity," says MVE analyst Superka, several interrelated problems persist.

The major problems include (1) the confusion and conflict about the meaning of the key terms used in values education—values and valuing; (2) lingering doubt on the part of many teachers, administrators,

14 H. Kirschenbaum, *Advanced Value Clarification*, p. 151.
15 L. Kuhmerker and D. Cochrane, "From the Editor's Desk," *Moral Education Forum*, vol. III, no. 1 (February 1978), p. 1.

and parents concerning the role of the school in teaching values; (3) classroom norms among the students that discourage open, trusting value activity; (4) uncertainty of teachers as to how self-disclosing, probing, and accepting they should be; (5) a generally inadequate level of teacher training in values education; (6) a tremendous influx into the values education movement of relatively inexperienced persons as conductors of workshops and developers of materials; (7) a lack of reliable, valid, and usable evaluation procedures and instruments to measure values developments in students; and (8) the difficulty of intelligently and systematically selecting from the overwhelming amount of curriculum and teacher background materials being produced and disseminated.[16]

Kevin Ryan mentions another concern: "We need to surround children with a number of moral exemplars and individuals of character and moral sensibility, but we are keeping very quiet about this need."[17]

5. How much each of us cares to look into the particular directions MVE is taking in our own area is a matter for personal conscience. In this respect, the percentage of knowledgeable voters vis-a-vis educational candidates is extremely disconcerting. In 1978, a city newspaper persuaded the husband of their education reporter to run for the office of school board member. Their intent was to indicate the weakness of the present system in which voters do not know their candidates. Mr. Smith "attended no election meetings, didn't advertise and didn't answer any questions or questionnaires."[18] Yet he polled more than 8000 votes. Eight thousand people supported and voted for a board of education candidate whose views on education were entirely unknown to them.

16 D. Superka et al., *Values Education Sourcebook*, p. ix.
17 Kevin Ryan, "Is It Going to Be Just a Word Game?" *The Humanist* (November/December 1978), p. 21. This article first appeared in *The Humanist*, and is reprinted by permission.
18 Rudy Platiel, "No Ads, Speeches, but Candidate Wins 8000 Votes," *The Globe and Mail* (Toronto), 16 November 1978, p. 1.

It is self-evident by now that moral values education is too important for us to make blind choices about it, or fail to meet our obligation to form our own considered opinion. Somehow I picture "out there" a vast army of educators and parents who really care about children and the morals and values they will eventually adopt. But so many of those educators and parents are no longer really communicating. This failure to come to grips with each other appears to be reflected in varying degrees throughout the system. Often board members are out of touch, to any meaningful degree, with superintendents, who may, in turn, be out of touch with what is actually happening in the classroom under their jurisdiction, and so on up and down the line. Recognizing the need to co-operate in this critical area of moral values education could form a rallying point for all these groups. Is it sheer naivete to believe that people—all citizens, whatever their function inside or outside the educational system—care enough about the youth of North America and their future to participate as never before, in order to make this a local issue, a state, provincial, and federal issue and, where necessary, a legal and political issue?

It is long past the time for acting on reasoned judgment and as the following passage points out, long past the time for being embarrassed to make those judgments.

> ... judgment is not bigotry; and indiscriminate sensitivity and tolerance may just be other terms for indifference. If to make judgments of better and worse, good and bad, fit and unfit, sound and unsound, competent and incompetent is to be judgmental, then there is a need to be judgmental and no need to apologize for it. For people, the ordeal of judgment cannot be shirked; to try to do so is not to be sensitive or tolerant; it is to avoid responsibility. One judges Nazism, Communism, and the teachings of the Ku Klux Klan; teachers judge the work of their students, students the work of their teachers, deans their faculty, the faculty the administration. A department chairman who will not judge the performance of his colleagues may condemn students to endless semesters of in-

competence. People judge fallibly, with uncertainty, on the basis of the facts; but if they will not judge, they do not want their convictions to make a difference. And people without convictions cannot be counted on.[19]

THE BOTTOM LINE[20]

Perhaps the ultimate paradox in MVE is the passionate way in which we indoctrinate *teachers* that they must be utterly *dis*passionate in speaking with students about moral values such as justice, honesty and compassion. If they indicate enthusiasm or support for these moral values they are told they will be "flirt[ing] with indoctrination."[21] We recall Robert Hall's caution:

There is an important but subtle difference between teaching values, such as justice, honesty, or benevolence, in the sense of promoting or inculcating values, and teaching about values in the sense of helping young people to appreciate the fact that certain values are commonly held in the society in which we live.[22]

In this approach, morality is reduced to a socio-cultural phenomenon, denuded of excitement or personal challenge. Andrew Oldenquist objects: "If children are introduced to moral principles by a discussion in which a teacher says, 'In our culture dishonesty is disapproved,' they will note that as a dry sociological fact, much as 'in the Bongo

19 Edwin J. Delattre and William J. Bennett, "Where the Values Movement Goes Wrong," *Change*, vol. 11, no. 1 (February 1979), p. 42. Reprinted with permission from *Change* Magazine. Copyrighted by the Council on Learning, NBW Tower, New Rochelle, New York, 10801.

20 The following section is adapted from a paper presented by the author. See proceedings of The World Congress In Education, *Values and the School*, Serge Fleury (ed.), C.P. 668, Haute-Ville, Quebec, G1R 4S2, pp. 316-320.

21 Robert Hall, "Indoctrination Revisited," *The Humanist* (November/December 1978), p. 23.

22 Robert Hall, "Moral Education Today: Progress, Prospects, and Problems of a Field Come of Age," *The Humanist* (November/December 1978), p. 12.

Islands it is wicked to eat jub-jub berries.' "[23] Similarly he observes, moral principles are reduced to mere "personal 'values:' my values, your values, Charlie Manson's values."[24]

In capsule form, these two positions reflect the considerably entrenched polarization which abounds in MVE circles regarding questions of autonomy, inculcation, freedom and indoctrination. Out of a somewhat compulsive aversion to reaching into the "bag of virtues" which—validly or not—is portrayed as being synonymous with requiring students' mindless and unquestioning conformity to a list of moral ideals, we somewhat indiscriminately reach into the "bag of MVE techniques" to experiment with yet another moral dilemma or classroom simulation. In addition to "games and values exercises which may involve an invasion of the students' personal and family privacy, which may be seen as emotionally manipulative in certain circumstances, or which are conducive to moral relativism,"[25] the "bag of techniques" approach, as we have observed, can constitute an equally glib and piece-meal approach to MVE.

I would like to suggest the construct of "moral vision" as a bridge between those educators on the one hand who are, understandably, opposed to a purely intellectualized "moral ideals" approach to MVE on the grounds that such an appeal may always and only remain that; personally detached: and those, on the other hand, who concentrate so exclusively upon the personal preference, affective domain that the rigors of critical analysis become irrelevant. I am suggesting that the construct of moral vision and the objective of developing in students the capacity for moral vision incorporates both cognitive and affective components of learning and at the same time avoids indoctrination. As such, one is hopeful that this may offer a constructive alternative and even serve to break through a measure of the

23 Andrew Oldenquist, " 'Indoctrination' and Societal Suicide," *The Public Interest*, Number 63, Spring 1981, p. 87.

24 Ibid., p. 88.

25 The Hon. Bette Stevenson, M.D., Ontario Minister of Education, "Memorandum to Directors of Education and Principals of Schools Re Privacy of Students and Values Education," Ministry of Education, Toronto, April 2, 1981.

entrenchment and polarization which characterizes much current debate.

MORAL IDEALS AND MORAL VISION

There is a crucial difference between a moral ideal and moral vision. An ideal is essentially a concept. A vision is essentially an experience. A moral ideal—however much one may "look" to it—remains "outside" oneself: an objective toward which one may (or may not) strive. Moral vision, on the other hand, by its very nature, denotes involvement: one "sees" with the inner eye; one is touched in the inward person. An ideal can be dismissed as *simply* that: too ideal of attainment, too far removed from the realities of life in today's society. But a moral vision cannot be dismissed for it has been experienced. It is alive. It is personally compelling. It is the real stuff of morality, for moral vision has its roots in both cognitive and affective insights and these roots necessarily give life to moral incentive and commitment. A moral ideal can be taught. There are various methods of teaching ideals—some meaningful and some exceedingly non-meaningful—to which point we will return. Moral vision, on the other hand, cannot be taught. It may, however, be "caught."

Perhaps one should state that the construct of moral vision as put forward here is, quite clearly, based on the premise that certain attitudes and behaviors in relationship with students—and indeed with people in general—are more growth-enhancing and humane than others. Justice and kindness are more humane than injustice and cruelty and so on. While most values educators would agree with this premise, as we have noted, the major controversy is over whether teachers should be seen to be promoting or in support of them, due to the danger of indoctrination. With this in mind, the following section will examine the distinctions between a moral ideal and moral vision as they translate into teaching methodologies; first of all in relation to the teaching of mathematics and then in relation to obvious parallels in the teaching of MVE.

A MATHEMATICAL "SENSE"

Conscientious Math teachers, whether they are working with students at the elementary or advanced level, seek above all, to inspire in their students a "feel" for Math; a mathematical "sense." Some teachers do this well for they enjoy the subject and their enthusiasm is catching. They are challenged by Math, not simply because they want to find the right answer, but because they are excited by the discovery of relationships and because they have a sense that they are grappling with fundamental realities. They have caught a "vision" of Math as a wholistic endeavor—and they readily transmit this excitement to students. At the same time however it would be unthinkable for such a teacher to teach, for example, that 4 plus 4 equals 8 "because it is simply a fact" or "because I say so." Rather, he or she seeks to provide an experience for students within which they are able to uncover and discover this reality themselves.

Whereas the Math teacher knows very well that there are mathematical theorems and objective mathematical truths which pertain, he or she will not present these theorems to be learned by rote. After all, being able to recite formulae and theorems does not constitute a grasp of the subject on either the part of the teacher or the student. The teacher realizes that if this is the extent of learning, students will be unable to apply these "models" creatively when it comes to the "unexpected" questions of advanced problem solving. Theorems will remain isolated parcels of memory work which ultimately disconnect and alienate the student from both the relevance and the excitement of Math.

It is only as students are given the opportunity to test these theorems in the sense that they may visualize and personally experience their reality that they may be able to validate them genuinely and know why and to what end they may apply them meaningfully and creatively in problem solving. As this occurs, the individual moves beyond a purely mechanical problems-focused perception of Math to "connect" with its fundamental and universal nature. The student experiences Math as an integrator influencing both self and the environment.

But is it really important to develop such a mathematical "sense?" Students who, for one reason or another, do not catch a vision of its wholistic nature or get a "feel" for Math become increasingly disenchanted with it and give it up as soon as possible. They believe that they were never good at it and that it cannot be relevant to their lives.

A MORAL "SENSE"

By now, educators fear that the parallels with moral values education are quite clear. Educators fear, and validly so, that if moral principles or theorems such as honesty, justice, compassion are inculcated on the basis of being "obvious fact" or "because I say so," these principles will be regarded as ponderous rules or abstractions outside the self, divorced from real meaning. Again, validly, we hold that it is only that which a student personally elects to value that he or she will actually value or apply in his or her life: that it is only as the student is given the opportunity to test these moral theorems or principles in the sense that he or she does (or does not) experience their reality, that the student may be able to validate them genuinely and know whether or not, or why, and to what end he or she will live by them. As educators then, there is a need to identify a vehicle which might offer such an experience for testing relevance and validity.

Relationship as vehicle:

This vehicle, I would suggest, is first and foremost, relationship: not exercises or simulations (although some of these can be useful), but relationship between persons or in a community of persons.

It is, for example, primarily through relationship that one really "knows" compassion. For one has experienced it and can, therefore, "connect" with it as having reality and validity. Beyond intellectual appreciation of the moral ideal of compassion, in relationship one emotionally understands and feels (i.e. experiences) the fundamental distinction, for example, between Looking Out For No. 1[26] and:

---

26 Robert Ringer, Looking Out For No. 1. (New York: Fawcett Publishing, 1978).

I shall pass through this world but once. Any good therefore that I can do, or any kindness that I can show to any human being, let me do it now. Let me not defer or neglect it, for I shall not pass this way again.[27]

One moves beyond the perception of morality as a list of ideals or, conversely, as a series of dilemma-focused exercises, to uncover and discover personally, its universal and wholistic nature. One catches a vision of morality as an integrator of self and society.

Parents and teachers are surrounded by children and youth who are constantly testing out the reality and validity of compassion; of honesty; of justice. And they are testing these out in the parent-child and in the teacher-pupil relationship. Courted by the media and solicited by rock bands, street gangs and cults, all of whom compete for their vote, youth faces a bewildering kaleidoscope of conflicting facts, values, opinions, hypotheses. They wrestle with the issues of drugs, sex, alcohol, crime and, often suffering the fall-out from broken homes, students hold parents and teachers up as prime targets against which to test out what is real and of any value. (While we are focusing on the teacher-pupil encounter here, this focus should be understood within the context of the family relationship as the most fundamental vehicle for experience and the importance of the educational system giving support and active re-inforcement to this context.)

The teacher as a role-model-in-relationship.

Most teachers are very aware that the teacher-pupil relationship can be a key factor in a student's life. They know that especially when a student is, for example, lacking in compassion he or she desperately needs to experience compassion personally, to be able to test and validate whether it *can* be real. But for teachers to be prime targets on that testing ground: to respond to students with compassion—to mobilize continuously the psychic energy

27 These words have been attributed to many authors, among them Etienne de Grillet. However, the author is actually unknown. See John Bartlett, *Bartlett's Familiar Quotations* (Boston: Little, Brown & Co., 1968), p. 531.

necessary to cope with dislike of some students, anger, threat and frustration is exceedingly demanding and emotionally costly. Yet this is moral values education at its best and most powerful. It is alive. It is relationship. It is not a hypothetical moral dilemma or a contrived exercise *about* compassion or honesty or justice; it is seeing and feeling a teacher *being* compassionate, honest, fair, *especially when it is difficult to be so*. This is offering opportunity for moral vision through relationship, and in my view, it is the essence of genuine moral education and provides the basis for building a "moral community" in the classroom.

However, just as a teacher's raw dictum to students to "be honest" may provide little meaningful or genuine support for the heat of the day, so edicts to teachers to "be exemplary in relationship with students" may offer little solace in the heat of their classrooms.

Example: From an experienced teacher speaking about MVE courses:

> We are given lots of MVE tools—more often we are given too many—but no-one really focuses on *us*: except, by way of introduction to the course, to raise our consciousness to the fact that everything we say— verbally or non-verbally transmits our values. Very quickly sessions move on to concentrate on the use of various MVE techniques in the classroom. It is the rare MVE instructor whose major objective is to actively help us to grapple with our conflicts about the fact that we are role models to students whether we really wish to be or not. Even more rare is the instructor who will openly acknowledge with us the fact that there are students we actively dislike, that we are unfair, that we mark them down regardless, that we stereotype; that losing one's temper, playing favorites, feeling hostile, then guilty, then apathetic, occupy and color varying portions of every teacher's day. Exceedingly preoccupied with students' problems, no-one seems to want to talk about where *we're* at.

Illustration: In the past decade in Nursing literature and elsewhere, there has been heavy emphasis placed on recognizing and meeting "The Needs of the Dying Patient."[28] No-one—least of all the nursing profession—challenges the fact that this is important and long overdue. However in practical terms, in order to affect and change practitioners' treatment of dying patients there is considerable evidence that emphasis needs to be simultaneously, if not initially, placed on the "Needs of the Nurse who is Nursing the Dying Patient." In fact, in an extensive self-study of the nurse-patient relationship, experienced nurses vividly document that irrespective of the patient's medical problem, it is only as nurses are specifically and purposefully helped to come to fundamental terms with themselves, their humanity, their conflicts, their negative and "unprofessional" feelings—that they are able in any meaningful sense to enter into or contribute in relationship to the stressful world of another.[29] In the same way, teachers' most fundamental conflicts are not met by MVE training sessions which are simply a mixture of theories, sheer logic, selected psychosocial concepts or a bag of assorted techniques. Again, the vehicle which carries these and brings them to life is the relationship between the teacher-educator and the neophyte MVE teacher. It is the experience of this relationship which, more than any other factor, can inspire a vision of what teaching MVE can mean. For, "teachers teach the way they are taught, not the way they are taught to teach."[30] Elsewhere, I have spelled out how pre-service and in-service courses based on this premise, may be conducted with professonals,[31] and I will not re-iterate them here.

A "MORAL COMMUNITY"

The fundamental truism, of course, is that we all need to feel part of a community—hierarchical or otherwise—upon

---

28 See for example, Elisabeth Kübler-Ross, On Death and Dying (New York: Macmillan, 1970).

29 Kathleen Gow, How Nurses' Emotions Affect Patient Care: Self Studies by Nurses, (New York: Springer Publishing Co., 1981).

30 Thomas Lickona, "Preparing Teachers to be Moral Educators: A Neglected Duty," Newer Directions for Higher Education, 31, 1980, p. 62.

31 K. Gow, How Nurses' Emotions Affect Patient Care, Chapter 16.

which we can draw and depend for support. This does not mean that there will always be agreement. Men and women of goodwill may disagree, but they have a choice as to whether or not they will strive together for a sense of community. The immediate support system community for the teacher is, of course, the staff and the principal of the school. As one teacher put it:

> When you walk into a staff room, you immediately sense whether this is a school where it's every one for him- or herself, or whether it is a genuine community of people who care about each other.

Across the educational system, principals, superintendents, directors of education, state and federal educational officials echo similar descriptions of their work environments and its direct effect on the level and quality of their work with employees as well as employers. It is difficult, for superintendents, for example, who feel no sense of community with and from their superiors not to project a similar "ethos" to the principals under them: equally it is very difficult for those principals not to project the same to their teachers. Thus it can be seen that moral values education, at its root, and helping to create and maintain a moral community, is not only the function of the teacher in the classroom, but the mutual responsibility of every individual across all echelons of the educational system.

Question: It is easy enough to agree with this concept. But an actual and active moral educational community requires far more than intellectual assent. It requires hard work. It asks each individual to confront the issue at a very personal level: to ask, "Are there any moral principles which *I* have experienced and tested and found to be valid: honesty? justice? compassion?" That is, "Do I 'connect' with any of these moral ideals as being essential integrators within my person and in my relationships with others? (i.e. "I will be compassionate even when it is difficult to be so.") Have they become for me deep and consistent convictions of mind and heart; in fact, integral to my moral vision? For example, do I *feel badly* when I am not compassionate?"

If the answer to these questions is "yes," then each attitude, each behavior, each situation, each relationship will attempt to reflect such holistic integrative principles. At the same time, that individual will not be indoctrinating others. For one cannot indoctrinate a moral vision; one can only catch it through relationship. He or she will simply offer, as consistently as is possible, an experience of honesty, benevolence, etc., through which others may test the validity of these ideals.

If the answer to the above questions is "no," then each attitude, each behavior, each situation, each event in a relationship will be a law unto itself—disconnected from any holistic or integrating principle (i.e. "I will be compassionate if I feel like it.") For the teacher, the endeavor of being a role-model-in-relationship will be rejected as invalid because there is nothing fundamental or consistent to offer to students. There is no basis for moral vision.

The question may be difficult to ask: the answer may be even more demanding. Still, both are critical to pursue. For, at its very root, moral values education is not talking about honesty, justice, compassion, or doing simulation exercises about them. Essentially, at least in my view, it is people who, despite the fact that they often fall short, are committed to *living* them. They have dared to risk the cost of caring, and they are open to the possibility of catching a moral vision.

Arnold Toynbee has amply documented that throughout history, civilizations which relinquished their commitment to core moral values, which lost, if you will, their moral vision, have not survived.[32]

This is the bottom line we have to consider in moral values education in our schools.

---

32 Arnold Toynbee, *A Study of History*, (London: Oxford, 1934-1961), twelve volumes.

Appendix (Chapter 8)

ILLUSTRATIONS OF THE TAO*

The following illustrations of the Natural Law are collected from such sources as come readily to the hand of one who is not a professional historian. The list makes no pretence of completeness. It will be noticed that writers such as Locke and Hooker, who wrote within the Christian tradition, are quoted side by side with the New Testament. This would, of course be absurd if I were trying to collect independent testimonies to the *Tao*. But (1) I am not trying to *prove* its validity by the argument from common consent. Its validity cannot be deduced. For those who do not perceive its rationality, even universal consent could not prove it. (2) The idea of collecting *independent* testimonies presupposes that 'civilizations' have arisen in the world independently of one another; or even that humanity has had several independent emergences on this planet. The biology and anthropology involved in such an assumption are extremely doubtful. It is by no means certain that there has ever (in

*Source: C.S. Lewis, *The Abolition of Man* (London: Geoffrey Bles, Centenary Press, 1947), pp. 56-64. Reprinted by permission of Wm. Collins.

the sense required) been more than one civilization in all history. It is at least arguable that every civilization we find has been derived from another civilization and, in the last resort, from a single center—'carried' like an infectious disease or like the Apostolical succession.

I. The Law of General Beneficence

(a) Negative

'I have not slain men.' (Ancient Egyptian. From the Confession of the Righteous Soul, 'Book of the Dead.' v. *Encyclopedia of Religion and Ethics* [=*ERE*], vol. v, p. 473.)

'Do not murder.' (Ancient Jewish. Exodus xx. 13.)

'Terrify not men or God will terrify thee.' (Ancient Egyptian. Precepts of Ptahhetep. H.R. Hall, *Ancient History of Near East*, p. 133 n.)

'In Nastrond (= Hell) I saw . . . murderers.' (Old Norse, *Volospá* 38, 39.)

'I have not brought misery upon my fellows. I have not made the beginning of every day laborious in the sight of him who worked for me.' (Ancient Egyptian. Confession of Righteous Soul. *ERE* v. 478.)

'I have not been grasping.' (Ancient Egyptian, Ibid.)

'Who meditates oppression, his dwelling is overturned.' (Babylonian. *Hymn to Samas. ERE* v. 445.)

'He who is cruel and calumnious has the character of a cat.' (Hindu. Laws of Manu. Janet, *Histoire de la Science Politique*, vol. i, p. 6.)

'Slander not.' (Babylonian. *Hymn to Sama. ERE* v. 445.)

'Thou shalt not bear false witness against thy neighbor.' (Ancient Jewish. Exodus xx. 16.)

'Utter not a word by which anyone could be wounded.' (Hindu. Janet, p. 7.)

'Has he . . . driven an honest man from his family? broken up a well cemented clan?' (Babylonian. List of Sins from incantation tablets. *ERE* v. 446.)

'I have not caused hunger. I have not caused weeping.' (Ancient Egyptian. *ERE* v. 478.)

'Never do to others what you would not like them to do to you.' (Ancient Chinese. *Analects of Confucius*, trans. A. Waley, xv. 23; cf. xii. 2.)

'Thou shalt not hate thy brother in thy heart.' (Ancient Jewish. Leviticus xix. 17.)

'He whose heart is in the smallest degree set upon goodness will dislike no one.' (Ancient Chinese, *Analects*, iv. 4.)

(b) Positive

'Nature urges that a man should wish human society to exist and should wish to enter it.' (Roman. Cicero, *De Officiis*, I. iv.)

'By the fundamental Law of Nature Man [is] to be preserved as much as possible.' (Locke, *Treatises of Civil Govt.* ii. 3.)

'When the people have multiplied, what next should be done for them? The Master said, Enrich them. Jan Ch'iu said, When one has enriched them, what next should be done for them? The Master said, Instruct them.' (Ancient Chinese. *Analects*, xiii. 9.)

'Speak kindness ... show good will.' (Babylonian. *Hymn to Samas. ERE* v. 445.)

'Men were brought into existence for the sake of men that they might do one another good.' (Roman. Cicero, *De Off.* I. vii.)

'Man is man's delight.' (Old Norse. *Havamal* 47.)

'He who is asked for alms should always give.' (Hindu, Janet, I. 7.)

"What good man regards any misfortune as no concern of his?' (Roman. Juvenal xv. 140.)

'I am a man: nothing human is alien to me.' (Roman. Terence, *Heaut. Tim.*)

'Love thy neighbor as thyself.' (Ancient Jewish. Leviticus xix. 18.)

'Love the stranger as thyself.' (Ancient Jewish. Ibid. 33, 34.)

'Do to men what you wish men to do to you.' (Christian. Matt. vii. 12.)

II. The Law of Special Beneficence

'It is upon the trunk that a gentleman works. When that is firmly set up, the Way grows. And surely proper behavior to parents and elder brothers is the trunk of goodness.' (Ancient Chinese. *Analects*, i. 2.)

'Brothers shall fight and be each others' bane.' (Old Norse. Account of the Evil Age before the World's end, *Volospa* 45.)

'Has he insulted his elder sister?' (Babylonian. List of Sins. *ERE.* v. 446.)

'You will see them take care of their kindred [and] the children of their friends . . . never reproaching them in the least.' (Redskin. Le Jeune, quoted *ERE* v. 437.)

'Love thy wife studiously. Gladden her heart all thy life long.' (Ancient Egyptian. *ERE* v. 481.)

'Nothing can ever change the claims of kinship for a right thinking man.' (Anglo-Saxon. *Beowulf,* 2600.)

'Did not Socrates love his own children, though he did so as a free man and as one not forgetting that the gods have the first claim on our friendship?' (Greek. Epictetus, iii. 24.)

'Natural affection is a thing right and according to Nature.' (Greek. Ibid. I. xi.)

'I ought not to be unfeeling like a statue but should fulfil both my natural and artificial relations, as a worshipper, a son, a brother, a father, and a citizen.' (Greek, Ibid. III. ii.)

'This first rede thee: be blameless to thy kindred. Take no vengeance even though they do thee wrong.' (Old Norse. *Sigrdrifumal,* 22.)

'Is it only the sons of Atreus who love their wives? For every good man, who is right-minded, loves and cherishes his own.' (Greek. Homer, *Iliad,* ix. 340.)

'The union and fellowship of men will be best preserved if each receives from us the more kindness in proportion as he is more closely connected with us.' (Roman. Cicero, *De Off.* I. xvi.)

'Part of us is claimed by our country, part by our parents, part by our friends.' (Roman, Ibid. I. vii.)

'If a ruler . . . compassed the salvation of the whole state, surely you would call him Good? The Master said, It would no longer be a matter of "Good." He would without doubt be a Divine Sage.' (Ancient Chinese. *Analects,* vi. 28.)

'Has it escaped you that, in the eyes of gods and good men, your native land deserves from you more honor, worship, and reverence than your mother and father and all your ancestors? That you should give a softer answer to its anger than to a father's anger? That if you cannot persuade it to alter its mind you must obey it in all quietness, whether it binds you or beats you or sends you to a war where you may get wounds or death?' (Greek. Plato, *Crito*, 51A, B.)

'If any provide not for his own, and specially for those of his own house, he hath denied the faith.' (Christian. I Tim. v. 8.)

'Put them in mind to obey magistrates. . . .' 'I exhort that prayers be made for kings and all that are in authority.' (Christian. Tit. iii. I and I Tim. ii. 1, 2.)

III. Duties to Parents, Elders, Ancestors

'Your father is an image of the Lord of Creation, your mother an image of the Earth. For him who fails to honor them, every work of piety is in vain. This is the first duty.' (Hindu. Janet, i. 9.)

'Has he despised Father and Mother?' (Babylonian. List of Sins. *ERE* v. 446.)

'I was a staff by my Father's side. . . . I went in and out at his command.' (Ancient Egyptian. Confession of the Righteous Soul. *ERE* v. 481.)

'Honor thy Father and thy Mother.' (Ancient Jewish. Exodus xx. 12.)

'To care for parents.' (Greek. List of duties in Epictetus, III. vii.)

'Children, old men, the poor, and the sick, should be considered as the lords of the atmosphere.' (Hindu. Janet, i. 3.)

'Rise up before the hoary head and honor the old man.' (Ancient Jewish. Lev. xix. 32.)

'I tended the old man, I gave him my staff.' (Ancient Egyptian. *ERE* v. 481.)

'You will see them take care . . . of old men.' (Redskin. Le Jeune, quoted *ERE* v. 437.)

'I have not taken away the oblations of the blessed dead.' (Ancient Egyptian. Confession of the Righteous Soul. *ERE* v. 478.)

'When proper respect towards the dead is shown at the end and continued after they are far away, the moral force

... of a people has reached its highest point.' (Ancient Chinese. *Analects*, i. 9.)

IV. Duties to Children and Posterity

'Children, the old, the poor, etc. should be considered as lords of the atmosphere.' (Hindu. Janet, i.3.)

'To marry and to beget children.' (Greek. List of duties. Epictetus, III. vii.)

'Can you conceive an Epicurean commonwealth...? What will happen? Whence is the population to be kept up? Who will educate them? Who will be Director of Adolescents? Who will be Director of Physical Training? What will be taught?' (Greek. Ibid.)

'Nature produces a special love of offspring' and 'To live according to Nature is the supreme good.' (Roman. Cicero, *De Off*. I. iv, and *De Legibus*, I. xxi.)

'The second of these achievements is no less glorious than the first; for while the first did good on one occasion, the second will continue to benefit the state forever.' (Roman. Cicero, *De Off*. I. xxii.)

'Great reverence is owed to a child.' (Roman. Juvenal, xiv. 47.)

'The Master said, Respect the young.' (Ancient Chinese, *Analects*, ix. 22.)

'The killing of the women and more especially of the young boys and girls who are to go to make up the future strength of the people, is the saddest part ... and we feel it very sorely.' (Redskin. Account of the Battle of Wounded Knee. *ERE* v. 432.)

V. The Law of Justice

(a) *Sexual Justice*

'Has he approached his neighbor's wife?' (Babylonian. List of Sins. *ERE*. v. 446.)

'Thou shalt not commit adultery.' (Ancient Jewish. Exodus xx. 14.)

'I saw in Nastrond (= Hell) ... beguilers of others' wives.' (Old Norse. *Volospa 38, 39*.)

(b) Honesty

'Has he drawn false boundaries?' (Babylonian. List of Sins. *ERE* v. 446.)

'To wrong, to rob, to cause to be robbed.' (Babylonian. Ibid.)

'I have not stolen.' (Ancient Egyptian. Confession of Righteous Soul. *ERE* v. 478.)

'Thou shalt not steal.' (Ancient Jewish, Exodus xx. 15.)

'Choose loss rather than shameful gains.' (Greek. Chilon Fr. 10. Diels.)

'Justice is the settled and permanent intention of rendering to each man his rights.' (Roman. Justinian, *Institutions*, I. i.)

'If the native made a "find" of any kind (e.g. a honey tree) and marked it, it was thereafter safe for him, as far as his own tribesmen were concerned, no matter how long he left it.' (Australian Aborigines. *ERE* v. 441.)

'The first point of justice is that none should do any mischief to another unless he has first been attacked by the other's wrongdoing. The second is that a man should treat common property as common property, and private property as his own. There is no such thing as private property by nature, but things have become private either through prior occupation (as when men of old came into empty territory) or by conquest, or law, or agreement, or stipulation, or casting lots.' (Roman. Cicero, *De Off*. I. vii.)

(c) Justice in Court, & c.

'Whoso takes no bribe . . . well pleasing is this to Samas.' (Babylonian. *ERE* v. 445.)

'I have not traduced the slave to him who is set over him.' (Ancient Egyptian. Confession of Righteous Soul. *ERE* v. 478.)

'Thou shalt not bear false witness against thy neighbor.' (Ancient Jewish. Exodus xx. 16.)

'Regard him whom thou knowest like him whom thou knowest not.' (Ancient Egyptian. *ERE* v. 482.)

'Do no unrighteousness in judgment. You must not consider the fact that one party is poor nor the fact that the other is a great man.' (Ancient Jewish. Leviticus xix. 15.)

VI. The Law of Good Faith and Veracity

'A sacrifice is obliterated by a lie and the merit of alms by an act of fraud.' (Hindu. Janet, i. 6.)

'Whose mouth, full of lying, avails not before thee: thou burnest their utterance.' (Babylonian. Hymn to Samas. *ERE* v. 445.)

'With his mouth was he full of *Yea*, in his heart full of *Nay*?' (Babylonian. *ERE* v. 446.)

'I have not spoken falsehood.' (Ancient Egyptian. Confession of Righteous Soul. *ERE* v. 478.)

'I sought no trickery, nor swore false oaths.' (Anglo-Saxon. *Beowulf*, 2738.)

'The Master said, Be of unwavering good faith.' (Ancient Chinese. *Analects*, viii. 13.)

'In Nastrond (= Hell) I saw the perjurers.' (Old Norse, *Volospa* 39.)

'Hateful to me as are the gates of Hades is that man who says one thing, and hides another in his heart.' (Greek. Homer. *Iliad*, ix. 312.)

'The foundation of justice is good faith.' (Roman. Cicero, *De Off*. I. vii.)

'[The gentleman] must learn to be faithful to his superiors and to keep promises.' (Ancient Chinese. *Analects*, I. 8.)

'Anything is better than treachery.' (Old Norse. *Havamal* 124.)

VII. The Law of Mercy

'The poor and the sick should be regarded as lords of the atmosphere.' (Hindu. Janet. i. 8.)

'Whoso makes intercession for the weak, well pleasing is this to Samas,' (Babylonian. *ERE* v. 445.)

'Has he failed to set a prisoner free?' (Babylonian. List of sins. *ERE* v. 446.)

'I have given bread to the hungry, water to the thirsty, clothes to the naked, a ferry boat to the boatless.' (Ancient Egyptian. *ERE* v. 478.)

'One should never strike a woman; not even with a flower.' (Hindu. Janet. i. 8.)

'There, Thor, you got disgrace, when you beat women.' (Old Norse. *Harbarthsljoth* 38.)

'In the Dalebura tribe a woman, a cripple from birth, was carried about by the tribes-people in turn until her death at the age of sixty-six. . . .' 'They never desert the sick.' (Australian Aborigines. *ERE* v. 443.)

'You will see them take care of . . . widows, orphans, and old men, never reproaching them.' (Redskin. *ERE* v. 439.)

'Nature confesses that she has given to the human race the tenderest hearts, by giving us the power to weep. This is the best part of us.' (Roman. Juvenal, xv. 134.)

'They said that he had been the mildest and gentlest of the kings of the world.' (Anglo-Saxon. Praise of the hero in *Beowulf*, 3180.)

'When thou cuttest down thine harvest . . . and hast forgot a sheaf . . . thou shalt not go again to fetch it: it shall be for the stranger, for the fatherless, and for the widow.' (Ancient Jewish. Deut. xxiv. 19.)

VIII. The Law of Magnanimity

A.

'There are two kinds of injustice: the first is found in those who do an injury, the second in those who fail to protect another from injury when they can.' (Roman. Cicero, *De Off.* I. vii.)

'Men always knew that when force and injury was offered they might be defenders of themselves; they knew that howsoever men may seek their own commodity, yet if this were done with injury unto others it was not to be suffered, but by all men and by all good means to be withstood.' (English. Hooker, *Laws of Eccl. Policy*, I. ix. 4.)

'To take no notice of a violent attack is to strengthen the heart of the enemy. Vigor is valiant, but cowardice is vile.' (Ancient Egyptian. The Pharaoh Senusert III. cit. H.R. Hall, *Ancient History of the Near East*, p. 161.)

'They came to the fields of joy, the fresh turf of the Fortunate Woods and the dwellings of the Blessed . . . here was the company of those who had suffered wounds fighting for their fatherland.' (Roman. Virgil, *Aen.* vi. 638-9, 660.)

'Courage has got to be harder, heart the stouter, spirit the sterner, as our strength weakens. Here lies our lord, cut to pieces, our best man in the dust. If anyone thinks of leaving this battle, he can howl forever.' (Anglo-Saxon. *Maldon*, 312.)

'Praise and imitate that man to whom, while life is pleasing, death is not grievous.' (Stoic. Seneca, *Ep.* liv.)

'The Master said, Love learning and if attacked be ready to die for the Good Way.' (Ancient Chinese. *Analects*, viii. 13.)

B.

'Death is to be chosen before slavery and base deeds.' (Roman. Cicero, *De Off.* I. xxiii.)

'Death is better for every man than life with shame.' (Anglo-Saxon. *Beowulf*, 2890.)

'Nature and Reason command that nothing uncomely, nothing effeminate, nothing lascivious be done or thought.' (Roman. Cicero, *De Off.* I. iv.)

'We must not listen to those who advise us "being men to think human thoughts, and being mortal to think mortal thoughts," but must put on immortality as much as is possible and strain every nerve to live according to that best part of us, which, being small in bulk, yet much more in its power and honor surpasses all else.' (Ancient Greek. Aristotle, *Eth. Nic.* 1177B.)

'The soul then ought to conduct the body, and the spirit of our minds the soul. This is therefore the first Law, whereby the highest power of the mind requireth obedience at the hands of all the rest.' (Hooker, op. cit. I. viii. 6.)

'Let him not desire to die, let him not desire to live, let him wait for his time . . . let him patiently bear hard words, entirely abstaining from bodily pleasures.' (Ancient Indian. Laws of Manu. *ERE* ii. 98.)

'He who is unmoved, who has restrained his senses . . . is said to be devoted. As a flame in a windless place that flickers not, so is the devoted.' (Ancient Indian. *Bhagavad gita. ERE* ii. 90.)

C.

'Is not the love of Wisdom a practice of death?' (Ancient Greek. Plato, *Phaedo*, 81 A.)

'I know that I hung on the gallows for nine nights, wounded with the spear as a sacrifice to Odin, myself offered to Myself.' (Old Norse. *Havamal, I.70 in Corpus Poeticum Boreale;* stanza 139 in Hildebrand's *Lieder der Alteren Edda.* 1922.)

'Verily, verily I say to you unless a grain of wheat falls into the earth and dies, it remains alone, but if it dies it bears much fruit. He who loves his life loses it.' (Christian. John xii. 24, 25.)

Index

ABOUT THE AUTHOR

Kathleen M. Gow, Ph.D., is eminently qualified to document the questions most crucial to values education. Her experience in international research dates from 1957, when she was awarded a scholarship to undertake advanced work at the Tavistock Clinic in London, and to conduct a two-year study of problems involving children and youth in Scandinavia, Central Europe, and the Middle East.

Dr. Gow's expertise spans three disciplines: mental health, sociology, and management studies. She has received numerous scholarships and awards in recognition of her important contributions in these fields. In each of these disciplines, Dr. Gow has been directly involved with the "consumer," the front-line practitioner, administration, and research. She has taught at several universities and is internationally known as an author and consultant to government, voluntary organizations, businesses, and educational institutions.

Dr. Gow was invited to join a U.S.-sponsored delegation of scientists and professionals to the People's Republic of China. In August 1984, she presented a paper to Unesco on "Values Education in North American Schools."